DOLPHIN
DOLPHIN

DOLPHIN DOLPHIN

Wade Doak

SHERIDAN HOUSE

Copyright © 1981 by Wade Doak.
First published 1981 by Hodder & Stoughton Ltd, Auckland, New Zealand.

First published in the United States of America 1982
by Sheridan House Inc., New York.

Library of Congress Cataloging in Publication Data

Doak, Wade.
    Dolphin, dolphin.

Includes indexes.
1. Dolphins — Behavior. 2. Human-animal communications.
3. Mammals — Behavior. I. Title.
QL737.C432D59 1982   599.5'3   82-10355
ISBN 0-911378-43-X

Printed in Hong Kong.

Contents

		Page
	Acknowledgments	9

PART ONE
Approaching the Ocean Nomads

1	Seeds are sown	13
2	Preparations	18
3	Testing communication channels with common dolphins	24

PART TWO
Delphinic Acceptance

4	Interval: new preparations	67
5	Meeting old friends	72

PART THREE
Dolphin Approaches to Humankind

6	The ambassadors	99
7	Children of the Gods: a history of the DINTS	114
8	Dolphins aid mariners	130

PART FOUR
With Larger Minds

9	Meeting with bottlenose dolphins	141
10	Simo and the keeper's wife	156

PART FIVE
Towards a Global Network

11	Project expansion	165
12	The film "Dolphin"	174
13	Interlock accounts from surfers, swimmers and mariners	178
14	Interlock Base II	186

15   Playing with whales   191
16   Cetacean intelligence and the ethics of killing them   205
17   Dolphin journey   214

APPENDICES

A   Strandings   229
B   Care of the dead   231
C   Dog/dolphin episodes   231
D   Iki: a lesson for mankind   234
E   Scientific revolutions   235
F   Reading list   237
G   The Interlock theory and Gaia hypothesis   240

INDEX

To Simo and Tatters, Notchy and Amazing Grace
and all those cetacean beings whose freedom of the seas we seek to
establish,
before it may be too late.

"We need another and a wiser and perhaps a more mystical concept of animals. Remote from universal nature, and living by complicated artifice, man in civilization surveys the creature through the glass of his knowledge and sees thereby a feather magnified and the whole image in distortion. We patronize them for their incompleteness, for their tragic fate of having taken form so far below ourselves. And therein do we err. For the animal shall not be measured by man. In a world older and more complete than ours they move finished and complete, gifted with extensions of the senses we have lost or never attained, living by voices we shall never hear. They are not brethren, they are not underlings; they are other nations, caught with ourselves in the net of life and time, fellow-prisoners of the splendour and travail of the earth."

— Henry Beston, *The Outermost House*

Acknowledgments

"But every man is not only himself; he is also the unique, particular, always significant and remarkable point where the phenomena of the world intersect once and for all and never again."
— Herman Hesse, *Demian*: 1960.

To acknowledge the assistance I have had in preparing this book is an infinitely humbling task. I feel like a fish that has been swimming through a benign ocean, encouraged and aided at every turn, recipient of unstinting generosity, open-heartedness and deep personal trust. Wherever dolphins and whales have impinged upon a human mind it seems a deep and resonant chord is struck, something that is bringing our species closer together perhaps than ever before. So, from the outset, I would like to acknowledge the spirit of cetacean consciousness that links the names placed here, ever mindful that the network is extending as each mail delivery brings Project Interlock fresh anecdotes and photos of cetacean/human encounters from all over the world.

My heart goes out to David Harvey, Dr Walt Starck and Hal Chapman who first listened to and encouraged an obsession; to Barry Fenn, Quentin Bennett, Bob Feigel, Meda McKenzie, Les Grey, the Tana family, Peter Munro, Eric Kircher, Toni and Dr John Lilly; Drs Bernd Wursig, Jeffery Mishlove, Ron Nolan, Avril and Tony Ayling; Drs Lyall Watson, Peter Beamish, Nicholas Webb, Robins Barstow, Ricardo Mandojana, Richard Gierek, Horace Dobbs, Allan Baker, John Yaldwyn (director National Museum); the Mobius Group, Jim Hudnall, Jim Loomis, Jim Nollman, Judy Weigel, Margaret Bingham, Joan Aldrich, Anna Horne, Cindy Slark, Rebbekah Lee, Sue Jolly, Ingrid Orbom, Claire Peacock, Grant Middleton, Anne and Jean Paul Fortum-Gouin, Val and Graham Mosen, Donna and Mike Baker, Joyce and Graeme Adams, Susie and Dexter Cate, Mikki and Ray Kleiman, Hazel and Wilfred Mason, Penny and Herman Otto, Morgan and Michael Wiese, Ros and Allan Rowe, Alison and Terry Goodall, Ruth and James Wharram, Trevor Williams, Vic Belcher, Eric Wellington, Ross Cotterill, Malcolm Pitt, Bill Shanks, Claude Thomas, Robin Solomon, Witi McMath, Waipu Pita, Elaine Smith, Te Rina Sullivan-Meads, Penny Whiting, Sam McHarg, Val Walter, Grant Couchman, Gary Tee, Ted Boehler, Michael Taylor, Harold Phillips,

Project Greenpeace, Project Jonah, Professor Pat Hindley, Colin Lee, Des Crossland, Ramari Stewart, Alan Fouts, Eric Morris, Bernard Moitessier, Rob Woollacott, David Pardon of *Sea Spray* magazine, Rob Lahood of *New Zealand Dive*; Dave Stalworthy, Laurie Brett, Dave Munro, Nigel Croft, Chris McLaughlin, Pat Selby, Syd Raines, Cliff Knight, Graeme Thomson, Hec Yates, John Denzler, Laurie Beamish, Mike Bradstock, Chris Sharp and the *Pirimai* crew, Jill Smith, Terry Johnson, Don Armitage, John Donahue, Estelle Myers, Carolla Hepp; Allan Fisher and Jim Burton, Whangarei C.B. Club; Hildegard Corbett, Patrick Wall, Steve Dawson, Hardy Jones, Bob Tillet, Jacques Mayol, Carter Haven, Jill Gray, Ian Briggs, Chi-uh Gawain, Malcolm Pullman, Gary Dods, Christine Johnson, Jody Solow, Roger Kempthorne, Peter Rippon, Peter Saul, Murray Brighouse, Marilyn West, Mathew Conmee, Stan Minasian, Anthony Lealand, Jan Brewer and Edwin McCaffery.

I would like to make special acknowledgement to the financial assistance given Project Interlock by the McKenzie Foundation and the Lottery Profits Scientific Research Distribution Committee; the generous assistance with scuba diving equipment from Allan G. Mitchell; to P.G.H. Industries for marine paints; and the dolphin suit made and given to Project Interlock by Moray Industries.

To my editor, Neil Robinson and his wife Flora I owe immense gratitude for the encouragement and perspective they have given over the years.

Lastly I wish to point out that without the total involvement and collaboration of my wife Jan and the help of Karla and Brady Doak both at sea and on land this project would still be a pipe dream.

PART ONE

Approaching the Ocean Nomads

"Whales and dolphins are the most likely
intelligent non-human life with which man
might seek to communicate."
— Dr Sterling Bunnell

1

Seeds are sown

ALWAYS, WHEN SHE put on her dolphin suit, Jan had a strange feeling of expectation; as if it was not only the colour and form of the creatures that she was assuming. On this day, as she dived down from our boat into the familiar sea, the feeling was stronger than ever, and it was with exhilaration but no shock that she saw five dolphins swimming beside her. They moved slowly at her speed, making it easy for her to keep up with them, but in spite of this disciplined restraint there was a smooth joy, a lively curiosity about them as they studied her. Now Jan's body and legs undulated as a graceful unit, curving up and down through the water in long sweeps. The five dolphins stayed with her. She swam effortlessly, adapting to an inner rhythm, careless of where she was heading, forgetting the world above the water; just swimming in great curves through shimmering cones of light.

Five years before we would have thought an incident such as this could only have been a fantasy: wishful thinking, perhaps, or the result of brooding too long over Greek legends. The setting, of course, helped to strengthen the fantasy. From the seacoast near our North Auckland home we looked over the ocean to the Poor Knights Islands and beyond. The coast, with its steep headlands and myriad islands, stretches far to the north. Here was the migratory trail for whales from the Antarctic to tropic Pacific seas. A great ocean river sweeping across the Tasman and along New Zealand's eastern shore brought life to the coastal waters. Pelagic fishes were there in abundance; reef fishes colonised niches in the underwater cliffs; and dolphins made it their ranging ground.

During our first twenty years of diving in many parts of the South Pacific, Jan and I had very little experience of dolphins. We enjoyed watching them as they frolicked at a vessel's bow. Occasionally, but not very often, we had glimpsed them underwater just long enough to realise that the sleek forms were *not* sharks. And then they were gone. Once or twice we had been with groups of divers who tried leaping in among them when dolphins were around. They always vanished into the blue.

Then, on 5 April 1975, it all began to change. Not just for us, as it first seemed, for we now have accounts from other divers who had similar encounters around that time.

That autumn day our "deep vee" was bucketing homeward from the Poor Knights over a switchback sea, running so fast that we just clipped the wave crests, virtually airborne, and all five of us totally exhilarated after the day's diving. With me were two young biologists Tony and Barry, Cathy who came from New York and big, gentle Les from Ngunguru.

Suddenly there were dolphins ahead of the boat. They raced to meet it, arcing from the water as they rose to breathe, making their presence known. The machine slowed to whale speed and the dolphins adjusted their tails to the pressure wave. They surfed ahead of us, cavorting from port to starboard; rolling on their sides to eye the glassy white and red hull and its occupants hanging over the bow shouting encouragement and slapping the hull with staccato rhythms. Both species, man and cetacean, had begun gamesplay.

I described the encounter in the last pages of *Islands of Survival*, not fully realising then just how it would change our lives. Looking back now, I feel that I acted in a predetermined way. I recall that our fast ride had begun in the cathedral quiet, green twilight of Rikoriko, Cave of Echoes, the eighty-foot-high dome inside Aorangi, chief of the Poor Knights. After diving we had taken Cathy, the New York photographer, in there to view its vastness. We had grown silent and thoughtful as we studied the vaulting roof, with delicate ferns clinging to it, marvelling at the sight.

Maybe my mind skipped back then to my only previous significant encounter with dolphins. In May 1971, I had been sixty feet down where white sand lies in drifts at the foot of the Rikoriko cave wall. Suddenly everything went black. I glanced up in fear — the cave portal, usually a blaze of blue fire, had dimmed. It was seething with huge shapes — sharp fins, fast tails and jaws. Dolphins! One of them, in silhouette on the surface, smacked its tail and a pair of curving forms glided down in a spiral, circled me and rose. Each time the games leader smacked with his tail a pair spiralled down, curving on their sides to gaze intently as they passed me. Enchanted, for some time I forgot I had a camera. Then with the last two frames left on the film I took my first dolphin picture: *Tursiops truncatus*, the bottlenose.

Now, on this April day in 1975, as the dolphins moved to meet our fast-running boat, it seemed I knew exactly what I wanted to do if I ever met dolphins on the bow. I would slow to a crawl, put the boat in a wide circle and leap into the centre. With my camera. I wanted dolphin photos, perhaps to satisfy a publisher's request. Tony took the wheel and I plunged in. My strategy worked: dolphins were frolicking around the bow like circus ponies, with me as ringmaster. I fired off my dozen photos. Then I became aware that roles were changing. The boat had stopped and I was now at the centre of a cyclone of dolphins. I called to Tony and the others to join me, but "one at a time; and let's all do the dolphin-kick". I can't recall why I should have said that, but it was probably an important factor in what ensued.

As an exercise in relativity it is interesting to imagine those dolphins' viewpoint. A diver bursts through the heaving mirror and points a third eye at them. He passes the camera up and starts to mimic the dolphin way of swimming. One after the other two more men join him, diving down in their wetsuits. Then — a subtle variation — a bikini-clad girl. Suddenly, a large nude male appears. Had this been planned we could not have designed a more effective introduction. Poor Les! He was supposed to look after the boat but our enthusiasm was too much for him. And the wind had died down. Almost! Barry and I saw the boat start to waft away — faster and faster. We only just caught it, averting an embarrassingly long swim home.

During our dolphin games each diver in his sealed-off world became aware that the dolphins were demonstrating new tricks. I was weaving among them with a fluid dolphin drive, my fins undulating together like a broad tail in a movement that began at my head and rippled along my body. A dolphin drew alongside me. By counter-opposing its flippers, like the ailerons of a plane making a spin, it barrel-rolled right in front of my mask.

Maintaining the dolphin-kick I imitated this corkscrew manoeuvre, counter-opposing my hands held close to my chest. The response was slow as my pseudo-flippers were tiny and my speed a fraction of theirs, but I found myself rolling wing over wing. Then something startling happened. The moment my spin was complete a formation of six dolphins, abreast of me and on the same side as before, repeated that trick, in unison, reinforcing my newly acquired mimicry pattern. And so it went on, the sea wild with energy, a maelstrom of dolphins, their shrill echo-ranging whistles dinning in our ears.

We gambolled with them for about an hour until utterly exhausted. Then one by one we hauled ourselves in over the stern. Around us we could now see salvoes of dolphins leaping in symmetrical pairs and singly for a mile in every direction. We must have met a whole tribe of bottlenose dolphins on their passage along the coast.

As we towelled ourselves warm I said how marvellous it was that such huge, sharp-toothed animals, each as heavy and as fast as my boat, had not even buffeted us by their swirling movements. "Only once," said Tony Ayling who had been the last on board. Just as he was approaching the stern one dolphin had rushed to within a metre of him, stopped short, vertical in the water, with flippers flung wide as if imploring us to continue. We felt we had let them down. I gave the hull a resounding thump. From a short way off a tail smacked on the surface in answer. I thumped again. Eight times we exchanged signals, and that was it.

A few months later, I was told a story that could almost be described as a sequel. Bill Shanks was rowing his dinghy up the Ngunguru River not far along the coast. To his amazement a large group of bottlenose dolphins passed beneath him. When they reached the first mangroves on an island in the river, they began to dart in all directions, almost stranding themselves, while a dozen large ones swam slowly in a ring. Then they all gathered together and swam back out to sea.

Later, I discussed the encounter with Jan and our two children, Brady and Karla, sitting in our snug little house tucked down beside a mangrove estuary at Matapouri Bay; out of sight of the open sea but within hearing of its restless energy.

Dr John Lilly, in one of his books on dolphin research had coined the word "interlock" for interspecies communication. I little realised then, and nor did Jan, how much our first interlock would change our lives. I could no longer continue exploring the sea and ignoring questions arising from that encounter.

How limited is man when it comes to communicating with an aquatic, games-playing creature! Even with body language we were no match for its speed and manoeuvrability. Was there a way in which, by using sound we could show the dolphins that humans could, like them, indulge in games for the sheer joy of such activity? Were there other ways in which we could bridge the present gap?

Not long before, Jan and I, with Brady (11) and Karla (9), had travelled through remote parts of the South Pacific on the undersea research ship *El Torito*.* While our children learnt to scuba dive and handle canoes we formed close bonds with saltwater peoples wherever we anchored, bonds that were in no way fashioned from shared language. Especially with the village children, our family learnt that mimicry, music and dancing can remove cultural gaps between human beings of greatly differing backgrounds. Was it too fanciful to hope that something similar could happen between humans and dolphins — oceanic nomads, a company of wandering villagers with a completely alien culture?

Over-fanciful or not, this concept was our launching pad — the working hypothesis, unashamedly anthropomorphic, on which we base our research because until it is proven otherwise, nobody knows just what would happen if complex brained cetaceans were treated with the same courtesy and ethics we find essential when meeting our own species on strange ground.

Synchronicities

It was eight months after that initial interlock that I had an experience which increased the flexibility of thought. I have never been religious. This was my first experience of another reality.

On a sweet summer's day at the end of January 1976, I was standing on a cliff top overlooking the Pacific listening to music. I became aware of the rotundity of the Earth and then I remembered that my sister was out there, on the other side of the globe, painfully ill in the isolation ward of a Paris hospital. Suddenly with a tearing sensation somewhere in my chest and a sudden surge of intense joy, I knew she had died. When I got home a cable call had just conveyed the news to my family. I checked it out. The times corresponded exactly. I have since found that a great many people have had similar intimations of the injury or death of a loved one. Since for obvious reasons such events are rare, the phenomenon has not yet entered the body of accepted knowledge. But in the ensuing years of dolphin research this was to influence the scope of my thinking. The possibility of some ESP factor operating in communication with cetaceans often occurred to me, especially after reading that famous passage in Sir Arthur Grimble's *A Pattern of*

*Voyage narrated in *Islands of Survival*.

16

Islands, when he witnessed the "calling" of dolphins to Kuma village (Gilbert Is.) by a man in a trance state.

Then one day I received in the mail four items, each containing news about cetaceans. They fell into my lap while I was writing a piece for the *Listener* magazine begun weeks earlier, but only picked up now on a whim, or so I had thought. The article, titled "Ocean Nomads", was about the plight of dolphins and whales.

There was a letter from Cathy Drew in New York, the girl who shared our dolphin dance: "Did you see 'Body State Communication Among Cetaceans' by John Sutphen? In this paper he proposes (and has done a lot of the appropriate biochemistry and biomechanics to back it up) that with the three sonar 'channels' available to them, cetaceans can 'see-read-hear' into each others' hearts and brains. There would be no lying. Rates of heat and pulse are continuously monitored by each member of the group. Cancers, swellings and inflammations in the remote internal organs are public information. Health and wellbeing, maybe anger, certainly fear. No bluffing, no faking it. Think what it would be like — so hard to imagine and yet so easy to believe."

I opened *National Geographic Magazine* — an article on the playfulness of right whales in Patagonia, by Dr Roger Payne.

From Italy, *Mondo Sommerso* magazine with a horror story on the butchery of cetaceans in Japan and the Faroe Islands, wholesale slaughter for meat.

And from my publisher, a proof copy of Lyall Watson's new book *Gifts of Unknown Things*. I opened it and read: "Dolphins rely on their oil channels for precise echolocation but sound still impinges on all parts of their bodies with the same high energy and turns every inch into a functional sound receptor. It is not just the surface that is involved either, because sound passes easily through the skin and muscle and bounces back only from bone and air-filled cavities. The internal workings of all bodies about him are a normal part of any dolphin's external environment.

"When you swim with one he is constantly aware of your health and general wellbeing, of your physiology and the level of your emotional arousal. There is no hiding or lying and no possibility of denial."

That day's mail did it. I wrote back to Cathy that I'd decided to prepare a book on the existing knowledge of cetacean minds, allied with our diving knowledge of their environment and speculative runs exploring the possibilities of a non-materialistic oceanic culture.

I decided not to publish this manuscript as our research overtook the fantasy, but putting it together helped enormously in modelling our approach: a communication model.

2

Preparations

MEANWHILE THERE WAS much to occupy and expand our minds. It is surprising how, when one embarks on a certain course, all sorts of details manifest themselves to support and encourage the journey. And so we were constantly stimulated by points cropping up in conversation and letters, seemingly casual comments and discoveries that helped us to gain knowledge and understanding.

For the next year I devoured every written word I could find on cetaceans. Most important to me were the books on dolphin research by Dr John Lilly. His three-volumes-in-one tome, *Lilly on Dolphins*, lays down a whole new framework for understanding cetacean sensory systems and their acoustic capabilities. It was in his "Programming and Metaprogramming in the Human Biocomputer" that Lilly coined the word "interlock" for interspecies communication. There, in language that was deliberately obscure (Lilly explains why), I found a clear expression of the objective towards which I felt drawn. You can read it in appendix G.

Knowledge of dolphins, I found, was based almost entirely on captive animals. How much could be learned about our species from a study of people in jail? Jane Goodall had shown what could be done through behavioural field work with wild dogs and chimpanzees. So much more was learned about these creatures when they were studied in their natural surroundings; but gaining acceptance of terrestrial mammals is easier by far than if they are ocean-dwellers.

I discovered there had been many problems when first attempts had been made at communication. Back in 1969 when he wrote *The Dolphin: Cousin to Man*, Robert Stenuit pointed out that wild dolphins refused to associate with man underwater. For the most part when divers encountered dolphins swimming free in the ocean and attempted to film them, their plans were cut short. The dolphins simply swam away. In his own book, *Dolphins*, Jacques Cousteau openly admits defeat in his attempts to study dolphins in the wild. In order to complete a film at all, Cousteau had to capture dolphins and restrain them in the sea with nets and buoys. He has declared he would never try to capture dolphins to film again.

In some ways, as time went by, I felt daunted by the size of the task we were setting outselves. True, we had already seen a way through the problem that defeated Cousteau, but where did we go from there? How to break through the barrier sealing off two different environments, to prove to the dolphins (was this a crazy thought?) that humans were also creatures of some intelligence — if that indeed needed to be proved?

Then came a meeting with a young Hamilton lawyer, David Harvey. Ever since a childhood encounter with Opo, the celebrated dolphin of the Hokianga Harbour, he had been drawn to them and had had two experiences similar to mine. Sometimes the mind works with a heightened power; and this seemed the case when David and I began sharing ideas and the fruits of our experience. Sometimes, too, I felt sure that thinking underwater brought inspiration and deeper insights; perhaps an unfamiliar space jolts the mind. But, when I look back now, I realise that I had started diving all over again; that, with my head crammed with cetacean research, I was, on occasion, able to take a dolphin's-eye-view as I dived.

Many theories would come to the surface in our discussions and then, maybe, disappear again. One line of thought that persisted concerned music and sound. What capacity did these dolphin friends of ours have to "read" our music, to accept the sounds we made? I found myself talking animatedly to David about my theory that western music might become meaningful to dolphins if we danced to it during interlock with them. Otherwise it might be too slow — like a record playing at 16 rpm. Normal human speech is at the same frequency as all the mechanical sounds in the ocean. But if we were to dance to the music they might mimic us, join our game and grasp that we were tuned to the low frequency pattern being transmitted.

John Lilly's research establishes that the frequencies dolphins use are four and a half times faster than those used by man. This corresponds to the difference in the speed at which sound travels through water compared with in air. To the dolphins we may appear to be stone deaf. The frequencies we use correspond to mechanical frequencies all around them in the ocean. Through dance it may be possible to demonstrate to them that certain low frequency sounds we make within the medium of air have recognizable patterns and rhythms.

They may then distinguish our music from the field of low frequency ocean noise and realise that humans can play complex sound games too. This was certainly an idea to play with and to test as our research developed. Our excitement mounted; life was going to have all sorts of fascinating spinoffs.

Our music-dance theory, so confidently elaborated, did not come unasked out of thin air. I have been looking back in our journal to an entry with the title "Cave Bay, 15 May 1976." Reading it again I see that I have set down something that I still feel has significance: sight, sound, movement — an interlocking series of impressions that stimulated my mind and, having done that, assumed relevance and meaning.

Cave Bay is on the eastern side of Tawhiti Rahi, northernmost of the Poor Knights group. It faces the southern ocean, and all the signs one sees when diving there indicate heavy water movement. On the bottom of the bay huge boulders gleam like freshly sculptured rock, scraped clean as the storm waves stir the great stones. With each storm, sea plants are torn loose from the underwater cliffs, leaving bare patches on which settle the larvae of any cliff-dwelling species happening to spawn at that particular time. Clumps of anemones, sponges and ascidians are arranged in a random mosaic determined by the removal of the kelp holdfasts. The patchiness of the encrusting life provides stability through diversity; it also allows the establishment of a vital link — that between plant and animal — in a relationship that benefits both parties.*

At first I dived and swooped around the perimeter of the bay, hoping to pick up the northern entrance to the arch, but missed it completely. It is concealed from the submerged explorer who has to swim up over the lip of the reef crest in only eight feet of water to enter the arch. It deepens magnificently to the south, opening into a great vault; but the shallow northern entrance is a series of sculpted alcoves where great boulders rest in the rollrock craters they have hewn. For the cetaceans, I thought, the sound vibrations from rocks rumbling in a storm must be an incredible orchestration.

Approaching the head of the bay I came upon the entrance to a new tunnel extending southwards. An incredible tunnel, in only ten metres of water, with wave sculpture of such excellence that it was like visiting an art gallery. The exhibits were laid out for inspection: every grade and hue of rock strata, giant eggs and cannonballs, buns, gourds grained and polished, no weed adhering in the half light. A silver drummer thudded for the entrance. I made towards the faintest point of light, reasoning that I could safely penetrate that far into the darkness without losing the entrance. Overhead the surface extended into the cave, surging and sucking with the swells. In the deepest recess I stopped and looked up. The end of the cave was bulbous. The smallest surges pulsed up and down the curved wall, arousing a faint glitter of bounce light in the gloom.

But the sound waves were amazing. A complexity of gurgles, thuds, dripping water and inrush. I turned to face the entrance. This, to my kindled imagination, was a sound trumpet — the music of the cave would be spiralling out into the bay and beyond. Maybe, out there, a whale was tuned into this space — a good location to test a sonar interlock device. . .

All through this dive, as I later wrote in my journal, I was listening for those ultrasonic sounds which might be on the threshold of hearing. When my exhaust gas had stopped its rumbling ascent and my mask quit venting tiny pearls of air, I had a moment of silence. In this brief interval I heard high-pitched whistling sounds such as I have never known in the sea. But I couldn't hear the fish schools as the old Indonesian fisherman did in Lyall Watson's book, *Gifts of Unknown Things*. Perhaps there were none around.

The message tape

I needed a special tape recording on which dolphin sounds were slowed to our listening speed and frequency, stage by stage so they could

*Theme of my sixth book, *The Cliff Dwellers — an Undersea Community*.

20

appreciate what was going on. Then a piece of western music would be recorded four times faster than normal, to communicate its patterns at their level of perception.

Both man and dolphin are surrounded by an extraordinary chaos of informational noise, thousands of bits of data quite irrelevant to survival or even to personal competence. The signal-to-noise ratio is low and it takes complex circuitry for us to scan incoming signals for pattern. With refined sensory systems an ability to discriminate between signals and noise becomes increasingly important. Both man and cetacean have evolved as social animals. In a complex social context generating a heavy static of irrelevant noise, selection favoured the group with the big brain, with its bulky cerebral circuitry, noise limiters, fine tuner and pattern-reading apparatus. But therein may lie the tragedy: when it comes to interlock between minds in media as different as air and water, both parties have missed the bus. Anyway that was the theory I wished to test.

To my delight a tape cassette arrived in the mailbox from Hamilton. David had used two reel-to-reel recording machines to produce exactly what I had outlined. Furthermore he had put on the rest of the tape a long recording of humpback whale songs and the vocalisations of twenty different cetaceans.

I decided to try listening to the message tape while immersed in warm water — a situation in which my main input would be from alien minds. Perhaps in this way I could gain an insight into the cetacean's sonic world. As I listened to the cetacean recordings replayed at one quarter of their normal speed I imagined these were scanning beams of sound, like the pencil of *El Torito's* radar beam outlining a coastline. With each call I visualized an image that persisted once it died away to be replaced by a successive phonation — a dissolve into another picture. Does each sonic pattern, perhaps a portion of the aural tradition, establish a scanned sonar picture, stereoscopic because of the twin sound emitters. . ?

It came to me, that for man, reality is a mental construct built up by senses which are predominantly visual. It can be extended with special lenses from micro to macro, from electron microscope to radio telescope. Sonar reality for the dolphin is another province. A diver's bones and scuba tank would reflect sound like an echo sounder pulsing off rock bottom after penetrating various densities of mud and schools of fishes. The total reflection of light is white; total absorption is black. I tried to visualise a white skeleton curving through black space, enmeshed in a complexity of orange organs, blue flesh and yellow arteries. The cetacean sonargram could convey as much information as x-ray, infra-red and hologram photography all combined in one system.

Listening to cetacean sounds in warm water, a series of thoughts flowed through my mind which enabled me to explore a hypothetical model and led to a series of practical experiments I could not have conceived otherwise.

Body language

Following the Cave Bay dive and the thoughts it provoked I decided to take body language much further. I had already made a series of behavioural experiments on fishes, using models. I'd found that there are special markings and signal patterns which reef fishes* use in court-ship, aggressive display and parasite removal. Certain ritualised movements or dance routines communicate messages between members of the same species and from one species to another. A black angelfish turns its back and extinguishes the white ear marking on its head, to appease a dominant invader of its territory. Many wrasses bear signal flags on their fins, and some have signature markings on their bodies for personal recognition. Coral shrimps wave their six long, white feelers from beneath ledges to attract customers for parasite removal. The sabre tooth blenny mimics the swimming pattern and colouration of the cleaner wrasse to approach unsuspecting fishes and nip pieces of their skin.

Assuming that dolphins are at least as intelligent as fishes in observ-ing such signals and body language, what would be their response if I were to mimic them in colour, form and movement; to turn myself into a model dolphin? At least they might enjoy the charade, but I hoped they might accept it as an attempted communication from an alien ter-restrial mind, perhaps something beyond the limits of cetacean belief.

I reasoned that something must have triggered the intensity of our April interlock and served to prolong the dolphins' interest in us that day beyond all our previous experiences. Perhaps there was some factor in the way it just happened quite spontaneously. By increments, as if to reinforce the point, three wetsuit wearers one after another enter the water while the boat circles, slowly maintaining the bow-surfing game. Then a female in bikini and a large naked male. Each of the five begins mimicking the dolphin mode of swimming, wearing very large fins and radiating enjoyment. Joy was communicated between human and dolphin and the charge recirculated and increased to a cyclone of play energy.

So I decided to take it all one stage further. I would try the same thing but this time the humans would have dorsal fins fitted to their weight belts. They would wear special wetsuits modelled on the dolphin body: black above and white below, both legs enclosed in a sheath of neoprene and terminating in jet-fins or ideally a model rubber tail-fin, with peduncle keel.

As swimming bipeds we instinctively use an alternating kick, but the sinuous waving of body and tail-fin is a much more effective and widespread mode of water propulsion. Instead of just increasing the power of our kick with rubber fins, why not copy the fish, as the ceta-ceans have done? Besides, this would be an indication to the dolphins that we too are intelligent observers of convergent evolution and have not permanently overlooked the fish's advantages. Propelled by transverse waves flowing through its musculature, the fish penetrates the sea with minimal disturbances or cavitation; a highly efficient transfer of body energy to wave motion and mass propulsion which the dolphins have emulated.

Midway along the dolphin's body the dorsal fin serves as a keel, providing lateral resistance about which the body can turn or pivot.

*My book, *Fishes of the New Zealand Region.*

Its function can be seen when the bow riders suddenly swerve aside and leave the ship. Such a fin attached to the centre lead weight on my belt, might assist dolphin-swimming. Certainly it would help me get the feel of it while watching them. My whole body has to become a swimming organ.

The dolphin's flippers serve as ailerons for rapid diving, ascent and spiral turns. They are also important for touch communication, an essential part of social activity. I would wear a pair of handfins made from plywood and covered in foam neoprene. I made a rough mock-up of my concept — just enough to test its practicality for swimming.

3

Testing communication channels with common dolphins

FROM THIS POINT the narrative of our dolphin research would best be done through the journals we both kept after each ocean excursion. While there may be defects in this method, I hope the immediacy and enthusiasm the journals convey will be some compensation.

More than this however, the journals provide a step-by-step record of our growth in understanding those areas of our dolphin research which we found hard to believe. For in setting out to study dolphins in the wild as if they were an alien nomadic people, we came across a great deal more than we bargained for. Few readers could be expected to accept the discoveries we are now making about human/dolphin relationships if they were presented with them out of context. Unless we provide a record of the gradual acquisition of insights, the quiet parts of our research, the slog of many hours at sea, the mistakes, disappointments and encouragements, and the growth in our attitudes and goals, the high points of our discoveries would be difficult to believe.

Testing the extensions
Journal, 4 November 1976: For dolphins it would be far easier to move around than remain motionless. I came to this conclusion today when I tested the dorsal fin, handflippers and dolphin suit.

On a calm spring day Jan and I boat-bounced fourteen miles over the southeast swells towards Aorangi, island of the cloud chief. Two puffs of vapour, the only ones in the entire sky, hovered above the Poor Knights. Recent rains had discoloured the sea as far out as three or four miles — but the ocean around the islands was sparkling clear, a fresh upswelling after the storm. We were hopeful of finding a spawning invasion of paper nautilus, the small pelagic octopuses that secrete an eggshell-thin case in which they lay their eggs. But there were no signs of bird activity — just huge rafts of petrels bobbing on the swells — the new water was low on plankton life as yet. We cruised around the cliff faces searching for signs of nautilus and anchored for lunch on Landing Bay Pinnacle — opposite Taravana Cave, an ideal place to test the gear.

Getting into the water presented special problems without the use of hands and legs. I set myself up on the stern, steadied my mask with one flipper and plunged headlong in. The momentum of my fall carried me completely through the surface and I found myself flying around the boat in an effortless arc. Thinking back on it the sensation was very curious — as if I had left my body. My mind was still, as if contemplating the body's action from apart — like the first time I flew a hang-glider. The dolphin motion was autonomous: I didn't seem to be consciously striving. Maybe some cellular blueprint for undulating movement was triggered by the "memory" extensions I had made to my form. In a situation where survival would instinctively depend upon a kicking action I was a legless monopode. Perhaps the physical suppression of a habitual pattern released some vestigial spermlike wriggling pattern. Because my legs were hobbled I had to move like a dolphin all the time and this forced me to perform better — just as when, dressed in regal garb, an actor assumes the bearing of a king. Maybe I could achieve the same with a leg strap, as the one-piece dolphin suit is a makeshift outfit I glued up from neoprene scraps and really needs to be properly tailored to preserve body warmth.

The dorsal-fin keel attached to the centre lead weight of my belt fitted snugly to my body. It made it very easy to move around in curving pathways and stabilised yawing movements, with a consequent saving in energy. The snorkel enabled me to breathe like a dolphin. I was well ballasted and very soon I could glide around just beneath the surface using my new body to rise and descend, turn and twist like a fish.

But the stinging cold sunk in and I found myself losing body heat too rapidly to maintain the pleasurable aspect of the performance. The more I moved the colder I became — a punishment syndrome that spoilt the previous, and essential, spontaneity of movement. Approaching the boat to climb aboard I learnt how hard it is to tread water with one leg and no arms.

Lying on my back I soon warmed up in the midday sun. Pohutukawa blossoms were starting to redden the terraced heights. Like scarlet spears the blooms of rock lilies, indigenous to these islands, hung from ledges and outcrops. Kingfishers and green parakeets fluttered among the crags and over every vertical surface sparkling clean forest water was sluicing from recent rains. A significant contrast with the streams of yellow porridge disgorged into the inshore waters from eroding coastal hills stripped of native bush.

Basking in the heat it occurred to me how the dolphin mind might experience this same calm and tranquility even while buckling through the sea. Whereas man breathes autonomously and swims by conscious effort, the sea mammal must choose each breath according to the opportunity presented by wave crests and troughs, flashing to the interface for a fleeting lung exchange and curving below to rejoin its companions.

For the next test, Jan climbed in while I operated a stereo cassette player, shifting the speakers to various positions around the hull. I played her the sounds of cetaceans as she swam about or dived down the anchor rope, to determine the effective range of our gear. I lowered my tape-recorder housing to test it for leaks and we tested out a prototype underwater speaker which, I decided, might work better if I filled it with oil and put a rubber diaphragm across the front.

For some weeks I've been preparing equipment to realize the ideas that occurred while reading, reflecting and writing imaginatively about

25

dolphins. My task now is to test the hypotheses I have devised, to see what will happen when we meet the dolphins again with conscious mimicry and body language. I wonder if we could ever establish an interlock involving dolphins, divers and a rock band, to see how they react to our soundgames, and tune to our frequencies?

"But *why* a rock band?" music lovers have asked.

What my journal does not bother to explain is that around that time I came *out of the sea*. Up till then my outdoor life and photography had been focused underwater. My first diving journal was begun in 1953 when I was thirteen and ever since I'd been oriented towards the ocean in every respect. Even marriage (Jan and I met because of a friend's introduction to her as a keen diver; she'd learnt with her mother and brother!): our courtship only began after a lot of time together underwater, when I learnt she was as capable a partner as any I'd known.

During our days in the little cottage at Matapouri Bay Jan and I, Brady and Karla became friendly with local people whose family roots penetrate deepest into the soil of Northland — a group of young Maori folk whom we reluctantly taught to skindive (training should be a formal process) and whose favourite relaxation was to play music outdoors. With them a day's adventure was to set out for a remote spot on the coast which had special acoustic qualities and play musical games there for hours on end. When the sea was too rough our family found itself traipsing over coastal headlands and staring into forest pools while flute and trumpet echoed through the valleys.

For me it was a mindjolt to discover patterns on the forest floor which reminded me of those beneath the sea. I began land diving; with the same techniques and lighting that I used underwater I zeroed in on orchids, lichens, insects and flowers which I could match with my large collection of undersea photos. I even found myself holding my breath to avoid bubbles as I squeezed the trigger.

Listening to music in an unfamiliar surrounding provided a "discontinuity", a detachment from the familiar way of looking at the forest to seeing the trees in form and structure as they really are. I bought two carousel slide projectors and put together a matched programme of forest and undersea pictures which culminated with human and dolphin.

In the Whangarei Town Hall the Maori musicians and one pakeha flautist gave a concert. They called their music "Headland Haze" because it was generated by the energy of a headland coast, like the haze of salt-laden air that sets the headlands aglow at dawn and dusk. While they played their music I projected around them pictures of twilit headlands, wave energy, rock patterns and then a matching sequence from the two worlds.

To critics of our music I respond: find me a group of classical musicians willing to play on land and sea and I would be delighted to join with them. Our relationship with the rock band reached a new height when they played in the vast dome of Rikoriko Cave. In my book *Sharks and Other Ancestors* I described the event, when Dr Walt Starck invited the Maori musicians aboard *El Torito*, his undersea research vessel, for the filming of the final sequence in his Poor Knights documentary "Islands of Friendly Fishes".

It was a fantastic experience then, in 1974; now, when I read the words I wrote, the excitement is still there, for the words give the mental link between music in that echoing sea dome and dolphins. Beneath the water, music had become physical, a column of sound that seemed to touch me as I dived and played: in a cave at night, weightless, surrounded by fishes and music, each in tune with the other. Listening, feeling and swimming, I had been taken back to that other day when I was diving alone in Rikoriko and the whole cave had suddenly filled with dolphins, a circus of graceful forms dancing around me.

Within Rikoriko I'd first met dolphins in their own realm and lost any fear at their presence. In there I first experienced live music while beneath the sea and realized it can be a touch sensation and a pacemaker for water movement. And so my strivings to bring the two experiences together. I like the Maori word "rikoriko". At once it means the sparkle of light and the echo of sound: the dancing of energy waves.

South Harbour jam

10 November 1976: A whale crossed our path and six dolphins briefly rode the bow wave as *Marco Polo* and *Rikoriko* bounced over the northwest swells towards the Poor Knights. The cetaceans were plankton feeding in the same area I had photographed them this time last year: an intensive swirl of activity, gannets, petrels, dolphins and a whale, and huge upheavals whenever the whale sounded. Its spouts were short and diffused and it was heading north.

Our hearts were set on playing music in the huge sea cave but weather conditions forced us to seek the shelter of South Harbour. With us was a television camera team. For the past week they had been interviewing me in various coastal settings, mangroves, headlands and around home, for a documentary on ecosystems; to round things off, a voyage to the Knights, some Headland Haze music and possibly some dolphin experiments.

Steve said he knew it would be hopeless in Rikoriko Cave — the forecast was for southwest winds but nor'westers had blown for days and that creates a short, jobbly sea which runs along the lee side of both islands.

"I had some pretty white Maoris on board," Steve said, nodding at the band, "so I figured it would be calmest in South Harbour."

The two charterboats, both thirty-five-foot, semi-planing wooden hulls with matching diesels, dropped anchor stern to stern, a deft manoeuvre that worked out very nicely; *Rikoriko* anchored with her bow towards Aorangaia; Ross Cotterill nosed *Marco Polo* close to the cliffs of Aorangi. His grapnel dropped in fifteen feet, he backed off, keeping a tension on the warp until within six feet of *Rikoriko*'s stern. From alternate cleats two ropes linked us, acting as springs to keep the boats in moving equilibrium.

The weather closed in during our crossing and yet I'd thought things boded well for us. At our departure Dan and Rose Tana, the Maori elders, had farewelled us fondly at the jetty, and dolphins *had* crossed our path. But the dark clouds rolling out of the south threatened rain. Twenty-four people hated them. Sizing things up the Hazemen left their instruments down in the hold for the time being and very soon they were hauling fish. By the time Janet Pitt had caught three snapper, Robin Solomon was peeling spuds while a pot bubbled on the primus. The snapper were scaled, gutted and cut into chunks, head, tail — the lot.

"They're just like Luaniuans," Brady said to me, "the way they catch fish and eat it."

The least improvement in the weather was enough. Just a lifting of the cloud cover, and the hatch lid was raised. Amplifiers, speakers, mike stands, guitar cases, congas and cymbals. I rigged the 1500-watt generator on the bow hoping it wouldn't be too noisy up there. They were all ready. The television team, Peter the producer, Dave the cameraman and Tony the soundman — "I'll just get a buzz track of that" — had sorted themselves out. They would use *Marco Polo* as a vantage point to film the Hazemen playing on *Rikoriko*'s afterdeck. My tape recorder was ready to roll. Dennis Tana gave an explosive volley on his drums that bounced off the cliffs like cannon balls and then continued as a rattle of raindrops on the stern canopy. By the time it had really set in the boys were rapidly stowing everything below again.

Only a brief wetness but driving in under the canopy it was enough to wreck their gear and electrocute us all. The sky continued to pour over the island ridge. Rain could resume at any moment and our anchorage in the lee of the island prevented us from seeing what was coming. Diving gear started to appear and pretty soon sacks of kina (sea urchins) were being hoisted aboard and eaten on the spot.

The teleteam got us to do a few things for them. Jan and Brady leapt in with me. I taught Malcolm and Jan to use the dorsal fin and we practised dolphin-swimming. I was getting more proficient and found I could do it very well without the one-piece suit, although it heightened the delphinic feeling. For the film team I shot a roll of movie underwater using my own housing and camera, sequences of Jan and Malcolm using the fin and other takes where I held the camera in front of me while I dolphin-swam, the lens alternating from above to below, as I cruised along the cliff edge and circled the boats. We were all enjoying ourselves; the teleteam had material to round off their interview with me, and things flowed on with no dejection, even though music-making was out.

Snug in my tailored wetsuit I'd been making long circles around the harbour when I came back into the stern for a spell. A voice from above said, "If you hang on a minute you'll be able to hear them in the water." I glanced up — the sun was shining, and Headland Haze were tuning in: all their instruments were rigged up again on the stern deck and guitar notes began vibing out and charting the cliff faces. The island responded with a sonic template of its form.

When they started to play it was their own number: "Dance to the Music", a tribal chant in which they encourage everybody to join in percussingly. At water level the music was powerful for twenty yards around the boats. I found I really could dance to the pulsing beat — my swimming muscles were tuned to the Hazemen's, linked by marionette cords of sound, sinew to sinew, and the music took possession of me. It flowed through my body so joyfully that prolonged exertion was sweet and painless. I could move swiftly with less effort than ever in my life — curving in steady arcs. I found myself involuntarily closing my eyes and swimming blind. My mindscreen sparkled with kaleidoscope pictures as my head rose and fell — each time the brightness strobed across my facemask, kinetic images flashed on the red screen of my eyelids, mandalic patterns and fast-moving geodesics like Karla's crochetwork. Vision seemed unnecessary: it was too deep to see the bottom and my eyes were getting such brief glimpses of the air world it felt more pleasant to shut them. Yet I found I could navigate quite easily around the boats.

I experimented. The sound was almost lost once my head was fully immersed. Except beneath the boat hulls or close to them there was little to hear underwater. Even right beneath the band the sound was nowhere near as powerful as it had been beneath *El Torito*'s broad steel hull. I found I could dive down and lie beneath the hull, floating there in a relaxed state, analyzing the sounds I was hearing. Strangely it was very like the sounds of whales — so much of the music was being lost at the interface. There were strange moanings that didn't seem to be any part of the music, wandering at random over the beat. When I raised my head above water they resolved themselves into instrumental sounds of which I was only hearing the lower frequencies. Maybe it's the same with the whales. Without Rikoriko Cave as a sound shell and better sound transmission through the hull we could not expect to attract cetaceans from afar. There was a small chance dolphins cruising around the islands would chance upon us, as they frequently approach Steve's boat, so I remained in the water, ready to play if they arrived. I knew that if I were to get out I would chill rapidly, losing flexibility and energy.

To my surprise I still felt no fatigue — my body just wanted to dance. The freedom it enjoyed in responding to the Headland Haze music was greater than it had ever known: no gravity, no overheating, just a weaving motion that followed all the subtleties of the music. The beat paused. I poked my head out. "This next number's coming straight from the sea. It's from nowhere else," Pete Munro was saying. A new beat — a different rhythm — it was like a second lease of life; a new group of muscles seemed to respond, fresh and ready for fun.

In her journal Jan wrote:
"For the filming Wade tried to teach Malcolm Pitt and me the dolphin-kick. At first I kept holding my breath. With my body curving up and down, I thought the snorkel would fill up. But no water got in and I found I could breathe freely even though my body was going through this wave motion. Once I got into breathing rhythm with the kick it got easier and easier. When I dived down to swim past Wade I found the dolphin-kick was even less effort under water and I just wanted to keep on going and going but to my frustration I had to come

29

up for a breath. Besides, I was getting deeper and my ears started to hurt. How beaut it would be if we didn't have to bother about coming up for a breath.

"Doing the dolphin-kick is so much better to music. I remember that very first time when I was with Wade and we had the tape recorder in a housing between our heads. We swam out for ages side by side doing the dolphin-kick to Pink Floyd. With music you never want to stop. . ."

The highest point of the whole performance was the recording cruise. For the TV camera and sound gear *Marco Polo* upanchored and circled slowly around her musical sister. South Harbour was a huge sound circus, every cliff face and rocky crag pounding out "Straight from the Sea" and we cruised through new versions of the theme refracted and transposed by the island masses. At the centre, the floating loudspeaker, the Hazemen blazing out with all their funky best — a cyclone of energy that set everything rocking with acoustic delight.

It was very late in the day, far later than normal charterboat hours, when the band played "Show me the way to go home, over land or sea or foam. . ." And that was their last number. Good music, I thought, to bring young and old together — a simple melody everybody knows which the Hazemen explored and tossed about playfully, always preserving runs of melody to keep it together.

We all stood there at the end of Tutukaka jetty, a circle of happiness, tinged with sadness. Like the last time when *El Torito* took us all out to play, we didn't want to draw apart and go separate ways after a day's shared adventure. Those who could prolong it came home and we listened to a replay of the tapes.

And that's when they told me I'd been burning around in the water for about forty-five minutes! I must have swum a mile or so and yet I felt no fatigue. Heavy exertion in water, to music, is like dancing gaily at a party all night — or a funeral dance at Laulasi. Rhythmic action to a sonic pace-setter; another step towards mimicry of the dolphin.

Our second interlock
16 November 1976: It was weighing heavily on me, such a long lapse of time since my last contact with dolphins — months of research and writing about them — all based upon that initial cavort, the day we danced. With this ticking over in my mind Jan and I headed the Haines out of Tutukaka Harbour for the Poor Knights this morning — a rare day of good weather in a bad year.

The inshore water was green with plankton. Over to the north of our path a cloud of seabirds hovered, wheeling and plunging into the sea — gannets and petrels working a school of baitfish. We veered over, my heart surging with expectancy. This time in readiness I was wearing my snug-fitting, farmer john wetsuit pants and all my gear was close at hand.

Dolphins leaping. Common dolphins. *Delphinus delphis*. Our bow was flanked with curving shapes. We slowed and headed towards the school activity. Jan took the wheel while I got the cassette player going: something to interest them, the message tape, side two. Cetacean sounds, *Tursiops truncatus*.

30

The boat circling slowly, we cheered and drummed on the hull while through the fibreglass came the sounds of their big cousins. I was scrambling into my gear — the dorsal fin on my weight belt all set to don. The dolphin sounds ended so we switched over to the song of the humpback whale. I slipped in with the movie rig to record anything odd that happened.

While I was in the water and Jan was steering the boat round me in circles she could see the dolphins passing me from all sides and knew that I couldn't keep track of them all, my field of vision being so small wearing a mask. She noticed that the dolphins were coming in and riding on the front of the boat for a while; then they would peel off and go back to feeding where the birds were continually plunging in from great heights. Some would then leave the boat to have a look at me, diving under and around me.

There were dolphins weaving everywhere, around me and below. Silver black bullets in the green haze. I could see only twenty feet because of the plankton bloom but groups of dolphins kept whizzing by within ten feet of me, twisting on their sides, or leaping out of the water and plunging back. When one made a shuddering burst past me, I managed to keep within range of it a while before, just on vanishing point, it whisked around and returned to circle me. From time to time the numbers around me would disperse, and eventually, after about fifteen minutes, contact was lost. Jan pointed to the bird activity a few hundred yards away — the dolphins had all resumed feeding.

I climbed over the stern and we moved nearer to the feeding frenzy — again the dolphins responded to our presence with frolicsome behaviour, leaps and tailslapping. I slipped back in and began diving down and circling about. They seemed to react even more when I descended but I needed more weight on my belt to do it with ease. The damned camera housing was buoyant.

I was surprised at the frequency with which they were defaecating right in front of me. Was it a signal? Dolphins swallow each other's faeces, I had read, but the way the emissions break up in clouds of tiny particles, all they would get is the taste — a form of chemical communication. Did they expect me to respond in the same way? The least I could do was grab at a cloud as if in acceptance of their gesture.

As a dolphin passed me I heard an extra loud whistle and saw a string of bubbles emerge from its hole just afterwards. I took the snorkel from my mouth and screamed "ruuaark" at the bunch as they headed directly at me. They veered slightly and passed at close quarters, turning on their sides to eye me as they zipped by.

This session was much longer and more intensive than the first. Jan had stopped the boat and was drifting nearby. It was full interlock in that no other stimulus than my presence was now keeping the dolphins from their feast. The birds working the fish school were some distance away. How I wished I had some comparisons to reinforce gamesplay, the exchange of body language. After about twenty minutes the numbers around me diminished. For another ten minutes I played with a pair of the largest in the group, while others came and went sporadically. Were these the oldest in the group? They seemed very curious about my performances with the fin. Whenever I put on a good

31

demonstration of swimming and diving there was a noticeable surge of vigour. I had improved greatly since my session with the rock band but I wished they were here. The more I increased my activity the closer the dolphins came.

I yelled out for Jan to get in but first she had to make sure she had a rope over the side to hold the boat. As she got ready there were two dolphins that kept coming over to the boat looking up at her as they turned on their side and then returned to me.

She was just about to enter when they disappeared. They must have satisfied their curiosity and resumed feeding. I got back in the boat at a quarter to eleven and we headed for the Knights. We didn't take the time I was actually in the water with them but the whole period they were in contact with the boat was forty minutes.

About two miles from the islands a string of leaping dolphins passed us on a parallel and opposite course. Careering along at top speed in a series of arcs like a rippling rope, they took no notice of us. I have often seen this leap-swim progression when schoolfish are about and on all such occasions the dolphins have ignored the boat, intent on their rapid passage.

During the day we hunted for signs of paper nautilus shells, and tested the underwater loudspeaker again. This time I'd filled the housing with thin brake-fluid oil retained by a rubber diaphragm. It worked about as well as the speaker had, pressed against the boat interior, but it was only half the size so the sound transfer seemed to be quite good. At least it would be a pressure-proof component for the submersible tape replay unit my friend Allan Kircher had built me, slicing the end off an old scuba tank and fitting it with a three-quarter-inch plexiglass port.

In Rikoriko Cave we sat and listened to the song of the humpback whale. In that huge echo chamber even the twelve-volt car stereo could set the echoes ringing. The deep notes were most effective in producing resonant echoes that filled the island interior with sound colour.

At the entrance a gannet plunged into the interface between light and dark to bob up with a tiny maomao in its beak. Swallows flitted across the light and bird calls wafted in from the surrounding cliffs to blend with the whale's song. I was hopeful we could set up another rock music session in this cave, playing the whale songs for the Hazemen to emulate.

Homeward bound we were skittering over the crests of a rising easterly sea twelve miles out when we saw birds working near the Pinnacles. Closer in dolphin fins appeared. I'd left my wetsuit on for the return journey, just in case another opportunity arose. It was much quicker this time to approach the dolphins. Our tape was transmitting the humpback song and in no time we were with the nomads again. Out there the water was oceanic blue and the countershading of their bodies looked quite startling against the backdrop.

With the whale sounds playing we approached and I leapt in. One dolphin sprang out and thwacked the water with its tail as he re-entered. He seemed excited at what he heard. There was a baby with its mother. The mother leapt out of the water and there beside her in mid-air was the baby. Only about twenty-four inches long, a miniature of its parent.

It was incredible to think that such a tiny thing could not only keep up to the speed of its mother, swerve and dive in perfect time, but it could leap out of the water at the same level as its mother too. It seemed to be glued in place by two invisible rods. Its position beside her never altered a fraction as far as I could see.

Jan was circling me in the water with the boat, yelling over and over "Too much! Too much!" as she watched the activity around me and knew I must be out of my mind. From the boat she had a much better view of how many dolphins there were. She could see them circling me at times when I couldn't. She was not sure whether it was the same ones that kept going back to the feeding frenzy and then returning to circle me or ride on the bow wave or whether they were different dolphins each time.

In the end there was no need to keep the motor going to attract them. They were coming in anyway and seemed very curious about my dorsal fin. Down below I found the schoolfish activity was frenetic: a white line of foam zipped across the surface hotly pursued by birds and crisscrossed by dolphin fins. The hunters seemed to be divided between me and their quarry. I felt honoured at the attention they gave but was not surprised when they hurtled back towards the melee only to return for another series of circuits.

After fifteen minutes of such antics I left them to it. I felt I was encroaching. What creature would abandon a high feast to play games as they had done? Schoolfish activity has been very lean this season with all the lousy weather and low temperatures (only 15 degrees C. inshore this week). I was glad the dolphins were having such a picnic.

Why didn't they snap up the odd seabird? From below I could see webbed feet and feathers all over the surfaces — sitting target for a poultry-minded dolphin. But I never saw any attacks, drifting feathers or injured birds. Maybe the fish herders have a partnership. Nor is it likely that a common dolphin could swallow a seabird.

In her excitement Jan forgot to time this interlock but it was longer and much more intensive than the morning's one.

Interlock III

22 November 1976: One week later we met the dolphins again. This time Jan had her first experience of playing with them, and Claude our neighbour too. Another day of calm, a brief break in the weather following a southeast blow, we set out for the offshore islands, hopeful that the stormy weather might have brought the nautilus in. The ocean seemed deserted — there were no signs of activity until we were within three miles of the Knights. Then to the north of our course we sighted gannets wheeling and plummeting. We homed on dolphin fins. Soon they were gambolling around our bow. While the boat circled I leapt over wearing the dolphin fin. The tape was playing dolphin sounds (*Tursiops*) at half normal speed, decreasing exponentially until they were as slow as human vocalisations. Once I was accepted, Claude joined me. We tried to stay together in a pair like the dolphins but it was difficult to match their synchronised swimming. For a while we tried towing each other with a special yoke arrangement in hope that the dolphins might follow suit, giving us a high speed ride. But we have not yet won such acceptance and they divided their interest between us and the schoolfish activity in the vicinity.

By now the plankton cycle had progressed from the initial bloom of tiny plants to the animal stage: mauve jellyfishes, translucent, wriggling larval fishes and pink krill, all heading into the gentle current which, at this distance offshore, flows warm from the north. Somewhere beyond the verge of vision kingfish, kahawai and sprats would be raiding each other and the plankton.

With my Pentax camera and 35mm lens I was trying to get pictures of the group in hope that we might find body marks and scratches from which to recognise them in future encounters. The concentration on taking photos wrecked my relationship with the dolphins. (It was much more demanding than the super 8 movie rig which is automatic and doesn't even need to be sighted.) Squinting through the viewfinder and adjusting the aperture I lost the spontaneity of play and failed to respond to many of the cues they offered, the body language gestures which, if I took the trouble to imitate, heightened their excitement and demonstrativeness.

Claude decided to slip on his aqualung. By this time the boat was playing moog music which Ian Briggs had sent me because he thought it simulated cetacean sounds. Perhaps because of my camera the dolphins' attention had turned more towards the boat than me. As it cruised around slowly I could see Claude forty feet below and 300 feet above the seabed, the centre of a dolphin circus. Later he told me he agreed about the faeces signal. It was a definite gesture he felt. From down there he had a three-dimensional uninterrupted view of the situation compared with a surface-oriented snorkeler. He saw two dolphins peel off from bow-riding and spiral down to his level. At ten and thirteen feet distances respectively they both released faecal clouds and rejoined the group.

Claude and I were exhausted after forty-five minutes' frenzied activity. We climbed out. The dolphins resumed feeding nearby. We were adrift with the music playing and Jan was getting into her gear when over the calm sea came what seemed to be the entire tribe — some thirty or more dolphins, lolling about slowly in groups, a playful indirect movement towards the boat about which they sported, occasionally lifting their heads out of the water briefly.

Jan hurried into her gear and leapt in. They were immediately all around her. She didn't know how many there were altogether but was mainly conscious of a group of five that stayed with her.

She dived down and dolphin-kicked. Straight away they mimicked her with exaggerated movements. She couldn't believe her eyes. This was the first time she'd been in the water with dolphins. Surfacing, she stuttered with excitement to us in the boat and then took a deep breath and dived down. Again she did the dolphin-kick and again they responded with an exaggerated version. Round and round they circled. There were two pairs and a single one. Every time it was the loner, perhaps lacking a mate, that came closest. She extended her arm and it seemed only a foot away from her outstretched fingers.

The dolphin wagged his head at her and seemed to want her to dive deep and follow his antics. She had to go up for a breath for the next dive. She could see them faintly far below, their white undersides flashing as they turned, so she knew they were still there. As she dived again the five dolphins came hurtling up from the depths like five spaceships taking off, with all their noses pointed straight at her. It was a cylinder of dolphins. They were close together, almost touching it seemed. Just before they reached her they peeled off. The pairs reformed and the loner spun around her very close, defaecating as he swept past with his exaggerated dolphin-kick and wagging head. She rolled over and over. One couple slapped each other with their fins and let out a shower of faeces as they streamed past her. They seemed to want her to copy them. She felt they were disappointed because she had to keep breaking off for air and was unable to dive deep. So it went on for half an hour; every time she descended they would come rushing up vertically to frolic around her.

These dolphins came in of their own accord. The boat was not running to attract them. When they arrived the music was playing and nobody was in the water. That lone dolphin sticks in her mind very clearly. He seemed to want her to be his playmate and she will never forget looking into his eye as he made his slow, close passes. "It was a friendly intelligent look; understanding, playful and wise all at once." All the time she was conscious of other dolphins circling at a distance. Towards the end of her dive she played with the dolphins just under the bow of the boat so we could see what was going on. Then she began to feel seasick and it impaired her performance — most frustrating for her! All she had wanted to do was forget everything and swim away with the dolphins, copying all their actions.

Afterwards it seemed like a dream. Jan wrote in her journal: "I'd listened to others raving about their experiences but hadn't really believed them — I used to think silently to myself that they were exaggerating because they were excited. But honestly — this was no dream — it was *very real* and I feel humble that I was able to have such an experience during my lifetime.

"Thinking it over I feel certain that when Wade is in the water with the camera in his hands they are unsure of him with the strange object he keeps pointing at them. They have every reason not to trust humans and Wade's interlocks with dolphins seem much better if he doesn't carry anything. For the most part of their dive the dolphins played with the boys but when Wade swam back to the boat for his camera they became suspicious of him."

When Jan got out I decided to vary our plan with some boat manoeuvring games. I found the dolphins grew excited when I did crazy things with the boat; figure eight patterns, sudden bursts of speed and wake crossing. While some rode the bow wave others enjoyed surfing the wave curling apart from our stern. At 1500 rpm the boat was only semi-planing and the wake reached maximum size. On either side a pair of dolphins could be seen through the curve of the wave.

I did tests to find the optimum speed for bowriding. For lengthy sessions 2000 rpm was best but they showed frenzied excitement if I speeded up for a short while. At 3000 rpm if I manoeuvred around in their general vicinity they came flashing in like comets, hit the bow wave at a tangent and ricocheted off at high speed. For brief bursts they would have been doing at least 25 mph and clearly enjoyed such tactics.

When Claude lay on the bow and leaned over close to the water yelling and thumping the boat they showed obvious delight and more dolphins rode the bow wave than at any other time. They came rushing over and turning on their sides, looked up at Claude. He managed to touch a dorsal fin but felt that this frightened the dolphin. He recognised an individual from the regular scratch marks on its back as one we'd been diving with earlier. I noticed another with an oval white marking in front of its dorsal: Grill Patch and White Patch.

I gained the impression that some were reluctant to play except at peak interlock periods. These were large animals and would hang back on the fringe of the group while others frolicked with us. Perhaps the oldsters were trying to get the group's attention back on to the job at hand: herding the baitfish. I also wondered whether they might not be controlling the whole situation by actually shepherding the plankton animals and so attracting baitfish to their vicinity. Earlier, while we were drifting south, it seemed strange how they concentrated their activity around us, as did all the diving birds. Baitfish and krill normally whirl about everywhere, a madcap pursuit and flight, whereas this situation seemed to include the boat on its perimeter. Further observation could lead to some surprising discoveries.

Eventually our manoeuvres brought us close to Rikoriko Cave. A mile off Aorangi we decided to run there in the hope that the dolphins might accompany us. For a time they did but as we neared the cliff faces, now crimson with pohutukawa blossom, we looked back. The birds and dolphins were still working in the same area.

In the cave we waited, music playing, but no audience arrived. We donned lungs and roamed the cave underwater. Eighty feet down I checked the music range — not a sound — it took too long for my bubbles to reach the surface for silence to intervene between breaths.

The nautilus are late this season. On our return journey we had another brief dolphin encounter but could not spare the fuel to prolong the game. At the wharf I met Peter Harper, the seabird expert, on his way to spend a week on Aorangi continuing his research. He invited me to spend a night ashore with the scientists when they were checking the night landings of the petrels.

Meeting White Patch again

Our experiments were shaping themselves. Variations were being introduced by random factors that sneaked into our world.

Journal, 3 December 1976: Today, when we got over to Tutukaka, the boat launched and ready to run, we tested the sound gear only to find the cetacean message tape was not on board and that the twelve-volt battery was dead flat. Coping with the logistics of these dolphin trips is always just on the verge of our capacity. We would not intentionally go without the message tape as our primary objective is to establish interlock and whether the dolphins get the message or not, it puts us in the right mood.

So I felt a bit depressed as we headed out — the weather didn't look as if it would hold — a blackening of the sky from the west and the wind rising from the same direction.

Midway we checked out a mixed flock of white fronted and black petrels, but there were no gannets and no dolphins. Then two miles off the Knights we saw a storm of white flakes wheeling above the sea — and homed on gannets and dolphins. They rode our bow wave a while but would not stay there when we circled in the boat. Our best technique for establishing a trusting relationship in the water, this appears to work better when we play the message tape to heighten interest in the boat. The dolphins didn't seem to want to stay around much — more intent on schoolfish in the vicinity.

Wearing both dorsal and handfins, I slipped in. The boat circled. No message tape. Whenever the bow crossed their path the dolphins briefly rode the wave. Jan stopped the boat at some distance. A dolphin appeared and inspected me briefly. I wondered — will he go and tell the others about my weird silhouette? But the ocean around me was empty, a small sphere of fifteen feet visibility, a green haze of micro plankton. Back aboard we pursued the dolphins. I leapt in again. Jan stopped the boat and watched. She saw about twenty dolphins approach me. When I dived down they all sounded after me and whisked away underwater. Despite my new appendages I could not follow. Were they testing my speed? We chased them again and the pattern was repeated exactly. While the boat drifted silently the dolphins approached me. I dived, they dived after me and disappeared. Viewed from the boat and in the water, the pattern was very clear.

We decided to wait and see if they would return. The wind had fallen and we drifted towards the Sugarloaf for fifteen minutes, watching the gannets and petrels working out to the east.

Six minutes at full speed and we rejoined the dolphins. This time I leapt in wearing an aqualung, in hope of getting some recognition photos. To my delight I saw White Patch! I managed to snap a few photos but with fast-moving dolphins the aqualung tank makes it hard to turn fast enough to maintain visual contact. As I hung there in the plankton soup the thought came to me: for these experiments we need more people — a bigger boat. Alone in the sea a man is hopelessly inadequate to interest dolphins; he is too clumsy and slow and his senses are too restricted to respond. We need gamesplayers, music, body language — everything we can muster to arouse their interest in man. In aquariums trainers do it with coercion and reward; in the wild interlock is its own reward.

During our lunch break the dolphins came around the drifting boat, and played for a while. Jan frantically scrambled into her gear but we failed to arouse interest and they left.

We followed them north to an area off Tawhiti Rahi, the northern Knight. A choppy northwest wind was rising when we fell in with a huge band of dorsal fins. This time it was Jan's turn.

She leapt in with the thought in mind to meet White Patch again while wearing the dorsal fin. This was a really big group of dolphins but by the time she was in, most of them had left to go on feeding. Five stayed close while a few others circled on the outskirts of vision. Amongst them was a mother and baby who inspected her three or four times then went away to join the rest.

Since she was on the surface, the five that stayed were beneath her and tilted their noses up to scrutinise her. To her delight one of them was White Patch — an unmistakable white circle just behind his blowhole and in front of the dorsal fin. It resembled a watermark and she wondered how he came to get it there. Maybe dolphins have birthmarks like us. She yelled to me that she had seen White Patch.

Like her very first interlock there was a lone one that came closest but not as near as that first day. She twirled round to keep him in vision as he circled. He may have thought she was trying to entertain him because he did a corkscrew too. When she let out a yell he gave a spurt of speed. Whenever she descended he came to meet her from below. The others did too but not so close, passing about ten feet away. She wondered if it was that same loner but she had nothing to identify him by, except that he seemed the same size.

Obviously they were much more interested in her when she dived down than when she just stayed on the surface. As she said after, "I don't think you would have much of an interlock if you didn't make the effort and dive down. Maybe they can examine us better acoustically away from the surface."

The interlock lasted ten minutes. The wind had come up and it was getting very rough. We stowed all the gear very carefully and bucketed off home.

As the boat skittered towards the coast I had time to think things over. White Patch. It now seems likely we have been meeting the same group of dolphins. Close study of individual markings will enable us to recognise each group and to determine whether we are building up a relationship through time.

The handfins. Trying them out for the first time amidst dolphins I really discovered how to use them. They control turns to left or right and enable the dolphins to descend or rise.

The fish has a rudder for turns. So has Walt Starck's submarine, but the dolphin doesn't need one. His flippers enable him to turn with incredible rapidity about the fulcrum of his dorsal — he just points both limbs in the direction he wants to turn and zowee, he pivots like a jet boat. His body and tail fluke are transfused with a flowing S-bend of energy, but it is the flippers which initiate the manoeuvre, deflecting him up or down, firing him completely out of the water in a high speed leap or corkscrewing down into the planktonic dark.

Murky water

8 December 1976: Visual contact is important. Today's murky conditions emphasized this lesson dramatically. Off the Sugarloaf we met the dolphins. For ten minutes they gambolled around the boat as it circled, playing the message tape. Since we now suspect we may be meeting the same group each time we have decided to use a cowbell to establish our own acoustic identity on every encounter. Unlike our previous

38

soundless expedition we had no trouble today interesting the dolphins in the boat. Everything looked good and I was eager to get some movie footage while Jan swam among them wearing the dorsal fin. I prepared the anchor rope as a lifeline so we would not lose the boat. Jan slowed gradually and switched the motor off. As we glided to a halt she rang the cowbell. The dolphins all turned and headed towards us. We began yelling, shouting, pounding the hull and bell ringing. The message tape was playing "Echoes" when I slipped in. Yuck — the sea was opaque. Topside it had looked oceanic blue but microscopic plankton screened all light beyond a hazy ten feet. I saw nothing.

After four days of calm sunny weather the plant-plankton was in full bloom. Even my hand at arm's length was slightly obscured by particles. From the boat Jan watched the dolphins circle me. Although I could hear their echo-location whistles, my eyes gave me no help at all.

Three times we repeated our attempt to establish interlock. Each time Jan hovered nearby and saw the dolphins surround me. When I called to her, "Come over", they took up position on the bow. I would take several deep breaths and dive to twenty feet where I hovered vertically, peering through the gloom for a glimpse of the whistling forms weaving around me. Once I caught sight of two bodies from the side, and suspect one of them may have been White Patch. In the murk it seemed body language was impossible and interlock could not develop beyond the initial phases. Jan had better luck, perhaps because by then we had established more trust.

After my third dive it was her turn. As soon as she descended I stopped the boat. We had sounds of the humpback whale playing on the tape. She wore the dorsal fin and had a cowbell in her hand. As she dived there were dolphins circling, swimming crisscross under her and as they rose for a breath they would pass by quite close before they broke the surface. They were all round the boat too. When she came up for air she lost sight of them, the water was so dirty with little particles. I yelled from the boat that they were still around her.

She dived again and sure enough, back they came. The dolphins below her were turning on their sides obviously trying to inspect her. All round she could hear high-pitched sounds from dolphins she couldn't see.

One large dolphin made several passes close to her. She turned to keep it in sight as it circled. The instant she rang the bell it slowed almost to a stop, obviously looking at her. It must have heard the bell. She stretched out her flipper and it was only another two feet from the blade.

She made a few more dives trying to see if she could recognise any individuals from other interlocks. The only time she could see them clearly was when they were passing on the same level. She couldn't see if White Patch was there because they were too far down for her to pick out any markings on their backs in the dirty water. It was hopeless to tell if they were mimicking her because they got out of sight too quickly in the murk.

All of a sudden they disappeared and she climbed back into the boat. They had stayed around five minutes this time. We followed after them again. They were on the move all the time continually feeding and covering a lot of ground. As soon as we caught up with them they immediately left off feeding to play on the bow. Jan drove while I lay over the bow, my leg hooked in the forehatch to prevent myself falling in. They seemed to enjoy that. I was excitedly ringing the bell and thumping the hull. I touched a medium-sized one and it came back. There was no sign of White Patch.

This went on for four minutes, then Jan leapt in for her second dive. I stopped the boat. Humpback whale sounds were echoing through the hull. She wore the dorsal fin and took the bell in again, alternately ringing it above the surface and below.

On this dive they didn't come as close; most of the time Jan heard their sonar squeals but couldn't see them at all. There was a pair that came past about ten feet away, one smaller than the other. She wondered if it were a mother and child or just a mating pair in which one was much younger. They stuck very close together.

This pair, along with a few others, made six to seven passes and then suddenly left. She recognised the dolphin I call Grill Patch amongst that group.

On her third dive when Jan got in, again wearing the dorsal fin and taking the bell, she dived three or four times and each time they circled examining her. One turned over, its belly facing upwards. This time they seemed more interested in the boat. She was startled when a big one came sweeping up behind her. She flinched briefly as it hurtled on its way. It had come from the direction of the boat. She wondered if it was the same one that had come very close on her first dive.

We were cruising along with the usual frisk of dolphins on the bow. The main group were feeding at some distance. Suddenly, as if summoned by a call, the bow riders all vanished. We saw no sign of them surfacing to breathe. We waited, searching the slight swells. Petrels paddled up close to our stern hopefully, dipping their heads regularly to see if there were any shrimps about. The dolphins must have rejoined the feeding group at high speed.

We ran over to the Pinnacles to check the cave for paper nautilus, the pelagic octopus. Once they enter such a large enclosure it seems they are trapped, unable to find the entrance, or afraid to venture out where kingfish and gannets await them. But this year we were not in luck. Outside the cave I reasoned: there's only one area we cannot scan for dolphins from here — between the Pinnacles and the Knights. . . Halfway across we came upon a flock of petrels feeding. No gannets. But in their midst were the dolphins, a large group of around a hundred. One leapt out and turned on its stomach in mid-air to re-enter backwards. Jan said she had seen a gesture like this underwater.

We attempted to engage their attention but they were feeding very actively so we decided to mind our manners and leave them to it. Circling around we began to study all their dorsal fins closely. Increasingly we became aware that every individual's dorsal was distinctively marked. There were the obvious variations caused by injury or old age. Stumpfin had lost the tip of his dorsal, which projected in a series of serrations. Others had ragged trailing edges — several nicks, possibly the result of cavitation and age. Then the fins themselves took on distinctive features. There were variations in shape: tall, squat, broad, narrow. On the fins there were white patches which could be sorted into four main categories: a narrow vertical band; a low sickle-shape patch; a complete coverage, or total absence. With experience we felt sure it would be possible to remember every individual, just as we recall human faces. As a Chinese friend once confided in me in a moment of intimacy: "There's one problem I have with Europeans — you all look the same."

At the end of the day, after some fast circuits and vigorous bow-riding games, we stopped and drifted. The tape was playing humpback whale songs. The dolphins came very close to the hull and for a time they were all twisting, turning and cavorting around it as if curious about the sound. Then one gave a vigorous spurt off the bow and they all vanished.

Homeward thoughts: The murky water has been our teacher. Unable to recognise individuals underwater we concentrated our attention on dorsal fins. Most significantly, the boat observer often saw dolphins circling the diver within fifteen feet but on many occasions the diver was quite unaware of their presence, apart from their whistles. Hence it seems they are scanning us by sonar in this dirty water and not bothering to establish visual contact.

Rough seas

13 December 1976: Such is our eagerness to join the dolphins, we put to sea at every opportunity. Sometimes the conditions are unfavourable. Interlock demands calm seas. Today we struck a strong southeast swell, decaying from a recent storm, with a stiff northwest wind running across it. Two miles out among a flock of petrels we sighted a pair of dolphins, but couldn't locate the group in rough water.

We found a sheltered anchorage in Nursery Cove so I took pictures of Jan wearing the dolphin fins for an article in *Listener*. She found a freshly shed nautilus shell, which suggested only a sporadic spawning took place this spring.

The pohutukawas, in full bloom on the cliffs, were interesting to explore with the telephoto lens. Then I examined the roof of Rikoriko Cave with it, zooming in on the delicate ferns clinging up there and the multihued patches of slime and lichen on the rearmost walls.

Always hopeful of another encounter with dolphins in the cave, we had the message tape playing when *Matira* came in, Fred Coterill's charter boat. The voices of whales echoing in there must have sounded odd, but those on board thought it was music.

"Turn it up and we'll have a cup of tea."

"It's whales, Fred."

"Could have fooled me."

Within the cave the echoing voices of the whales were at their best, because the whales pause long enough to give each echo its full range.

On our return we met the dolphins in the usual area, just abeam the Pinnacles, on a course for Tutukaka. But the seas were too rough for us to do more than make a circle, ringing the cowbell as a recognition signal.

Jan noticed they were bow-riding much deeper in these conditions, probably to avoid the plunging hull. Leaping from a wave crest a dolphin seems to be the very embodiment of mind and energy; directed force, perfect timing, joy at living: an act devoid of purpose.

Testing the big speaker
27 December 1976: Two days after Christmas the sea is alive with pleasure craft. Schoolfish activity is nil. Acres of petrels rock on oily swells, asleep, their heads tucked beneath wings. Around the Sugarloaf a huge carpet of gannets rests on the sea. No dolphins.

After prolonged and vigorous offshore winds and sunny conditions it seems all the nutrients have been used up. The water is clear and bare. We seem to get one good boat day a week, a calm between weather cycles.

We now have a twelve-inch speaker mounted in the bow. I wanted to see what range its sound output would have when focused through the hull by a bell-shaped washing-machine bowl. Anchored off Blue Maomao Archway I found I could hear the speaker within a fifteen-foot radius of the boat. Then I dropped to the bottom. To my surprise I could still hear it clearly at fifty feet — the sound must be reflected from the rocky bottom.

Dance to the music
11 December 1976: What passed through their minds as they hung there, ten feet from the stern, three dolphins huddled together apparently listening to Eric playing his flute?

We didn't think we were going to see the dolphins at all today although our hopes had been high when Jan and I set out, with four friends, to meet them on a smoky hot morning. Eric brought his flute and tenor sax along and Graham Mosen was eager to dive with the dolphins. With Val and Sharon aboard we were three sets of humans, a pleasant group with which to establish interlock.

The sea was a desert — bird activity nil. A long swell was flexing toward the coast even after a period of strong easterlies. Further south a cold storm must have stirred the Pacific sea mightily. It was so rough off South Harbour I paused before taking the boat through the arch- way. The swells heaving through the tunnel were almost touching the roof. We bounced through Labrid Channel into a pleasant lee, cruising slowly along the western cliffs of Aorangi enjoying the bellbird calls and the scarlet pohutukawa, now beginning to shed their petals, and just beginning to bloom over on the mainland coast. The rock lilies have finished flowering. I told the Poor Knights virgins to watch Serpent Rock as we approached Rikoriko Cave. Then swinging hard on the wheel we entered the huge black dome at full speed, cut the engine and glided to silence.

Delighted we stood there drinking it in, the echochamber alive with wave play, the delicate ferns on the roof overhead, the gannets circling at the entrance. I played the song of the humpback whale to show the others how the cave echoes fill the whale songs out as if they were intended for such spaces.

Then Eric began to play. The echoes were superb and we checked them right through the cave. Midway in there was a nice balance — not too dark for a boat audience and a rich blend of vibrations. Some day we must have a dolphin/human Woodstock in this spot. Our eyes kept turning out of the entrance — if only dolphins could hear this. What would they think of us then?

On Landing Bay Pinnacle we anchored for a scuba dive and I took pictures of Jan swimming with dolphin fin and flippers. She made a dive down the Pinnacle and found a very rare shell *Xenophalium royanum* which we decided would be safer if we put it out in deeper water.

By 3 o'clock we were complete — it was early, yet something tugged me to go. All day the sky had been bare of gannets except for lone birds that patrol the cliff edges and though we kept scanning the sea, not a fin showed.

Two miles on our home-run they exploded from the sea around us — rocketing out and cleaving the swells like salvoes of gunfire. We laughed and yelled as the boat circled. We rigged the tape to play dolphin sounds and Eric got his flute together. Then it started. At the outset about thirty dolphins sported with us. They seemed curious about the flute — but gradually their numbers dwindled and we saw the main school hovering nearby, probably herding their fish to and fro. Three that remained kept curving in and veering on their sides to look at the bow-watchers.

Jan leapt in wondering if she would recognise some of our playmates from previous interlocks. This time we had forgotten the cowbell and she couldn't wear the dorsal fin because it was broken. We try to keep a pattern so it is easy for the dolphins to know that we are the same people each time. But somehow we wouldn't have wanted to rattle a cowbell with Eric there playing the flute.

As she dived down, in they came — all in pairs — six of them and did a half circle round her before going up to the surface. Then they dived again, down and around following the same patterns as they have on other interlocks. I was still circling quietly in the boat and they were moving from the boat to swim around her — sometimes eight, sometimes six and sometimes a few more but she lost count. She was delighted to see Stumpfin: he was one of the dolphins that came in close this time to ten feet approximately. On previous occasions he has stayed with the group and not come close. There was another one with a nasty gash about six inches long down his right side that had healed, leaving a ridge of scar tissue: Sidescar should be easy to recognise again.

There was one in the group that always circled a bit closer and reacted most to her gyrations. She wondered if it was because she always singles out the closest to focus attention on. When she dolphin-kicks the one she is looking at immediately initiates an exaggerated dolphin-swim. She wondered too if this was the same loner that had come closer on other dives. He or she is a beautiful dolphin, about medium size with no marks or blemishes to identify it. On its dorsal fin it has a very regular white triangle so we have named it Even Patch. She can't say whether or not it *is* the same one but it seems strange that one always comes in

43

closer than the rest and reacts to our playfulness more than the others. But then we can't tell if some of the others are reacting too because it's impossible to keep an eye on them all. It's usually the closest one that we observe most. And for Jan this one has always been an extremely handsome mammal reminding her of a fresh and beautiful young girl. We'd love to know whether it is male or female.

I stopped the motor and Graham leapt in. The dolphins stayed around just on the very edge of perception (twenty feet visibility). We wanted badly for Graham to have them sweep past him so he could experience the thrill of seeing them close underwater. Jan dived down several times and each dive she caught a glimpse of them coming in but they never ventured any closer than twenty feet.

After a while they didn't come round us at all, but as we hung off the stern someone said, "They are coming back." But they didn't come near the divers in the water. They stayed off the opposite side of the boat where Eric was playing. While in the water Jan wanted to see how well she could hear the flute. She lay very still on the surface with her ears under, just like the dolphins. She could hear very well. If she moved the slopping of the water round her head cut the flute out. No wonder they hover in this peculiar manner essential for hearing above-water sounds.

I yelled for the divers to stick with the boat as it was drifting out of range. As they swam up to the bow the dolphins moved a bit further afield. This made Jan decide to get out and leave it to the flute. She felt pretty sure that they were more nervous when there were two of them in the water, perhaps more of a threat, and they kept further away. As she climbed out, Sharon, her face all animated said, "I touched one, Jan." She had been leaning over the bow.

Just about the whole time we were there, three dolphins hovered fifty yards away, sometimes coming closer. They seemed very interested in the flute.

Every time the boat started up to follow the main group these three flashed in to ride on the bow. Sometimes we didn't know they had been closeby. Eventually the dolphins all rejoined the main group still fishing vigorously only a short distance away.

Afterwards Eric remarked, "They didn't seem to show much interest."

Then it hit me. Had he realized that the hovering dolphins *were* listening to him, how would this feedback have affected his performance?

A new group

2 January 1977: With more powerful sound gear we were keen to meet the dolphins again. When at last we did make contact we found that our earlier friends, the group with White Patch and Grill Patch and Stumpfin, had moved on. Establishing contact with a second group, we had to start afresh and learn all over again to recognise individuals. And from their reactions it seems the dolphins had to do the same.

Robin Solomon and Brady were with us this day. We met the dolphins about halfway to the Knights. With the big twelve-inch speaker playing we circled in the boat until we seemed to have a large number interested. They were feeding on schoolfish but left off to play with the boat. I stopped the motor while Jan finished getting her gear on. Things looked good because even though the boat wasn't moving the dolphins were still around. They seemed to be interested in the sound from the loud stereo. Jan leapt in with the dolphin fin on. We had been ringing the cowbell over the side, with Brady hanging over the bow for a close look.

The dolphins were everywhere around Jan, under and alongside. She dived repeatedly and each time they dived down and past her. After a while only seven were left and they were interested in her. She had plenty of time to have a good look at them because they were slowing down when they passed, examining her closely in return. She was trying desperately to see if she could recognise dolphins from previous inter-locks. The visibility was fifteen to twenty feet and these seven dolphins were coming to within ten feet moving slowly, scrutinizing her very carefully. These were a different bunch — there was not one she had seen before.

Each interlock has been different and these dolphins were not trying to mimic her or do the dolphin-kick in an exaggerated way as others had before — nor did they give the feeling they were overly excited. They just seemed immensely curious as if they had never seen anything quite like Jan. This went on for about five minutes and then they went off suddenly to catch up with the others and resume their fishing.

Jan got out and we raced after them, each time circling until they were on the bow and then stopping before Jan got in. They only had a couple of looks and then went on their way again. Feeding was very intensive now. We were near the Sugarloaf. Jan got in and out about four times and the last time we were heading towards Auckland, south of the Pinnacles and they again made a couple of passes and went on with their feeding as if to say: "It's that *same* thing again. We've seen her before and she can't do much, can't even keep up with us. Not worth giving up valuable feeding time over."

We decided to call it a day and go over for a dive at the Knights. We were sure these dolphins were not any we had dived with before.

In Rikoriko Cave a tiny yacht was moored. Tom paddled over in his tractor tube inflatable. New Year's Eve, he told us, he'd sailed out to the Knights by moonlight. Dolphins surrounded him most of the way across. With luminous particles flowing over their bodies they looked like streaking comets.

Moonlit Knights

6 January 1977: Tom's story did it. On Thursday night the moon was full. Just on dusk about nine o'clock we raced eastwards through the harbour entrance. We had Bryan, Huia and Dennis with us, and high hopes of a dolphin meeting.

It was the most exquisite night of the summer, a warm wind, flat calm sea and the moon, newly risen, was hiding behind a line of horizon cloud a little to the south of the Poor Knights. As we zoomed out over the sea a huge hole appeared in the clouds with a star in the centre. The moon made a shimmering track on the sea and we sped along its path feeling really exhilarated. Looking back to the mainland, along the hills, the sky was red with the sinking sun. Then the moon found the cloud window. Such moments are unique. We were all feeling so fantastic and it was contagious. We made huge circles in the ocean with the boat and figure eight patterns and then just drifted with the motor off, hoping like anything that the dolphins would come along. To induce the right mood we played dolphin and whale sounds on the stereo while we drifted. Even at that hour seabirds were swooping low like giant moths. Jan supposed they wouldn't bother roosting when it was moonlight because they could see just as well as in daytime. We waited for a long time but no dolphins showed, to our great disappointment.

Not to worry, we will try again.

We sped on towards the Knights. We would have a dive in Rikoriko Cave and maybe with any luck the dolphins might come to us there. As we approached the Knights the great cliffs towered above us silhouetted in the moonlight, the pohutukawa trees making magnificent etchings against the sky.

Into Rikoriko Cave we zoomed in pitch blackness until our eyes became adjusted to the dark. We had only one torch so Jan, Bryan and I took turns to dive. We had the stereo going all the time echoing round the cave.

Inky blackness met Jan's eyes and a moment of uneasiness as sinking down the torchlight picked up nothing but water. Soon the beam settled on the bottom and she felt relieved at the sight of something familiar. The encrusting life on the rocks lit up by torchlight was much more beautiful than by day: every brillant gemstone imaginable; tiny emerald and ruby trees and demoiselles of gleaming opal quivering in each crevice.

Pink maomao with their night-time blotched bodies were resting peacefully until disturbed and they would swim off all groggy as if hardly awake. The night-time predators were out: a large yellow moray eel waved out at her from a hole; a scorpionfish sitting ready on the rocks for any crab that scuttled by — his skin bright orange and red in the torchlight. There were snakelike brittle stars everywhere with their arms twined round the rocks and encrusting life or slithering over the white sand of the cave floor. Elaborate pieces of sculpture wobbled across the sand on the backs of tenant hermit crabs.

As she explored the darkness Jan was suddenly conscious of music in her ears. She must have reached a point directly under the boat where it was focused. She sat there for a while and listened, enjoying the sensation. It was incredible down there alone in such splendour, miles from nowhere. It made her feel very reverent and special until she almost choked with emotion.

When Jan got out we had ham sandwiches, chocolate and hot coffee. At 2 am we up-anchored.

Outside the cave we were surprised to find the wind had come up and it was now quite rough. We stowed everything securely and set off. The boat had turned into a submarine; as we sped across the top of the waves great slashes of spray drenched us. We felt so crazy speeding across the ocean on a choppy night in the moonlight, heading towards the winking light on Tutukaka headland. Huia said, "Put your head back Jan, and look at the land. It makes you feel like flying." Our laughter was snatched back and away on the wind.

Entering the harbour, we had to edge our way through hundreds of holidaymakers' boats moored for the night. The moon had gone behind clouds so we left the boat tied up and went home to a hot bath and bed for a few hours.

The next day we went over to get the boat and couldn't believe the human faeces and scum coating the entire hull below the waterline. We took her out and gave her a good scrub down. Tutukaka Harbour must be the foulest place at Christmas with hundreds of boats all shitting into the harbour. You would think they would enforce holding tanks with waste removal trucks coming down and pumping them out as they do in other countries. There were little kids playing in the water on the boat ramp; people complain that there are tummy bugs going round. No wonder.

Even though we didn't meet the dolphins we wouldn't have missed that night for anything. It would never be the same. We will do it again and it will be different in another special way. And maybe there will be dolphins next time.

The tuna boat

17 January 1977: One perfect Monday our ute pulled up alongside Grant and Claire at the Tutukaka store.

"Would you like to come to the Knights?"

"Would we what!"

The sea was oily calm and very clear. No gannets working, but then planktonic life was at a low ebb: after so many fine days the nutrients had been used up. We sped out from the coast over a mirror. I swung in an arc to run past the Sugarloaf so that Grant and Claire, local school teachers, could see the gannet colony on its naked heights.

Then we rounded the Pinnacles and headed north towards the Knights. No sign of dolphins anywhere. Ahead I saw something rather odd close in to the Southern Archway. As we closed in it resolved into a tuna boat — a purse-seiner, F.V. *Lindberg*. Her ten-man crew was busy winching the giant net aboard. Mackerel, the dolphins' diet, dripped from the net. A huge dory chugged at right angles to the ship, to maintain tension on the net bellying out from the other side. Men thumped the ship's side with a billet of wood to keep the fish out in the belly of the net.

I circled the scene snapping pictures to show clearly how close this commercial operation was to a high quality recreational area like the Knights. [In 1981 it was declared a marine reserve.] Closeby big schools of trevally were feeding so intently they didn't even mind if we buzzed right through them, taking pictures.

My fears as to the effects of tuna boats on dolphins are growing. The previous day dolphins had been sighted, as well as an orca. But the tuna boat had been working around the islands for the past week. The dolphins have no sanctuary from man — we compete for the same stocks.

We anchored in Rikoriko Cave. As an experiment I decided to float the twelve-inch speaker housing out on the surface within the huge dome. A child's plastic paddling pool served to support it. We towed the contraption around the cave beaming the voices of the whales directly up into the vaulting ceiling until we found the sonic centre — a point where the sound took on a specially lustrous quality — the echoes balancing from all sides. Examining the cave structure at this point I was surprised to see we were at the centre of a very special portion of the cave, not the actual centre but the most symmetrical point — about where *El Torito*'s wheelhouse had once sat.

The echoes were superb. Following the whales I played a tape of music recorded in the cave that memorable Labour weekend when *El Torito* had the musicians aboard. I found that a certain series of guitar notes made by Tama Renata created the best echoes of all.

Long, low attenuated notes. This suggested to me that the whales are making particular types of sound waves which create the most interesting echoes. Do they enjoy listening to these echoes, or are the echoes just a by-product of their sonic performance?

They may seek to create echoes because these either convey a sonic reflection of their surroundings or reproduce the sonic reflection of some environmental feature stored in their memory circuits. Even if they were passing on from one generation to the next a navigational picture, just as the Polynesians transmitted their star charts, this could have an entertainment value as well as being a means of annual migration. It would be nice to play to the cetaceans echoes recorded in various terrestrial surroundings, such as the forest valleys on our land. Maybe we could communicate along such lines?

Like a museum guide, Jan was showing Claire and Grant the cave walls with our diving torch, while I practised breathhold dives in the music field beneath the boat, wearing the dolphin fin. Overhead I could see our friends struggling like flies across the surface towards the boat hull. From fifty feet I rocketed up, spiralling as I rose towards them. They nearly took off when they saw the fin approaching out of the darkness. At least they got over their initial fear of sharing the sea with dolphins and I was pleased that the fin and mode of swimming were so effective as mimicry. (Next day they took their own boat out and played with the dolphins.)

Today I achieved a longfelt desire. I listened to a complete piece of classical music while gazing at the cliff face sixty feet down. To hear music in such an unusual setting gives a special relevance to every life form and note. It soon seems that this is the sound track in some spectacular movie. I saw a small section of rock face in infinite detail. Two golden nudibranchs beside a rosette of orange lace. One twice as large as the other — what an irregularity in size for spawning. The waving arms of brittlestars; a blue-eyed blenny in front of its refuge; the wisps of tubeworm gills, a cup coral with slender, fleshy stinging lobes, tiny rigid coraline structures of intricate design created by bryozoans, others of pliable substance, by sponges. Everything I looked at in that shaded recess was feeding on the water column adjacent, snaring tiny energy packages — stored sunlight; fuel cells.

As I dolphined about I found it easy to push my scuba tank in front of me like a torpedo, wearing the tape-recorder housing on my back. I had strapped a block of lead to the tank and it handled like a feather. A small pair of fins on the bow would have assisted turns. I could glide along to the rhythm of the music so effortlessly. I set out on a tour of the bay to perfect my swimming technique. Before the tape ran out I had swum through dozens of sunlit vistas, hedge-hopping over the kelp forests, swooping along sandy avenues and plunging over ridges, whatever manoeuvre a bird might make, and with as little effort. With music to give the timing it seemed as though my scuba tank had a small motor in it, towing me through the sea — yet with all my equipment I was propelling fifty pounds of extra mass.

Just as I was heading up the cove towards the boat, a song from "Hair" I'd fitted onto a gap at the end of the tape began to come through the system: "My body is walking in space etc". Below me an alien world unfolded every time I moved my form. What an appropriate song for a movie sequence like that!

As we left the Knights the tuna boat hove into view again — this time just off Rikoriko Cave, hauling their net anew. All around a flotilla of pleasure craft waited to witness the catch. I took some more photos and on the journey home composed a newspaper article about the situation: "The Giant Nets". An energy sink — all those men and machines — how would their productivity compare with atoll-dwelling Luaniuans in their canoes?

I speculated as to how we could best gather energy stores from the sea. Large-scale plankton sieves feeding into methane plants? Or should we just recycle our wastes on land and leave the ocean for recreation? No commercial fishery for wild stocks has ever proved to be sustainable. We are just nomadic huntsmen with helicopters and future generations may marvel at our idiocies.

Cold shoulder day

23 January 1977: Now that I've started shooting dolphin film I begin to see that it will develop in its own way. The day after I got the first batch back from the processors we set out to sea again, this time with Brady and Karla aboard — a fine summer's day with a light offshore chop and moderate southeast swells, the remnants of distant storms.

No sign of gannets until we reached the interface ten miles out with its line of floating seaweed and debris. I saw rock pool algae out there — I wonder where the drift line originates? Then to the south we saw some gannets diving and pursued them. There were only a few, and no dolphins. Continuing our run we spotted gannets to the north — quite a detour, but this time we were in luck — our dolphin friends were swimming vigorously amidst the birds. We yelled and thumped and shook the cowbell — so happy to see them again.

For a short while they rode the bow, rolling on their sides and looking up at us. The tape was playing humpback songs. But when I began to turn the boat in a circle, they disappeared to the south. Jan got her diving gear on and we set after them. Wherever the dolphins go it seems the gannets follow — probably because there is a school of fish amongst them.

We found the dolphins again. They danced on our bow, leaping high and arcing over to our cheers. Brady and Karla took turns clanking the cowbell. Fins were all around us. I cut the motor. Jan slipped in. The dolphins left. The visibility was about thirty feet and she didn't even get a glimpse of a dolphin. They had gone before she hit the water.

This was uncanny. We could not understand it. No longer would they ride our bow wave in a circle or allow any visual contact in the water. To put the matter to the test, we would keep trying to make contact with the dolphins.

We were catching up with them again when we noticed four dolphins turn away from the group and race towards the boat. We yelled, "They're coming to *us*!" I stopped the motor and Jan leapt in.

As she dived down one dolphin swept under her. He rolled on his side and looked up at her continuing on his way. She didn't see the others and they didn't stay around so she got back in the boat again and we took off after them.

This time I decided to keep the boat going. When we were well and truly up with them I slowed down and Jan leapt in while I took the boat round in a circle. This time she could see eight to ten dolphins weaving beneath her. She felt an excited surge. This time perhaps? She dived down towards them and to her utter dismay and disappointment they accelerated off, diving deeper, and didn't come back. Just before they took off she heard a high-pitched sonar call. It had an urgent tone to it. Was it a "warning" or a "follow me" call?

We decided to try yet again. Catching up, we yelled and thumped the hull of the boat. Jan said, "I get the feeling they don't like the thumping on the hull. They seem to veer off slightly."

She was thinking of the men banging on the fishing vessel to scare the fish and wondering if this was the reason we were getting the cold shoulder. All the week before that damned purse-seiner had been working round the Knights.

To vary our approach we made two attempts with the motor switched off, gliding to a halt with the message tape playing. No luck. Karla sat up in the bow hatch to be close to the dolphins when we reached them. Would they respond to a child's presence? Then Jan tried slipping in while we were still under way — chugging quietly through a large group of dolphins and gannets.

"I caught sight of a pair and as I dived they just took off, diving deeper themselves, going away under water. Not once did they stay around me and take a good look and every time I dived towards them they accelerated into the blue depths."

I decided to make a long run eastwards in the direction the dolphins were heading, to see how long they would stay with us before we attempted interlock. The whole group, about forty in all, raced along with us as fast as we dared travel across the short choppy seas.

Twice more Jan slipped in but the dolphins left. After the sixth attempt they disappeared. We could see no gannets anywhere so they must have gone some distance.

Looking around I realised we were exactly where we had been on our last expedition when we had noticed the fishing vessel close to the Southern Archway at the Poor Knights. Just as before, we sped across to Aorangi Island and thoughts raced through our minds. Dolphins had never treated us like this. The complete cold shoulder — not even the remotest chance of interlock. Certainly it was the group we had previously contacted, but what had happened out there to change things so much?

I headed for the huge archway where swells were thrashing the portals and bucking through the canyon. That boat! Could it have been the purse-seiner we'd seen there last time? It had spent two weeks around the Knights, netting some 260 tons of pelagic fish, its big dory buzzing for hours to keep the net under tension while they winched in their catches of schoolfish. Supposing there were dolphins in the area — what had happened to them? Surely the fishermen would follow the gannets too? Later I learnt that charterboat men had seen several divers with scuba gear on board — illegal on a registered fishing boat.

We skimmed through South Harbour, north around Aorangi, bouncing over the swells until we reached the calm of Nursery Cove. The summer flush of pleasure boats was over — just the usual half-dozen ocean lovers dotted around the bays. The cliffs echoing with bellbirds — a perfect day.

Could it have been the Christmas traffic? Did somebody maltreat the dolphins at that time? I had seen recent news reports of two pilot whales being shot over on the west coast of Northland and a dolphin shot off the Taranaki coast. When cities release their inmates in bulk, denatured man, an unpredictable creature, is liable to vent all the aggression his touch-starved, jangle-frayed mind has stored up, on anything that moves: signboards, beer cans, cows. . .

Whatever it was, the dolphins had demonstrated they were not having any more games with us.

In the cove conditions were ideal for filming. I shot footage to narrate our pattern of activities: Brady putting the message tape in the stereo cassette player, surrounded by speakers and wires, then setting up the underwater tape-player and closing the port on the housing. While Jan kitted up with the dorsal fin and handflippers I filmed her getting ready and rolling over the side; sequences of her dolphining over the surface and then a series of her underwater, swimming past my lens as I balanced on top of a submerged rock pinnacle.

While she took the children for a dive among the tame reef fishes of the cove, I set out on another test of the tape-player. This time I decided to try it without the little extension speaker strapped to my hood. I rigged up the housing as close to the back of my head as possible so that the sound might reach my ears. I strapped a one pound weight onto the scuba tank and leapt in with it in my arms. I could hear almost as well as with the extension speaker but to overcome swimming noises more volume was needed.

Out over the white sand, at sixty feet, I cruised with ease, the air tank thrust out in front of my mask like an extension of my body. The tall shape of Castle Rock loomed up and I circled it like a bird before landing at the base. A yellow moray leaned from a crevice. The music seemed to mesmerise it. I advanced my mask close to its head. The gulping jaws swayed towards me until they were opening and closing against the glass an inch from my eyes. To my surprise the interior of the mouth was very beautiful — like the fleshy body of an anemone. It was possible to see right down the gullet towards the stomach.

As I buckled around the cove in curving flight, pausing here and there to approach fishes the music created the sound track for a movie. I realised this would make excellent footage. With mobile sequences it is hard to avoid unsteadiness, which can be distracting to the viewer. But this rhythmic motion synchronised with music would make a virtue of necessity; a dolphin's eye view of the bay: waving kelp forests, sandy avenues, an eagle ray hovered with curving tail, fishes bright as jewels in the sunny shallows — a picture of the incredible range of activities within the small area of the cove — an interdependance of oceanic lifestyles that makes our terrestrial world seem sterile and harsh by comparison.

Beneath the boat Jan was showing the children how to stroke the fishes crowding around them. Our diving friends, the Slark family, arrived and joined us for lunch. Tony told me about a one-legged chap he had dived with who coped perfectly and for him the dolphin kick was his *only* choice. With only half the propulsive power one-legged divers often do better than bipedal companions — necessity forces them to adopt what may well be a superior mode of propulsion through water. For walking creatures struggling to survive in water, a kicking action is an instinctive response but if man truly wished to adapt to a liquid world, he might do better by emulating its oldest inhabitants.

In the forest at the foot of Magic Valley, a few days later, I traipsed through the bush as though on a dive, still dollying the camera mentally before me, gliding over fern heads, skimming past tree trunks, glancing up the slope at the diversity of life forms in silhouette — just like the gorgonian fans and finger sponges on the walls of Rikoriko Cave.

Thinking back over the past months of experimentation, how does the fantasy I wrote first, compare with what we have been able to learn? With no avenue to communicate with man other than through body language, could there be a significance in certain dolphin activities which we continue to overlook, blinded by our arrogance?

A recent newspaper report tells of a dolphin arriving on a beach, its body slashed and bullet riddled. Had it been injured by fishermen, caught in the power block of a purse-seiner, and shot to get rid of evidence? It wouldn't do for a lacerated dolphin to go loose on Christmas seas. Perhaps the dolphin eluded the fishermen and delivered its wounded carcase to our feet.

Dismiss this as the idle speculation of a water-logged mind, but one fact remains: bullet wounds testify to human violence wrought on a species which has never retaliated, no matter what the provocation. As a means of communication, body language cannot go much further than demonstrations of this nature.

52

Then, at Coopers Beach in the far north, dolphins flock into a bay full of swimmers and romp around them. Had they sensed the group playfulness and sought interlock only to find an edge of fear in the bathers and keep at non-contact distance? On many occasions I have seen that most people are not quite ready to trust the dolphins fully — man cannot easily believe that a creature more benign than himself exists. We project our own unpredictability onto the dolphin.

Was this first refusal of the dolphin to play with us an item of body language in itself, a demonstration as repeated and clearcut as any mother/child remonstrance and a direct pointer to the tuna boat (which removed about one-third of the resident trevally population from the Poor Knights, a fisheries scientist told me); or were those dolphins strangers to our antics, intent on hunting and unimpressed by our attempts to engage their interest? Reviewing all that has taken place to date determines us to continue our interlock experiments, until we can answer these ambiguities.

Footnote (1980): If the reader compares these dolphin/human episodes with those in subsequent years of our study it will be seen we were involved in a learning process and later found it much more conducive to interlock if, on meeting dolphins, we followed an ethic of establishing mutual trust with them, *before* entering the water. But mutual physical access is not easy to offer with a conventional boat and was a major advantage of the change to a catamaran with lowslung bow hammocks.

We also learnt to avoid repeating the same communication experiment, as it met with diminishing responses; to avoid pursuing or approaching dolphins involved in hunting and feeding. It was enough to enter the general area and heave to. They would come to us, when ready.

In the interest of dolphin/human relationships we hope others will not need to repeat our mistakes or read these early episodes out of the full context. Inasmuch as they record the growth in our understanding, we decided to include them, warts and all.

We call them killers

Around this time we obtained from the Canadian Embassy a film, "We Call Them Killers", that affected us deeply. Midway through the film, after two captive orca have demonstrated their physical prowess with leaps and graceful manoeuvrings, biologist Dr Paul Spong appears at the pool's edge. Placing his head between the gaping jaws of the seventeen-foot mammal, he says, "Fear is one of the principal barriers that exists between us, human beings and them, the killer whales. I feel and sense from my own experience that I know the greatest rapport with whales when I'm least afraid of them. When a person places his head in the mouth of a whale he's simply saying to a whale, 'Look, here I am. I trust you.'"

Stroking its head with a yellow feather: "Killer whales have obviously got highly developed sensory systems in a number of modalities. Their sense of touch is well developed. They're capable of sensing the presence of very small, very fine touches. Like the touch of a feather for example. They seem to derive some reward from sensory experiences.

Visual, touch and auditory or acoustic. They have basically the same senses that we do. The emphasis is different.

"We're predominantly visual creatures. Vision, so important to us, takes second place. With them the emphasis is reversed. Hearing is the primary sense, vision is secondary."

He rubs the rim of a wine glass to elicit a delicate humming sound. The orca hover close by and loll about in seeming ecstasy.

"Cetaceans have the most marvellous hearing systems that there are on the planet. Their hearing is exquisite. Ours is good, theirs is *exquisite*."

On a poolside movie screen a Red Indian dances in full regalia — the orca watch. The camera zooms into soft and sentient eyes. "Their vision is quite well developed. They see about as well underwater, for example, as a cat sees in air, although I doubt whether vision is of that great importance to them, living in the ocean. But we still know, I really feel, practically nothing about the creatures."

As the film shows Paul Spong in wetsuit, climbing onto an orca's back, his voice over says, "I really don't know what the possibilities are for exploring interspecies communication at the level of physical interaction. But I feel that this is a necessary step in the process. When I'm in the air, in my environment, presenting myself to a killer whale, I'm presenting a rather limited aspect of myself. I always, for example, have the possibility of withdrawing from the situation. But if I'm in the water with them, then they are in total control of the situation."

He is carried around the pool on the whale's back.

In the later part of the film the flautist Paul Horn sits at the pool edge and begins to play. (No words at first.) Dr Paul Spong comments:

"Sound is something that we certainly both experience and presumably mutually appreciate. Music more specifically is something that we know transcends language barriers in our own species. I see no reason why we shouldn't explore the possibility that it may transcend interspecies barriers. The more a musician can project himself into his music, the more responsive the whale is. Paul Horn, of course, is a fantastic musician — a fantastic person and the whales I'm sure appreciate him in both areas."

As Paul Horn plays, the orca experiments with its blowhole, attempting to imitate the flute, on the indrawn breath. The film closes with extraordinary close-up shots of the blowhole that exhibits all the expressiveness of a troubled brow. Eventually it masters airborne sound-making, but the notes bear little resemblance to the flute.

Paul's final comment: "If there were a process begun in which killers that have been in captivity for five years were released back in the ocean in the same area that they were captured, I think this would be a *totally positive* step in the direction of real interspecies relationships and understanding."

We are not alone

31 January 1977: The midsummer ocean was so calm. Five miles off shore the only sound was the distant rumble of Anniversary weekend traffic. Our runabout drifted over a translucent plain. The tape of the whale songs had played right through.

Bob Feigel let out another shrill whistle. The dolphins we'd been following were moving off now. They were working about half a mile to the south. We found ourselves listening to their breathing and splashing sounds. Then it happened. Our ears thrilled to a raspy, hollow whistle — it came from amidst the dolphins. One had answered Bob. I saw a large dolphin surge off to the west. It sounded and emerged, whistled boldly and dived. We were hanging there, Jan, myself and the two girls. And Bob was standing at the grab rail, whistling across the water and listening to the responses, hardly believing each time that it was not one of us — that a sea creature was making such sounds. Our experiments had taken an unexpected turn.

From the outset it had been the most perfect day — not a breath of wind, the sky a cobalt blue to match the sea and the water so very clear. Boats were everywhere.

Halfway to the Knights with an American writer Bob Feigel, Karla and her friend Lisa aboard we had met the dolphins at twenty-five minutes past ten. This time there were no birds working. One or two gannets and shearwaters were sitting around on the ocean and occasionally taking off for a few circuits.

Jan donned her gear. We cruised along with the dolphins and they seemed very interested in the boat. We had whale sounds playing on the tape and the girls were ringing the cowbell.

Two days before we had read in the newspaper how dolphins had come in close to bathers at Coopers Beach further up north and frolicked and played, leaping high out of the water. And a friend had rung to say that the day before they had met the dolphins out from Tutukaka and had been with them for an hour. They swam with the dolphins without any diving gear and were unable to observe their responses other than peer down through the water and know the dolphins were still there.

After the cold-shoulder from the dolphin group we met the Sunday before we were hopeful of better things this day. Just before Jan got in, the small group of dolphins we were cruising with joined up with a larger school. Bob climbed up onto the bow and was leaning over close to the water. It was time to leap in: the dolphins were all around us.

As Jan hit the water and dived down dolphins came from all directions to have a look at her, sweeping in to within ten feet. She dolphin-kicked energetically until she had to ascend for a breath. There were dolphins on the surface only ten feet away. She dived again and they came in, circled once and withdrew. She could hear their sonar whistles all round when she was below. They were curious but didn't try to mimic her as on other occasions: once they had satisfied their curiosity they left. As she climbed out she felt a lot happier because they obviously were not avoiding her this time. From examining body marks and dorsal fins it seemed this was a different group from any we had met before.

The second time Jan got in with them was much the same as the first. They had a look at her twice before rejoining the rest of the group. It seemed that only some of the group would ride on the boat and check us out while the majority kept apart, possibly with the school of fish they were working. On every occasion that we have followed common dolphins this same thing has been apparent.

A large launch cruised past quite close. Two dolphins tore in to have a quick look at Jan. The dolphins did not go over to this boat to frolic on the bow wave as might be expected. Yet our boat was stationary with the motor off.

We caught up with them. I got in this time and shot some 16mm movie footage before they left. Filming is a problem. It destroys interlock playfulness. I can't frolic about spontaneously and shoot movie at the same time. But I badly needed some action shots — it would be my third roll for the film proposal. Each time I dropped in they would do one burst round me and leave. I wanted to film Jan in their midst wearing her dolphin fin but there was no way.

As I was returning to the boat after my second attempt I got a real jolt. From the depths airbubbles were rising in sparkling screens. "There can't be a diver down there! Gas? No, it's not coming up steadily."

At depths beyond visible range the dolphins had released large gulps of air which expanded as they rose and as pressure diminished, swirling silver bells exactly like the exhaust of a scuba diver. But out here it was over 300 feet deep. Was this an attempt at communication, a visual game, or just indigestion? Future observations may reveal its significance. At that time no dolphins were in sight — they'd all left the scene, I assumed. So maybe the bubbles had been released at some considerable depth.

I took some movie of Jan dolphin-kicking with the fin on and some of the boat approaching me in the water with the kids hanging over the bow. Then I made four more attempts to approach the dolphins with Jan and camera but they sounded and came up further away each time. We wondered if the boat motor drove the schoolfish they were herding deeper as we approached. It was twenty minutes to twelve. We had been moving with them for one hour and fifty minutes so far and we weren't getting anywhere. By this time we were sure this was a new group of dolphins. We decided to try a different approach, starting again from scratch to establish trust.

Bob, having been shown only a few minutes previously how to handle the boat, suddenly felt at ease with the controls. I was very happy at being able to concentrate on the dolphins and not the boat. In fact we were all feeling quite ecstatic. Karla and Lisa were leaning over the bow gliding gently in the midst of a dolphin parade. The taped dolphin sounds finished and Pink Floyd started. At twice its normal speed "Echoes" has a crazy carnival rhythm. Somehow it sounds just right in that setting and the dolphins all around us showed clearly they were listening to the tape: when the tempo increased a surge went through them and they began to frolic.

I never thought when David Harvey and I first tried that tape one winter's day on the coast, six months back, that we would ever manage to play the entire experiment to a group of dolphins and feel certain they heard the sequence of acoustic logic it expresses. From the outset

56

David and I had hoped that if dolphins ever heard these experiments they might realize that the communication barrier between man and dolphin is the great gulf between the wave bands which each species uses. We hoped there might be some significant response if ever they grasped the analogue message on our tape. So I was particularly interested in this quickening of pace with the Pink Floyd piece. They definitely responded to its jingly, dancing music — a festive mood was induced in dolphin and man. I felt as if we were in a Mardi Gras procession.

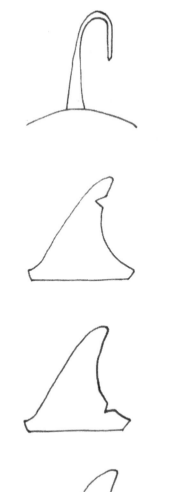

Bob was driving sedately, letting the dolphins lead us. When the humpback song came through the tape he began whistling the same whistle over and over again, mimicking the whale sounds. The dolphins were all round the boat, riding the bow, rolling over and looking up at the girls. Every now and again one would leap out of the water. It was so clear you could see every mark and scratch on their backs. We started to note in our minds things that we would be able to recognize at another time.

There was one with the top of its dorsal bent right over: Bentfin; another with a nick out of the top of his dorsal: Nicky; another with a nick out of the lower part; one with two grill patches on its left side in front and behind the dorsal; one with a diagonal scratch on the left side in front of its dorsal.

I saw one roll over on top of another as it went to get in front of the boat. I've never seen them actually touch like that before.

A rush of understanding: of course, every time we meet a new group of dolphins we have to start from the beginning and let them get used to us first. They seem to accept us as long as we are responsive. We must let the dolphins lead us and not the other way round. A new ethic: they are teaching us the rules.*

Speeding up to get on the bow the dolphins were defaecating as they passed alongside. We were only doing four knots, Bob whistling all the time. The dolphins were getting much more friendly, milling about under the boat, in front and behind in the wake. They seemed to be swimming in pairs or fours. We were now halfway between the Sugarloaf and the shore. There were a few gannets and shearwaters in the vicinity. They weren't feeding, just following the dolphins. Then the dolphins seemed to form a line which broke into three groups. We were 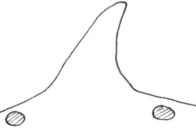 with the middle group, some were to the west and some to the east. They were leaping out of the water. It was so clear, we could see them coming up after sounding.

They sped up and Bob altered our pace to keep with them — another knot, letting out a shrill whistle as he did so.

Lisa said, "They made a whistle back!"

It was then we could hear their sonar peewees even above the boat motor. We had been cruising with them in this manner for twenty-five minutes.

*Even after the ESP hypothesis developed we still felt a mutually acceptable interspecies meeting ethic should be followed at all encounters. It would be rude to withhold courtesies involving mutual trust on the assumption of an ESP link. An overt display of body language ensures understanding and respect.

Jan said, "Look, I can see a couple together. One has its white belly pointing upwards. I wonder if they are mating?"

Broadside to the keel the dolphins were streaking under the boat rolling on their sides as they passed close to the girls' dangling feet. Then the three groups came together in one mass. All this time we had the tape playing the songs of the humpback. It ran out and Bob turned the motor off. We could easily hear their sonar squeaks. It was so calm and still with a continual low rumble coming from all the traffic on the land. It was now ten minutes to twelve. Bob continued to whistle like a whale. Then all of a sudden we looked at each other. What was that unearthly sound? We were all stock still, hardly breathing. Once more Bob whistled. We heard it again. It was a dolphin making an aerial sound with its blowhole, as if it was trying to master the whistle and couldn't quite make it. Blowing raspberries! Bob kept whistling and we noticed that the answering call seemed to be coming from one particular dolphin.

Dolphins in captivity have been trained to whistle with their blowholes but for a dolphin to attempt this in the wild was just too exciting for words. By now the dolphins were at quite some distance but we continued to drift silently listening while Bob kept up his whistling. Then we noticed they were getting closer. While Bob whistled they came nosing through the clear water right back to us. Defaecating as they went, hurtling under and around the boat. It seemed Bob's whistle had drawn them to us again. One group stayed close to the boat and others spread out around.

By 12.30 pm the dolphins were gradually moving away as they went about their business. It was so hot Jan got in the water to cool off. At 12.55 we turned on the tape and started the boat to move after them. We moved faster, in circles, and dolphins came to ride the bow and in the wake.

Bob and the girls were leaning over the bow. Bob whistling. Every now and again we would hear the return whistle. The mimicry was getting better and better until in the end it was quite perfect and we would look at Bob to see if it were he or the dolphins who had made the sound. Three times we stopped the motor and the tape and drifted while Bob whistled so we could hear the answering whistles.

We were looking at the group of dolphins ahead when Jan suddenly stopped jotting down notes. She felt as though she had been interrupted. She turned and her gaze joined ours. At that moment out of the water shot a large dolphin. A trio were travelling north very fast to join those ahead that we were concentrating on. As they approached the others we heard two more whistles. Both Bob and I felt this strange premonition too — that something was going to happen. We were all looking in the same direction just as that dolphin broke the water, whistled and plunged back in.

It was now 1.25 pm. We started up again. While we circled Bob was leaning over the bow with his arm outstretched over the dolphin backs riding on the bow, whistling to them gently. I saw one answer Bob ten feet from the boat. Bob touched one, lightly rubbing his fingers along its side. He said after, that he was amazed at the softness of its skin. The dolphin gave a start, splashing the water with its tail. It came back up

58

again, rolling on its side to look at Bob, then it did a sideways wriggle.

We kept cruising with them in this manner until 1.50 pm, heading towards the Pinnacles now. Each time we caught up with the dolphins we had whale sounds playing and would ring the cowbell. We wanted them to recognise and get to know us by introducing ourselves the same way every time. Then we would turn everything off and let Bob whistle.

We decided to try getting in with them again. I manoeuvred the boat until we were in front of them. Jan leapt in three times while I kept the boat circling. Much the same thing happened as in the morning. They went away after she had dived down twice but both times as she dived they came and circled and had a good look within ten to fifteen feet range. The second time one swept in close to about six feet and then went away. She got out at 2.15 pm and I decided I would get in on the end of a tow rope. We had various arm signals worked out: go faster, slower and stop.

I was towed behind the dolphins for half an hour but they were moving just a little too fast for me to catch up. More speed and I would lose mask and arms. It was unlikely they were aware of my presence behind the boat because of engine noise and the white water from the wake.

The tow proved more interesting than I'd hoped for; here was a way to move fast like a dolphin. At slow speeds I found I could still do the dolphin kick even though being towed. It relieved the strain on my arms. I could readily veer out from behind the bow wave by thrusting one arm obliquely ahead.

Eager to get amongst the dolphins I signalled Jan to speed up by stages until the water pressure was all that I could stand. Chain salps and jellyfish whisked by. Movie footage shot like this would be incredible. I was hurtling through innerspace — a giant marlin bait! Uneasy thought, but the dolphins ahead were a source of some comfort. Little did I know there *was* a mako shark in the vicinity. Aqua-sledding has its small risk factor but could be worthwhile. It would be possible to build an elaborate tow sled for this purpose with built-in scuba tank, tape recorder and movie rig.

They were moving faster by this time in a southeast direction so we decided we couldn't afford the fuel to follow them any more, even though we wanted to. We took off to the Knights and as we detoured to pass near the Sugarloaf, noticed a fin in the water. Preparing to leap in we slowed down and circled. It turned out to be a magnificent mako shark. The water being so clear we were able to see him very well. We watched for a while and then he swam off into the light. He looked tremendous as the sun lit up his huge blue-grey form. We could even see the gills opening and closing on his side. I had almost joined him! Mako sharks are deepwater animals and we were lucky to have seen it so close.

We continued over to Nursery Cove where the girls and Jan snorkelled and enjoyed the fishes. The demoiselles were thick in against the cliffs and they lay on the surface watching these little fishes spawning. There were newly-hatched demoiselles everywhere no bigger than a thumb nail. And males guarding nest against all-comers — other than dancing females of their own species whom they courted and whose eggs they accepted.

That night we all slept with dolphins before our eyes.

Thinking things over

On thinking it all over, it seems possible that common dolphins, *Delphinus delphis,* may be nomadic herdsmen, pasturing schools of baitfish along interfaces and thermoclines. There is so much of their behaviour that could only be understood if we studied the schools with side-scanning sonar and observed how they are being protected and husbanded.

Another factor in trying to interpret their manoeuvres is that in many instances only about half the dolphins would be surfacing at one time. Very often it seems there would be one group swimming near the surface while others spend longer periods submerged. The surface swimmers may be more available for play as some can be spared from fish-tending. They may even be detailed to distract the boat by playing on its bow. The surface swimmers are often younger ones and mothers with babies.

When we approach a dolphin group with a fish school under surveillance, they often sound. This may be because we frighten the schoolfish which they must then pursue and round up. *We must avoid this in future.* Another ethic.

Dolphins rounding up prey: One method seems to be to form a long line, which may then divide into three groups. I can visualise them driving the fish at five knots and then suddenly sending down three groups beneath the school to completely surround it. The preyfish form a "meat ball". Those dolphins on the surface rush together to close the gaps and feeding may occur.

Vocal mimicry, key to first stage of communication: Vocal mimicry is the first stage in communication between mother and child. The dolphins have now shown they can adapt to our low-frequency airborne sound signals with perfection. Physiologically it is not easy — see *Lilly on Dolphins*, chapter 14 — a highly consummate feat by an acoustic gymnast. But once the actual production of such sounds was mastered they rapidly perfected their modelling. Like a man first learning to make a sound on a trumpet and then playing a recognisable tune.

In captivity it took scientists weeks of reward/punishment training to elicit airborne sounds from bottlenose dolphins. But these were lonely, touch-starved creatures with little choice other than to comply with the research pattern imposed on them. In the wild the dolphins have the trump hand — they can withdraw at will. In this situation man can only proffer himself to be taught by the dolphins.

Our message tape is a logical acoustic statement. It may act as a rosetta stone, or a bridge between two acoustic cultures whole wavebands apart. I don't think the dolphins regard us as particularly interesting yet. We offer little diversity of behaviour. Our canned music can't communicate because the element of response is missing.

"OK — you're making cetacean sounds but that's no more intelligent than the wind whistling over wave crests if you don't respond to us."

First the tape establishes the concept of changing speeds through the four-stage recording of dolphin sounds, slower and slower until their whistle calls become much more complex to the human ear than the shrill whistles we hear normally. Next, a piece of western music which incorporates imitation whale sounds is presented at increasing speed until it becomes to us, musical nonsense. Then the humpback whale songs start and Feigel begins to copy the whales. "That's it," the dolphins may think, "they make meaningful sounds in air, at low frequencies. Let's try them out." (Maybe they tried for some time but we didn't notice until the motor stopped.) They pucker their blowholes experimentally, sometimes a bit too tight and the air is released in explosive clicks. Too loose, and a hoarse, rasping sound. Then they get it right and manage to whistle in air instead of the high-pitched calls they generate inside their heads. We respond with more whistles but it's hard to show them a patterned performance as yet because they're not on the surface long enough to hear a series of calls. I had the uncanny feeling they must have known when Feigel whistled, because immediately after, one leaps out and responds, but this is just a hunch.

At first we'd tried hard to engage them in the water. Each time we dropped a diver in they made a turn about him and left. Perhaps the preyfish school had been frightened and had to be overtaken. But once we motored along quietly at the same speed as the dolphins we got our first lesson. Bob had begun to notice certain signals which seemed to indicate which way the group would veer. It was this that enabled him to anticipate their turns and so keep right up with them. As long as we did this, dolphins that were surface-swimming came close around the boat and cavorted on the bow wave. They responded to changes of pace in our tape and inspected us closely through a mirror calm surface as they swam in at right angles to the boat.

At these times a wave of happiness seemed to cocoon the whole boat, all its occupants and those below: all moving through the same field of sound and light, the whale songs and the summer's day. I'd kept wondering whether I should get in but didn't want to spoil what was developing between Feigel and the dolphins. I'm glad I had the sense to refrain or otherwise we may not have learned anything new that day.

The dolphins showed us their hunting patterns, they inspected us closely alongside the bow and displayed a range of antics indicative of joy and exuberance. Even while the motor was going we heard some very loud sonar whistles which penetrated the hull. These may have been earlier efforts to communicate before attempting the airborne sounds. We are Brobdingnagians unable to see finer realities that underlie the coarse-grain world view our culture admits.

The dolphins have whistled to us on a fine summer's day. The eerie sounds still echo in my thoughts — the most uncanny and haunting I've ever heard — something alien, droll and utterly perfect — a comforting response from a mind in the sea — an assurance that we are *not* alone, that bridges can be built and both sides can cross them.

I recalled seeing a movie about hill tribesmen in New Guinea. When gifts were left on the track, they emerged from the jungle, unaware of a telephoto lens, gathered up the parcels and hurled them down the path. Mutual respect and gamesharing, self-effacement and flexibility are all essential for transcultural exchanges. We may be on the brink of something exciting if we develop a flexible, creative approach.

When we meet a group, if they respond to the boat manoeuvres by

61

following around in a circle, they are amenable to further interlock in the water. But if they only play on the bow when we head along their course, they cannot be induced to stay and play.

We've now tested this repeatedly, and it seems they have other duties to perform. In such situations only the surface-swimming dolphins are amenable to vocal interlock. It could be that, like the early explorer and missionaries, we are mainly encountering the young ones and mothers, rather than the acoustically more sophisticated elders, who probably manage the schoolfish. This may hinder the development of interlock, so we should be patient. In all cases observed it was the larger, older dolphins who learnt to whistle in air.

In conclusion: After months of experimenting with dolphins in the wild, we have just met a group who heard our message tape. And they have acknowledged it. The tape is an acoustic statement about the vast communications gap which may exist between air-dwellers and sea-dwellers.

In response they learnt to make low-frequency airborne sounds within our hearing range. Then they used the new wave length to mimic us perfectly. The ball is now in our court. Can we show them we are acoustic gamesplayers too? Can we offer them a diversity of interesting sounds? How complex could their responses become?

Had we known then what was to unfold exactly one year later with this same group of dolphins, we would not have been ready to believe it. Perhaps we had to grow in understanding.

Whistling dolphins

Later that same year Marilyn West was diving at Great Barrier Island — fifty miles south of the Poor Knights. She is an experienced scuba instructor who has had several dolphin encounters. She was aboard Murray Brighouse's fifty-two-foot ketch *Xanadu*.

"At some ungodly hour in the morning, someone yells 'Dolphins, dolphins!!!' Hearing the magic word I was jolted wide awake and my first reaction was to grab my Nikonos camera and off.

"Scrambling on deck so as not to miss anything I was greeted by the sight of six enormous bottlenose dolphins cavorting in our bay, egging us on to join them in their play. I was just about to leap over the rail, when I suddenly realised I was clad only in my flimsy nightie!

"After a lightning change into a T-shirt and a bikini I paused momentarily to grab a mask and snorkel before disappearing over the side into the nippy October waters. Swimming into the dolphins' path I hung back a few yards and waited with bated breath to see what they would do. As if on command they ceased their play and appeared to dive very deep. With visibility extremely low I kept my head under, scanning every inch of the water for acknowledgement of my presence. After waiting what seemed an eternity, out of the gloom shot these six dark shapes some twenty feet below me. They continued to bombard me, with every visit edging closer and closer until they were gliding just inches below my feet. Diving down every now and again I could hear the water alive with high-pitched shrieks and whistles and the clicks of the Nikonos seemed to draw them to me.

"About now Murray's son, Tony, had launched the dinghy and, rowing furiously in the direction of the dolphins, yelled to me that he would round them up rodeo fashion so that I could get some better photos.* He then proceeded to whistle a tune to them as one would whistle up his pet dog, all the time rowing round and round in circles. I then asked Tony if he would stop whistling so I could listen intently to the dolphins communicating and he retorted, 'I'm not whistling!'

"I answered, 'You were, so shut up!'

"With him still protesting his innocence I happened to hear the tune seemingly come from under the water. Jack-knifing down I paused motionless and, as God is my witness, here was this tune being relayed to me by dolphins.

"Lionel Coleman, an avid movie photographer, now joined me with his camera and it was not long after that the dolphins tired of us, took off for another part of the bay and carried on with their antics of spinning, tailwalking and backward falls.

"Exhausted and exhilarated after an hour's frolic with them we swam back to the boat, babbling like schoolchildren over the excitement of our encounter."

We checked with Marilyn as to whether they actually heard the sounds underwater. If so, this is quite incredible because dolphins don't normally make low-frequency sounds such as a human whistle pattern with their internal phonation organs.

Her reply: "I recall on two occasions diving down specifically to listen to the dolphins after telling Tony to stop whistling. I did this because it appeared incredible to me that dolphins were imitating the tune that he had been whistling from the dinghy!"

*We now feel that shepherding or trying to manipulate wild dolphins, like human village folk, should be avoided. Fortunately Tony's good-natured playfulness was the most important aspect here.

PART TWO

Delphinic Acceptance

"So many things fail to interest us, simply because they don't find in us enough surfaces on which to live, and what we have to do then is to increase the number of planes in our mind, so that a much larger number of themes can find a place in it at the same time."

— Ortega Y Gasset

4

Interval: new preparations

THE FIRST PHASE of our experiments culminated with the Anniversary Day responses to our message tape. An interval followed, of several winter months, during which we prepared a whole new approach.

At the outset we had wanted to see whether we could meet dolphins in the open sea and stay with them for extended periods. We had wondered whether creative gamesplay might provide the key. We knew that hitherto such events were rare, and even more important, seldom initiated by humans. Could a way be found whereby we could open up ocean meetings with dolphins ourselves?

And so we had embarked on our experiments, attempts at being more interesting to them through body language and musical gamesplay.

As we became able to stay longer with the common dolphins, *Delphinus delphis*, aspects of their oceanic behaviour patterns began to emerge. Once we learnt to recognise unusual fin patterns we found we could tell when we were with dolphins we'd met before, or a new group. From this basic knowledge a number of pathways led out. We started to get clues as to seasonal movements of dolphin groups, how some paid brief visits, while it was the "home range" for others: clues as to the size and age structure of groups began to appear, and so forth.

In sum, our "friendly approach" procedures could give scientists much the same sort of information as a conventional tagging programme would provide. It is neither as easy nor as precise; for example: some individuals have no recognisable markings. But we feel such a method is the only feasible one to use with cetaceans if the field study is to continue successfully. It is the same with chimpanzees, gorillas and elephants in the wild: if large-brain mammals are molested with tagging devices, objective, close-range study is no longer possible. They learn to avoid human contacts.

Besides this we learnt that the would-be scientific observer encounters another problem — like the anthropologist in a remote village, if he remains aloof and detached the dolphins may leave him staring into blue space with a blank writing slate. *He must interact.*

There is the case of orca under study in Puget Sound. Researchers* noted that one group of orca seemed "slightly less tolerant of human

---

*"Who is that Killer Whale?" Chandler, Goebel and Balcomb. *Pacific Search* Magazine, May 1977.

presence'' than others. Three years earlier a male in this group had been captured and two notches made in the rear margin of his dorsal fin.

Early in the piece we found our own problem in applying scientific method. After several public lectures about our dolphin experiences people came up to me and urged that I should read *The Structure of Scientific Revolutions* by Thomas Kuhn. (See appendix E.) I came to understand that an objective dolphin study would have to give way to something closer to social anthropology. Winning acceptance by a tribe and entering their culture is essential for understanding the folkways of human societies. Even with our own species it is hard for a researcher to retain his objectivity. As we perceive how the folkways of each human culture are an adaptation to the particular environment in which it must survive, western value judgements become relative.

So often the dolphins seemed to use defaecation as a greeting signal — a sudden voiding right in front of our masks. Could it be a threat gesture? But our goat seems to do something like this too — so often she urinates when I approach or just as I leave. Such signals must be considered in the total context. They are ambiguous and easy to overlook, but slowly a significance may grow. The question arises: how do we respond?

An ability to recognise individuals also led us to another path of thought. We could often sense that we were meeting a new group. But at times, although we realised these dolphins had not met *us* before, there seemed to have been an acquisition of experience, some sort of carry-over or transfer. This aspect was to emerge with greater clarity as phase two of our work proceeded.

The Anniversary Day experience brought things to a climax for the Doak family. From that time we began to face the need for a major change in our setup. A total committal of all our resources to the dolphin project was needed if we were to get any further, even if this meant selling up all our negotiable possessions: the Haines Hunter runabout, the utility wagon and even our Matapouri home. Jan was as convinced as I was: we could never rest now unless we devoted all we had to answering the questions suggested by the first phase of our study.

It was in May 1977 that I wrote a letter to Dr Walt Starck explaining the changes in our situation.

"Here it is a sunny, warm river valley domed with a crisp blue sky and I'm sitting beside Gavin who inhabits a pen at the end of our yard, a spot where I like to write on winter days when the sun is so low it barely reaches our cold little cottage. Gavin weighs about a hundred pounds now. For the past five months he has been undergoing a number of pig-raising experiments in preparation for when we shift on to the forest land we've bought at Ngunguru. As soon as my recently injured arms are strong enough again, Gavin will be deep frozen as the Doaks are shifting out of this house in five days' time.

"We've sold the Haines Hunter and ute and bought with the results a thirty-six-foot Polynesian-style catamaran (James Wharram design, fibreglass on marine ply) and a Volkswagen Kombie of ancient vintage but sound in chassis and kind on fuel. To get further into this dolphin project, it seemed essential to make some major changes. Running costs on the Haines were outrageous and even then we would have liked to have had much more time at sea.

"The more I thought on it, the more the catamaran format seemed to be a valuable component in the pattern of experiments we've been following. So now we've got two thirty-six-foot canoes bridged with a slatted deck, seventeen feet in beam. The day after I paid for it, I had a bad fall up on our land and fractured bones in my right hand and screwed up both my elbows. What an anticlimax but it did give me plenty of time to think things over.

"This catamaran will enable us to do a lot of experimenting in situations impossible with the Haines runabout. When we interlock with a group we'd like to stay with them through the night, keeping up the gamesplay as long as it can persist — a whole range of exchanges, recording and transmitting sounds, making physical contact, miming and just enjoying things.

"For filming action on the bow the dual set-up is unbeatable. I'd like to try skimming along in a hammock slung between the bows inches above water level, where a wider range of interplays would be possible. I feel that deeper communication must start from a position of greater trust where we place ourselves at their mercy and vice versa.

"Next month I'll be taking delivery of a twelve-foot Avon pneumatic boat designed for surf rescue work — it will be a perfect tender for the catamaran, fast and flexible, and useful as an auxiliary if our main engine breaks down.

"The catamaran will enable us to take out groups of people, young and old, who want to play with dolphins. I've had watertight fibre-glassed boxes made to house on-deck sound gear for musicians, so we can try playing music to the dolphins and see if they'll join in. This is the level of interlock I'm most eager to establish — a fun situation with groups of both species — sound games and physical games through which new avenues for communication might be tested and explored from both sides to the limits of belief and maybe beyond. . .

"Until we learn to sail we'll have to use the vessel as a motor-cat; she has a new 28hp Mariner outboard.

"Another facility I'd like to have is a good RT so we can keep in touch with the charter boats on dolphin sightings. We decided to call the craft *Interlock* to identify it with the project. On her bows Hal Chapman is painting rondels which depict man and dolphin in the 'yin yang' symbol. The same design will be attached to the bottom of the hulls both in relief and recessed, to provide an acoustic parallel. I have a set of big speakers which fit in the bow compartments. Stereo sailing is a superb way to travel — it makes a virtue of moving at a quieter pace, listening to music and wafting along with the world's wind. Puts us in a very receptive state for meeting the dolphins. How long will it be before ocean voyages on aerofoil windjammers again become attractive?''

The dolphin suit

The interval was a time for fresh assessments and preparations for a better equipped approach. A proper dolphin suit was designed and a

69

manufacturer of wetsuits consulted. Alf Dickenson of Moray Industries is a pioneer skindiver who made the first wetsuits on the New Zealand market — and gave me a sample one, when I was a teenager. Alf came up with valuable suggestions as to how a dolphin suit such as I proposed could actually be manufactured. His practical advice resulted in a one-piece wetsuit fitting both Jan and me, with a rear entry zipper running from waist to hood. Although the suit had separate legs to maintain body warmth, Alf sheathed it with a thin rubber skirt incorporating a panel of white neoprene material especially imported from Britain. This provided us with a contrasty *Delphinus* body pattern. Wire and neoprene were fashioned into flippers. With some aluminium sheet and a pair of fins I concocted a dolphin tail-fin to complete the outfit.

A powerful car stereo tape player was purchased and our best nine-inch speakers were installed in the bows and tested. Around the catamaran we found we could swim in a field of music — the effective range was not more than about forty feet, but to dolphins the music should be audible when they approached the bows.

Journal, August 1977: The catamaran has just been on her maiden voyage as a dolphin research vessel — a trip we've all been planning for months. The process of preparing is complete. The ingenious arrangements Malcolm Pitt put together, the eight foot by ten foot stern platform that hinges down into a diving ramp and the special steering system that gives tight control when people are in the water, have worked like a charm. He says he dreamt it up stage by stage, at night. I feel ashamed of my impatience as I pushed him a bit and will tell him so. I didn't realize how difficult it would be to design a system such as we needed.

Outside the harbour our sailor friend hoisted the mainsail and we headed along the coast towards Ngunguru in a light southwesterly. Then we went about and swooped north again. As wind squalls hit the sails I saw no stress on the rudders — Malcolm could just let her go and roll a cigarette as we knifed through the water. When gusts hit us the catamaran didn't react for a small interval and then she just surged ahead, with perfectly even keels as if I had pushed the accelerator lever on the deep vee. Now Jan and I must learn to sail — quite a hurdle ahead but sure to be a pleasurable experience.

Journal, 21 August 1977: In an energy field between two roaring jet engines I am soaring into the sky bound for Wellington. I'm comforted by my tape playing Santana to me through an ear plug. I always fear take-offs. This is a very bizarre occasion — my dolphin science fiction story "Interlock" has won first place in an international short story competition. I'm off at airline expense to collect a travel award for two people to any Air New Zealand destination in the world, expenses paid. I wonder what nudged me the day I noticed a spare manuscript lying around and suddenly recalled the competition which I'd heard of vaguely a month earlier and forgotten. A flash — send it in — if it wins, *Jetaway* the airline magazine will publish it widely — concepts about dolphins that need to be disseminated. And it won!

At the award ceremony I met the judges. It was quite unfair. Patricia Godsiff told me that some years ago she put her hand in a dolphin's mouth, felt its prickly teeth and a sudden readiness to enter the pool with it. She was a lover of horses and cats and quite convinced of the ESP capacities of animals. The other 215 entrants didn't stand a chance!

5

Meeting old friends

Bucklefin meets the cat

Journal, Thursday 6 October 1977: Stage two of our dolphin experiments began. For the first time we took the catamaran out to meet the dolphins. On board we had the new dolphin suit, the new tail-fin, flippers and dorsal. Between the bows we planned to sling a double hammock made of orange netting, a foot above wave level. The catamaran was newly outfitted with a large diving platform at the stern and a greatly improved steering system.

On board were Malcolm and his four-year-old daughter Rachel, Graham Mosen, Jan, Karla and Claire. There was no wind so we motored out through the entrance. It was flat calm with big glassy patches on the ocean. As we crossed them the boat and people were perfectly mirrored. Even clouds were reflected, like huge jellyfishes. We could see real jellyfish too: the water was full of plankton. Visibility was not going to be good.

I was gazing at a couple of gannets far off to my left and thought I saw fins but wasn't sure. Then Malcolm yelled, "There they are — dolphins. Over there." We all watched for a while and sure enough there they were. Malcolm steered towards them.

We thought these dolphins would be the bottlenose, *Tursiops truncatus,* that we usually see along the coast but to our surprise they were the common dolphins. We had never seen them in so close to the shore before. Usually we meet them about midway or nearer the Knights.

When we first met it was 10.15 am and we just motored along with them playing on the bows until 11.30 am. The catamaran was perfect with its two hulls; it meant that more dolphins could swim in front at one time. Rachel, Karla and Jan were leaning over one bow and Graham and Claire over the other. Malcolm was steering and I was downstairs frantically trying to get the stereo going so we could play the message tape to them from two speakers set up forward in the bows. There was something wrong with the stereo and we never got it going that day.

Rachel was singing "Mary had a little lamb", Graham was whistling and the rest of us were leaning over talking and singing. There were a lot of mothers with their babies in this group. The water was so calm we could see them very clearly playing to and fro. Malcolm had never been with dolphins like this before and Graham or one of the others took over the steering every now and then so he could be with them.

We were able to note some of their differences. There were two with scratches on their backs, right side, in front of the dorsal fin. One with a slightly bent fin angling gently to the right. We named him Bucklefin. He also had a little notch at the base of the fin. One had a perfect black triangle on the top of his dorsal — Black Triangle. One had a perfect white triangle to the right and behind the dorsal.

A few gannets and petrels began working with them at 11 am. At 11.20 I put on the dolphin suit and appendages and stood right on the prow of one hull so that the dolphins could examine me. All this time they were playing between the bows, defaecating as they went. At 11.30 we cut the motor and drifted. Until now we had been continually with the dolphins but because we had stopped, they just went swimming on about their business.

Claire was calling to them, Graham was whistling and I was all kitted up like a dolphin ready to get in if they should come back. Jan got into her suit too, just in case. Malcolm started the motor and took after them again, cutting it off when we caught up — but they moved on. I noticed a large one with no markings except for an oblique line behind the dorsal fin.

I had been planning to rig a hammock between the hulls up front so that we could lie in it just a few inches above the dolphins. Graham dragged it out and, with some help, got it slung. Then he climbed in to test it. Perfect. Now to catch up the dolphins and see how they liked it. I got into the hammock. It was 12.30 pm.

Here they were — one swam zigzag in front of the hulls eyeing me, but keeping its distance. Then others came in keeping quite clear of the hammock. They were also swimming deeper and were very cautious. We wondered if they were scared of the hammock, thinking it was a net. Then they started to come a little closer, even mothers with their babies. Three times Malcolm glided up to them and cut the motor. The first two times they avoided the space between our bows entirely.

Then all of a sudden, as if a decision had been made, they came up from behind us, between the hulls, to the bow. We didn't see them coming because they were underwater. They got really close to me, stayed for a while, then disappeared only to return from nowhere and move alongside me for a closer scrutiny.

Jan wondered if they might think I was a dolphin caught in a net, with the suit on. Twice they seemed to be waiting suspended as we approached and the fifth time they stayed in front of me much longer. Swimming along on the outside of the hulls, they would cross in front looking up at me as they did. Mothers and babies were doing the same.

The sixth time as we approached, I decided to try and get in with them but before the boat had slowed enough for me to slide in, the dolphins had moved on with their fishing and didn't get a look at the new suit.

The next time I slid in they actually did circle me but I saw only one when I dived down. The water was too murky for me to see the others

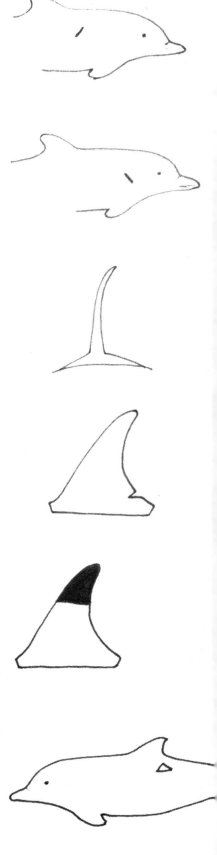

that those on the boat watched circling me. They went on their way. Feeding activity was increasing. It was now 12.55 pm. Gannets started plummeting in and we could see the dolphins were really involved in a feast.

Three times we approached their vicinity but I hung onto the hammock instead of getting in as they were much too busy feeding by now to take any notice. We stopped at 1.15 to leave them alone while we had our lunch too.

At 1.30 pm while we were drifting, we suddenly noticed the dolphins were with us. They milled around a bit taking a good look at us and then went on their way. I climbed out of the dolphin suit and we decided to put up the sails as a light northerly had sprung up. It was exquisite under sail and we managed to take her right into the harbour and up to the mooring without turning the motor on. A thrilling trial in every way — and we used only two gallons of petrol.

We were very excited about what might happen in the future, especially when we had all our equipment and sound gear working.

Barry arrives (after my fantasy. . .)

Journal: The new phase in our experiment is well under way now. It all really came together when I returned home one evening after giving another talk on sewage.

I burst in and there was Barry Fenn: the piercing blue eyes of a space traveller, a shining person who seemed to know where everything was. Hal Chapman had met him in Auckland while painting our rondels. Learning of his interest in whales and yachts Hal told him about all our experiments so far. An American, Barry had just cycled through New Zealand and was about to head home. On the spot he decided to join us. "I've come to look after your boat," were his first words. And in the months to come he took it apart completely, putting it together again in seamanly order and giving us sailing lessons.

Dear Hal. I had often fantasized with him that some day a young man would arrive to help us, with the practical abilities of a Walter Starck and his questioning mind. Over the past three days I have learnt enough of Barry to set him on a very high plane. Yesterday's sailing lesson and dolphin adventure all served to show him in action. Then there is his presence in the house with parents and friends about, gentle and loving, easy and thoughtful. Such circumstances do not usually occur so soon in an acquaintanceship and I already feel I have known him for a long time. A dolphin person.

It began the day we met the whales, four fin whales off the Knights. A windless, sulphurous day when the horizon was ringed with low haze. Plumes of whale spouts hung in spectral veils. . .

Whales, dolphins and sardines

29 October 1977: Malcolm was working on his garden, so Barry took over today as sailing master and steered us out of Tutukaka. Our mooring sank as we left. Curses! Peter Rippon, one of my oldest diving friends, was with us. I felt especially happy to be sharing this new venture with him after years of common experiences and mutual encouragement. Pete has always boosted my writing morale by registering enthusiastic comprehension. Karla and Brady, Graham Mosen and Pete Saul — a wonderful bunch of dolphin lovers. Astern trailed the new Avon inflatable on its first trial as an *Interlock* auxiliary.

Graham rigged the stereo, now in going order. With the motor cut and the sails spread, wafting along on a breeze of wind and music, it seemed no surprise, it seemed perfectly "Of course it should" when we sighted gannets wheeling. I enjoyed the novelty of an approach under sail, bowling along toward the Sugarloaf as the gannets grew larger. Graham switched over to the message tape. We all began digging out whistles and pipes. As the ship slid into their midst we put out a frenzy of acoustic nonsense — unworthy of intelligent consideration but an attempt to link our body actions, perched on the slender prows, or in the hammocks, with sound-making in air.

The response after several runs through, was an approach by a pair of listeners to hang motionless in that same curving, head awash posture we'd noticed the day Eric Kircher played the flute to them.

We caught up with them again at 1.50 pm. The message tape was playing "Echoes" sped up. A tremendous number rode the bows right across our seventeen-foot beam and along the sides. There was no hesitation this time at the presence of the hammock. One kept leaping out of the water and flapping on its side repeatedly. Another came speeding back underwater, turned behind us and raced up to the group. One had a nick in the top of his dorsal. There was another big powerful one with a large diagonal stripe down the right flank.

The dolphins went on their way and we noticed another doing side flaps: head out and then flap on its side; nine times we counted. They all sounded, not a thing to be seen. Then they came to the surface and the birds started diving again. We didn't recognise any from previous dolphin meetings.

The boys yelled that they saw four whales spouting in the vicinity. The dolphins split up into two groups and then came together again. Some dolphins continued playing on the bows while the rest were hunting. Those on the bow were really very interested in us now. The catamaran with her two hulls is so good for this. So many people can be with the dolphins at the same time.

Peter Rippon was standing on the bowsprit and the dolphins were turning on their sides looking up at him. Pete Saul and I got into the inflatable and motored quietly over to the centre of the feeding activity. It looked magnificent glancing back: people all lined up across the bows of *Interlock* with dolphins leaping about in front. The feeding activity was very intense. Dolphins, whales and birds all feasting frantically. A whale bobbed up within twenty yards of the inflatable.

At close quarters Pete and I saw the "meatball": a dense sphere of anchovies being devoured by gannets and dolphins. The gannets were no longer diving, just sitting on the water and gobbling them, thanks to the pressure of the dolphins beneath. We decided to return to the cat for a plastic bag to collect a fish sample. As we sped back minutes later Pete said, "They'll probably all be gone by the time we get there" — and they were!

We saw the last crumbs disappear. A dolphin seized a six-inch fish delicately in its jaws right alongside the boat. This was the most intimate glimpse of wild dolphins feeding we have ever witnessed.

When close to the whale we had an odd sensation of security. It knew we were there and could easily flatten us, but accepted our presence despite the hideous cruelty our species practises towards them. Why? Intelligent? Stupid?

Dolphin girl meets Sideband

17 November 1977: Last night charterboat skipper Ross Cotterill called in and said that he was going out to set a 100-hook driftline and would we like to come too. Eric Kircher and Sharon were visiting at the time and we asked them if they would care to join us. They jumped at the chance. It was a wonderful offer because Barry was off down to Auckland to hear Dr Paul Spong speak. At this stage we needed his help to handle the catamaran while we interlocked with dolphins.

It was a perfect day as we set off in *Marco Polo* towing *Interlock II*, the inflatable, behind. Jan, myself, Karla, Eric and Sharon and Ross. We soon noticed gannets working slightly to port as we headed out. Sure enough dolphins were working there too and we caught up with them at 9.30 am. A mother with her baby came alongside. They rode the bow while others approached from behind and in from the side. Ross stopped the motor and I heard Sharon say in a soft voice, "Don't go away — stay around."

The dolphins stayed, milling around the boat while Eric sat on the bow and played his flute to them. After showing interest for quite some time they rejoined the hunters. Eric and I set out in the inflatable to get closer without encroaching on the feeding. In their vicinity we cut the motor and drifted. Suddenly the dolphins were all around us and gannets plummeting through the surface in rapid succession like feathered missiles. One gannet hit the water right in front of Eric's nose. He looked at me questioningly but I was sure from past observation that gannets were much too adroit to hit us.

When the feeding frenzy ceased, probably because all the prey had been consumed, Eric began to play his flute. Jan could see the dolphin fins crowding around the inflatable. She struggled into the dolphin suit — just in case. I returned to the ship and picked her up. She finds the inflatable much easier to work from when she has the suit on and no legs. She just lay on the side and rolled in very gently.

While Eric played his flute a group of about two dozen dolphins circled the dolphin girl, inspecting her curiously for fifteen minutes as she dived and curved through the sea. After twenty minutes only three dolphins remained and then, just one. The rest resumed their fish-herding occupation with the main group.

The loner was so curious it came within four feet, spiralling slowly. When Jan descended it dived beside her, coming in much closer under-water than on the surface. When she ascended the dolphin rose too. Every now and then it would disappear but the water was so very green and murky with plankton it didn't have to go more than fifteen feet to be beyond her vision. With its sonar the dolphin could easily scan the dolphin girl as it circled in the fog. She knew it was closeby as she could hear its sonar whistle calls surveying her. Each time she dived, sure enough, into vision it came, circling very slowly.

"It was looking at me with that wonderful eye," Jan told us. She was quite overcome with emotion to have a creature like this come so close, scrutinising her with such interest over and over again. In these circumstances all she felt she could do was hang there motionless underwater gazing at the dolphin, taking in every part of its handsome, streamlined form so that she might recognise it again.

Sideband. It had a white vertical band on its left side behind the dorsal fin. It wasn't a scar but looked more like a watermark on a painting. A large dolphin, it was a paler grey than most.

Then she remembered to mimic it. The response amazed her. As soon as she began moving like a dolphin, Sideband responded by throwing its tail up and its head down, performing its own exaggerated version almost to the point of absurdity. Jan wanted to laugh for sheer joy.

Topside on the boat we watched the game with equal delight. You could have bet money on it — every single time that Jan ascended from a dive the dolphin would bob up alongside her, gasp and descend. We knew it had to be circling her out in the murk because every time she dived it would rejoin her.

After thirty minutes Jan was very tired and she rolled into the inflatable, now tethered to the big boat. She sat there alone, stretched along the side and to her delight right beside her in the water was Sideband. She extended her hand towards it as the inflatable glided forward under tow.

Her strength recovered when the original dolphin group returned. She slipped in again and dived. There were dolphins everywhere, sweeping beside, under and around her, all defaecating as they passed by. She performed a couple of rolls and noticed two dolphins do the same, their white bellies flashing.

After a while the majority withdrew leaving the same trio: Average White, Smallscar and her special friend Sideband. It swam along slowly with her and when she lost it in the murk, she dived. Always it would sweep in close, to surface beside her when she did. There was a definite pattern emerging. When she descended it always dived at the same time and came in closer to her than when on the surface.

She was unable to know its sex because she never caught a glimpse of its underside. It would pass her very close but always on the same level or slightly below. I shot a roll of film of the episode. I was itching to film it underwater but this might have upset the pattern emerging. Every so often the other dolphins would return for another look.

Twice Jan got out for a rest and each time Sideband swam beside the inflatable. The third time she got back in the water a fourth dolphin had joined the trio: Grillmark, with a grill pattern on its left flank just in front of its dorsal.

By now Jan was beginning to feel exhausted with continual diving and breath holding. She lasted only ten minutes, and remembers thinking, "If I black out now I wonder if this dolphin would come and support me?" She was getting dizzy from staring at the shafts of sunlight shining on the plankton particles, long rays forever angling down into the depths. As Hal Chapman told us after his very first, and very brief, dive, "I like infinity Wade, but not *that* close."

The moment Jan decided she would have to get out, unable to return, Sideband disappeared, as if it knew.

The total time this dolphin had bonded with her was four hours and twenty minutes. We were sure now that the dolphin suit must have had something to do with this because we have never had such intense interest before. In fact I have not been able to find any other account of a human/dolphin encounter in the open sea of such duration.

In our ordinary wetsuits common dolphins have come in and looked two or three times but always moved past pretty rapidly. This was much better. They were coming in slowly and sometimes just hanging there and, besides Sideband, the whole group stayed around for so long in comparison with previous interlocks. To round things off, when Jan got out, I joined the dolphins in my ordinary diving gear. Their responses were neither more nor less than I have found usual.

These dolphins did not appear to be the same group as we were with three weeks earlier when we met the whales. Quite a few had completely white dorsal fins and many were a paler grey than is usual, with hardly any cuts or disfigurements.

As we cruised homewards at sunset we wondered what would happen if we ever managed to meet the dolphins with more logistics: a whole team in dolphin suits, more musicians. Could we stay with the dolphins all through the night? Would we gain complete acceptance à la Jane Goodall? At least on this occasion it was our side that had terminated the interlock.

Touching

18 November 1977: So far this season, since our first interlock cruise on 6 October, we have made seven excursions and had four days of dolphin encounter of very high quality. On each occasion we have learnt important aspects of the communication game, distinct behaviour patterns have appeared and new equipment has been tested with surprising results.

We now know that the dolphin suit has especial interest for the dolphins, to the extent that a group of dolphins accompanied us for four hours twenty minutes after detaching from the main group, and that one of these virtually paired up with Jan over that period, never leaving her vicinity and diving with her every time she dived.

We know that the catamaran with its bow hammocks is especially useful in bringing a large number of people in touch with dolphins at one time. This has spin-offs in the quality of the contact as we are all communicating with each other on developments and so, probably, are they.

And yesterday both Malcolm and I *were contacted deliberately by dolphins* as we dangled our limbs amidst the bow-riders. While Pete Munro blew his trumpet on the port bow Malcolm extended his hand, fingers spread, from the starboard bow. A dolphin examined it in detail for some time, turning on its side about two feet from the hand.

I dangled a foot to offer an alternative — another human extremity.

Contact had been initiated by Malcolm who stroked the back of one which had been swimming close to his hand — it sped aside but not away. At that point he was in the centre of the net by the bell. He later shifted to starboard bow. I watched in sheer delight as the dolphin veered slightly and gave his hand a definite nudge. Shortly after I felt a dorsal fin glide sensuously between my toes. We continued, Malcolm with his hand on the starboard bow, me in the starboard hammock about three feet away.

Shortly afterwards I saw one sidle up to Malcolm's hand and give him another nudge. It was an unmistakable gesture. All the while the humpbacks were singing through the stereo in each bow and Pete was playing his trumpet to dolphins cruising just beneath the surface, two feet from the bell of his instrument.

During this encounter, each time the dolphins approached us, the first to arrive was Double Nick. When contact was broken this dolphin clapped his tail on the water very deliberately off our starboard bow. From there on the dolphins were hunting vigorously. After further attempts at contact we decided they were too busy with a small, fast-moving prey school so we hoisted sail and blew home on a path south of the Sugarloaf.

From the inflatable I took movie and stills of the ship gliding by, its sails adorned with our new dolphin insignia and Jan in the dolphin suit on the bow and Pete Munro blowing his trumpet on the stern.

On checking our notes three of the dolphins we met on this trip, including Grillmark who touched Malcolm, seem to be from the group we met the day before, two from Jan's close attendants.

Dolphin girl again

Journal, 2 January 1978: Several weeks elapsed before Jan had another opportunity to join the dolphins again clad in the dolphin suit. Once more their reception left her deeply moved.

With sweet flute music playing through the bow speakers, we met common dolphins out near the Poor Knights. It has become our practice to establish mutual trust from the outset by lying in the bow hammocks within their reach for some time before entering the water. In this way we are equally vulnerable to each other. Once they show an interest in the music and accept our presence close by, we feel we may enter their space.

Dolphin girl slid out of the net and clung to the leading edge for a while so the dolphins could see her. Two on the starboard bow looked across. She felt the catamaran slow down. She dived. Immediately five dolphins swam around her, moving slowly and showing great interest. She just kept swimming and diving as the dolphins circled, swooping under her, some coming up from behind, some straight towards her or in from the side. She was in ecstasy. The dolphins were keeping pace with her. She got the feeling she was moving in a set direction. She couldn't tell where, as she didn't want to raise her head from the water and break visual contact with her companions. She became aware that the dolphins were quietly leading her in their direction as she sought to stay with them. She just forgot about everything and became a dolphin.

Then she noticed there was only one dolphin left, a large one with the thickness toward the tail that denotes maturity. On the right side of its dorsal were two small scratches. All the others had departed. This dolphin kept surfacing beside her, sometimes on her left, sometimes on her right. Each time she caught sight of it again she would dive and beside her the dolphin curved its body in a very graceful arc and slid below too. In time with her body waves the dolphin performed a slow motion, exaggerated version of the dolphin-kick. Was it mimicking her or giving a lesson? Whatever, this was far from the usual behaviour of a dolphin and it was repeated maybe five or six times. Then it would go on ahead and slowly turn to the right or left to look back at her. She got the feeling it wanted her to follow. It was just as a dog runs in front of its master, frequently turning to see if he were coming. Body language. Then the dolphin would disappear into the haze only to turn and resume its position in front of her. Sometimes it came up behind her. Once it circled her steadily and she circled too, gazing in admiration at its form. She dived and rolled over. The dolphin didn't roll completely but spun on its side flashing its white belly at her. She was not quick enough to discern its sex. Then it took the lead, waggling its head in that slow motion dolphin curve again.

Jan noticed that each time it came back the period of separation was lengthening. During one of these intervals she suddenly realized she had forgotten the catamaran entirely, so absorbed by her companion and its antics. She was shocked to find us some four hundred yards away and could not believe she had swum so far oblivious of the boat, her own safety — everything. She saw us preparing to leave in the inflatable. With that momentary glance she felt as if a spell that had been binding her were broken.

The lone dolphin returned three more times and she dived with it repeatedly. Then it just didn't return. She wondered if the dolphin, sensing her distraction and concern, had decided to leave her. Its companions were afar.

As we hauled Jan out of the water she was raving, "It *must* be the dolphin suit, the fin and the dolphin-kick that fascinates them. I wonder what they think? A human trying to *copy* them! They kept swimming at my pace, not sweeping by fast as they usually do. I was able to stay with them and play. I wonder if I dreamt it all?"

Filming "The First Move"

9 February 1978: Last week the Doak family finished a thirty-minute television documentary about dolphins. But now I feel things have only just started to happen. When the film crew left I got a chance to search through my notes on the past two years' activity. I had a hunch that the dolphins who put on such a magnificent display for our film were not strangers. I felt sure we had met Bentfin and his companions before. . .

I read through every episode of our first year's activity. And yet it wasn't till I came to the very last chapter, Anniversary Day, January 1977, that I rediscovered Bentfin. There were even sketches in our notes of his fin pattern and those of his companions. Yet not one of us

80

remembered the link between those patterns. Not Jan, Karla, Bob Feigel nor myself who were all on board the Haines Hunter when Bentfin's group first rode our bows, and again on the catamaran when we filmed them, twelve months later.

This was more than any of us had bargained for. During our work we have encountered dozens of groups of common dolphins, maintaining contact with one over a period of six weeks. But Bentfin's group we'd met only once before. On that occasion, twelve months earlier, Jan and I had a dolphin experience so profound it prompted us to sell our home, car and runabout, to give up publishing, buy the Polynesian catamaran and devote ourselves to interspecies communication.

That exquisite day when we were able to play our cetacean message tape right through to them — a logical acoustic statement about the different sound channels used by humans and dolphins. The day the dolphins answered Bob Feigel's whistle calls with perfect mimicry, airborne sounds through their blowholes. . .

For a fortnight our journals tell of boat preparations, six days of filming at sea in a row, six of bad weather and then, the strangest dolphin day in our lives.

From the outset I'd had certain misgivings at making a television documentary about Project Interlock but the problems resolved themselves: first a young director turned up, Jason Olivier, with exactly the kind of sensibilities that would be needed in filming dolphins. And Jason enlisted cameraman John Longsworth and sound technician Bernie Wright, two men who we found could be trusted to treat our friends in the sea with high regard. Wild dolphins cannot be scripted into a preconceived narrative. All we can do is have all the gear ready and leave it to them. But such an approach to filming has its problems when it comes to paying the piper for his tune. Jason was quick to appreciate the situation. He had a small budget and only two weeks on location, but he would *not* follow a script — just take things as they came.

I figured the film would enable me to document something of our work properly (my own filming had served to set things in motion) and communicate our procedures to others who might try them. I was eager to share our discoveries and see how dolphins would respond to others who approached them creatively. A wild dream to stimulate a global interest in dolphins' games, the new interface.

But I wasn't to know just where the filming would lead us. Now it is over, I see it provided the energy to document a strange episode of human/dolphin communication exactly as it unfolded.

Since our last day together twelve months back, the day the dolphins whistled to him, Bob Feigel had been trying to put on paper the experience which first made him eager to know dolphins better and led to his coming to sea with us that Anniversary Day. Bob is a professional writer from Malibu, California but this was something almost impossible to put in words.

I once took a photo crossing Auckland harbour bridge on a wet night. Just resting my camera on the car window sill I made a time exposure of the city lights, neon signs, street lamps, buildings aglow, headlights and the wet roading with its reflections. My photo is a fantasia of light trajectories — a picture that records a third dimension: time. I showed it to Bob Feigel. That's just about what he saw the first time he experienced dolphins. Just before our film project he gave me an account. I titled it:

Bob encounters his first alien

On 12 November 1976 (see page 27) I was out on charter boat *Lady Jess* from Tutukaka heading back from a day of fishing around the Poor Knights along with some friends. There were probably twelve or so people on board and most of them were either aft or on the bridge with the skipper. I was hanging out one of the cabin doors on the port side thinking of nothing in particular when the inside of my head seemed to come alive with high-pitched sounds and something my mind's eye saw as multi-coloured dots zigzagging all over the place. If you've ever seen one of those electronic ping-pong games. . . It was like that, but in colour and multiplied by thousands, and the visual experience was connected with the auditory one. It wasn't a very pleasant feeling because of its intensity but it only lasted a few seconds when BLAM!, out of the water right in front of me jumped a dolphin.

It was huge and I've never been that close to any creature of the sea before, but of all things I remember feeling, fear wasn't among them. . .only a *very intense awareness*.

Its jump was a tight arc and when it reached the level of my face it seemed to hang in the air and look me straight in the eyes and then dive back in the water. It came up a short distance away one more time, and everyone on the boat ohhed and ahhed and then it disappeared. All in all I estimate the time involved to have been no more than sixty seconds.

The bouncing, multi-coloured dots were just as real as everything else. It seemed as if my perception had widened. The reality I had been experiencing a moment before was put into the background with this new overlay happening simultaneously — like a double exposure.

There was a hint of another dimension. The multi-coloured dots seemed to zip and zap all over the place, points of light moving infinitely away or close around without becoming larger or smaller, as if there were no up or down, or in or out, but a total 360-degree awareness.

There were more subtle movements too, slight changes in the colours and patterns of the "atmosphere" within which I seemed to be seeing the points of light. This atmosphere was crystal clear yet at the same time produced a sense of colour; a dimensional thing like layers of subtle, changing colours.

The discomfort was not caused by the intensity of the sound. It seemed I was not hearing in the usual sense but listening to sound registering in my head without coming through my ears. The sound was so beautiful, like some absolutely perfect electronic music. The discomfort came from trying to listen to it without hearing.

It would be like getting scared at going fast down a snow hill on a sled and dragging your feet and hands to slow yourself down. Then the thrill and excitement of going fast. Only I felt I was going downhill, afraid of taking off and going on forever. I felt that if I let myself hear and see then I'd disintegrate. It was not the sound or visual effects in themselves that produced discomfort and fear but my trying to handle them.

Both the sound experience and the visual seemed connected, just as the music and light at a rock concert can be connected, yet at the same time they were distinct and separate. Despite the intensity of the experience and discomfort, after it was over I felt as I would if someone I loved very much but hadn't seen for some time had come into my life for a short visit. I felt relaxed. . .I felt comfortable. . .and I felt full of love for everyone.''

Before any filming could commence aboard *Interlock* Barry Fenn issued us a friendly but firm ultimatum: The mast had to come down. On our last trip he had become uneasy. The top rigging had never been inspected since we bought the vessel and Barry had a hunch it was not safe. This meant beaching the catamaran near some strong trees to be used as ''deadman'' as the thirty-five-foot pole was lowered. We sailed *Interlock* around to Ngunguru River estuary and beached her on the firm sand in front of the Tana family piece of land.

This proved a perfect place to overhaul a Polynesian catamaran. The Tanas are a surviving relic of the traditional Maori extended family — a chip of Luaniua (described in *Islands of Survival*), the Polynesian village Jan and I had visited in the tropics; a warm, three-tier human group who accept us as their own and whose company we seek at the turning points of the year.

There were trees to tie onto, and many strong arms to haul on ropes. Raising a hull for repairs — twenty Tana men and women egged on by excited dogs and kids, heaved together and the thirty-six-foot wedge-shaped canoe rose high enough for baulks of timber to be jammed beneath the keel.

Once Barry had the vessel at his mercy he became a man possessed: the energy he released was cyclonic and soon he had whipped up an army of helpers. Some spent days sanding down the mast and brushing on four coats of varnish until it looked like coffee table legs. Others scrubbed down the hulls, mended the fibreglass sheathing and brushed on antifoul. Hectic days lying on our backs in the sand scraping and fixing and racing the tide.

Meanwhile Barry had another team strengthening the bridge deck, and most exciting of all, attaching the gleaming new twenty-inch rondels that Hal Chapman had painted for us. *Interlock* had eyes now: a pair on each bow, the ancient yin yang symbol of polar opposites such as Chinese voyagers to the Americas once bore on their junks.

And we *were* lucky: Barry's hunch proved true — the mast had been in a dangerous condition but when the tide again lifted our twin hulls afloat, the ship was ready for filming. Her old mainsail had been replaced with a new expanse of terylene that Jan had adorned with a pair of leaping dolphins. The film crew arrived and they, with a band of dolphin people, camped around us on our forest land at Ngunguru.

When *Interlock* left the Tanas one summer morning, the early river at low tide, kids drifting about fishing for sprats, a tern poised at the water's edge, the journey downstream was interminably long for twelve people yearning to reach the sea.

In the six days that followed not one was spent on land. At five each morning we all had to leap from tents and caravans so we could be on the sea as the sun rose over the bows. They filmed *Interlock* entering and leaving Tutukaka Harbour at sunrise and sunset, sailing around the Poor Knights Islands through archways, past tunnels and cave mouths.

It was a major adventure to take the catamaran into Rikoriko Cave. We knew the ceiling was much higher than our mast but nobody could be sure about the entrance tunnel. Barry rigged a bosun's chair and we hoisted Brady to the mast top. The vessel then backed up very cautiously to the cave entrance while some of us went off in the inflatable for a better angle on the situation. Tension mounted. Brady yelled, "We're going to clear easily."

So we went out, turned and entered bow first. High on the mast, nearly forty feet above the water, Brady watched the craggy ceiling glide past ten feet above him until we reached the soft cool darkness of the interior dome. When his feet hit the deck his eyes still sparkled with excitement.

Within the cave the yacht seemed like a strange yellow toy. Knowing we could negotiate the portal was quite a triumph as this was *El Torito*'s favourite anchorage during our six-month filming stint around the Poor Knights back in 1974 — a refuge from bad weather in the vast hangar.

While they filmed several exits and entrances and silhouettes of the ship framed in the portal Jan took the opportunity to scuba dive below us. She sat on the sandy floor of Rikoriko while a school of golden snapper folded around her head. As they swam through shafts of sunlight streaming from the portal, their bodies glinted gold. Looking up she could see through the lens of their bulging nocturnal eyes. She enjoyed the peacefulness of diving by herself, wandering at will in the cave space.

Another day was spent filming us diving with the dolphin suit and perfecting the undulating rhythm by wearing a tape recorder, and then, the improved version — an effortless flow.

The third day we were making a fast passage home when Hal Chapman saw two dolphins leap dead ahead. They held the pattern of the leaping dolphins on our sail. For five minutes they raced on our plunging bows while the film crew shot a few hundred feet. But it was too rough for interlock and they sped off into the wave crests.

The following day, by an immense stroke of luck, we managed to shanghai Bob Feigel. Poor Bob was in the throes of deportation (he has subsequently gained New Zealand citizenship) but when our friends, the Slark family, offered to whisk him out in their runabout to join us on the catamaran, Bob didn't hestitate. He knew we wanted to record his strange dolphin experience on film. I'll never know how Bob could sit on our sunny foredeck and give an interview with such vivacity and warmth twelve miles out on the ocean when ashore, for him, all hell was breaking loose.

When the film was in the can he turned quietly to me to say he had had a dream. He saw me up on the bowsprit of the catamaran (a foot wide plank that runs fore and aft midway between the hulls, between the foremost crossbeam and the next) surrounded by seven dolphins. In the dream he saw the interlock rondels fitted on our bows, although Bob knew nothing of them. One large dolphin communicated telepathically, directing towards me a Maori word, "tepuhi" or "tepuke". Now Bob is an American and knows no Maori. As it proved, this is a rare expression anyway.

"Find out what it means," Bob urged.

Then the runabout raced him back to the coast and his battle with bureaucracy.

For the next two days we sailed and sailed but not a sign of a dolphin — just superb weather and a deserted ocean — no gannets, no schoolfish, no action. The film shows us in Rikoriko Cave again, endeavouring to "think dolphin", calling the dolphins. . .

Then the heavens opened up on us and for the next six days we could not go to sea because of bad weather and strong onshore winds.

Meeting a Maori elder

Jason Olivier and I took the opportunity to drive up the coast to meet Waipu Pita, an elder of the Ngatiwai tribe and see if we could arrange a filmed interview with him. As we pulled up at his door Waipu was just getting off a horse. The stocky, silverhaired Maori apologised for the tear in his shorts.

"Just breaking in this racehorse," he explained politely, nodding at the sleek creature tethered to the fence. Jason and I were mentally reeling. We knew Waipu was seventy-six years old, but age had not diminished his powers.

We met his wife and their pretty five-year-old daughter. In their lounge we discussed dolphins with Waipu and later arranged to film our questions and his replies. Waipu told us that to him the dolphin was like a human in the sea. If a canoe or boat were in trouble, dolphins would appear and the distressed Ngatiwai would follow them.

"When they start to jump and dive you know you are clear. Our people once used dolphins as an echo-sounder."

He told us how dolphins would reveal new fishing grounds to them. "The Maori once regarded the dolphin as some kind of a god or influence to direct them to things they wanted to know. To me it is a human being in the sea," he repeated with conviction.

"I swim with them, I play with them. Where I live in Whangaruru Harbour just a chain from the water we hear a splash and then a pip and we know they are in the harbour. Early in the morning we get up and go out and all the family swim with them. You can ride on them. But no funny tricks. I've seen my uncle Hohepa Pita play a flute to them.

The dolphins may be spread out over the sea. When the flute is played they bunch together and frolic around the music.''

Jason asked, "Could you tell us about calling the dolphin?''

"We only call dolphins when we need help in a rough sea, or in difficulty or if there is something we would like to know about relatives at a distance over the ocean. If a relative is sick when the dolphin appears it will give a sign whether or not that person will recover or has already recovered. We can tell from the way it leaps.''

Jason: "Do you call dolphins as individuals or is it a general call?''

"You can't call a dolphin as an individual. The dolphin always swims in a group. Therefore you call them in a group. When you try to separate dolphins it's a sad moment for them. The Maori people nowadays mostly live in European society and to them it's just a story or a dream. It would not work for them any more — like a young animal, a horse, you train to suit you and then neglect. When you go to it again it will refuse to do what you taught it before. That's why calling the dolphins doesn't work for most people now. Some Maoris still have the gift — even a European may.

"Dolphins can always tell whether you're genuine in your feelings. I don't know whether you've noticed or not. If you are genuine in your desire they will do exactly what you want.''

Waipu explained to us that you don't call the dolphins directly but through a special bird that flies with them — Tukaiaia, the sea hawk. He sang us an incantation to the sea hawk. He showed us a sacred walking stick with a snake entwining the shaft and the seabird's head for a handle.

"That bird is the emblem of the Ngatiwai people.''

Then I put the question I had been longing to pose: "Waipu, we have a friend called Bob Feigel who seems to have the gift. He's had some interesting dolphin experiences. The other day he told me he had a dream and in that dream he could see me on the bowsprit of our catamaran with the dolphins around. He said there was a word in the dream that seemed very important — something like 'tepuhi' or 'tepuke'. Does that mean anything to you?''

The elder smiled gently. "That's the flowing out of the breath from the dolphin's blowhole,'' he told us. "It's not a dream when it's like that,'' he added. "It's real.''

Finally, Waipu explained, it conveyed a subtle point: the third syllable of the word "tepuhi'' was neither an 'h' nor a 'k' but a Maori aspirate something in between. Onomatopoeically "puhi'' mimics the rapid exhalation and inhalation of a dolphin. Try it.

Footnote: Maori attitudes and relationships with dolphins compare interestingly with those of the ancient Greeks. A Maori elder from Hawkes Bay told me later her people believed that if one reached a high level in this life, one became a dolphin or a whale. In the oral tradition the first two migratory double canoes to reach New Zealand were guided here by whales. Most families formerly had a dolphin that was their family member in the sea, a protective ancestor or "aumakua''.

Anniversary Day again

The camera crew had been with us for two weeks. Every aspect of our work on sea and land had been filmed. But no dolphins. Fair weather eluded us from the start. Jason Olivier, the director, got an extension of time from head office. The very next day had to be our dolphin day or the whole film would flop.

There were thirteen on board that Anniversary Day. As we sailed over the big swells those of us who had previous experience with the dolphins (our family, Hal Chapman, Eric Kircher, Bob Feigel, Barry Fenn, Karen Buckley) communicated a quiet confidence that they *would* appear. By contrast the film crew were getting pretty twitchy. Even the cool jazz from our bow transmitters couldn't dissipate all the tension on board. But the dolphin gamesters remained serene.

"They're here!" Jan yelled. She was holding the tiller and saw them gliding through the water from behind us. The motor was silent, our ship dancing down wind. Those dolphins were acting in a strange way. Not rushing in exuberantly and cavorting on the bows as usual. Just lying in the water quite still, and then moving gently into the ship's path and sweeping around in between her hulls. The games began.

The film crew dashed off in the inflatable to shoot our bow activities from dead ahead. This upset the usual pattern of interlock procedures, and from this point I realized that in documenting them it would be very difficult not to interfere. Yet somehow that day the dolphins seemed to be running the whole film show themselves. While Jan wriggled into the dolphin suit the film crew were surrounded by dolphins. I've never seen them behaving in such an intimate manner, really hamming it up: cruising straight towards the camera on the surface, several fins converging on the lens like a "Jaws" fantasy, making delicate arching leaps right alongside the inflatable — it was all happening at such an intensity they would have needed three cameras. It was as if the dolphins really knew our purpose.

When Jan slid in wearing the dolphin suit the slow pace changed to a frenzy of excited manoeuvres as dolphins whirled around her, imitating her actions, filling the sea with sounds and graceful forms. Waggling their heads and rolling on their sides they swept by her over and over only to turn sharply and come speeding right back, veering aside at the last second. As usual one particular dolphin seemed to adopt her, coming closer and staying longer.

"I've never felt such joyousness and excitement generated from the dolphins," she told us later. "I could hardly breathe."

In the water with her I felt an electric heat — my suit became too hot and I would have liked to swim free of it. I saw a dolphin with a bent fin — like one I'd seen before — but when? Another with the tip of its fin missing and one with a scratch on its left side.

At one stage the inflatable stopped suddenly. The cameraman kept going, just managing to toss his $25,000 Arriflex back aboard before he flopped on the dolphins. Normally with such a shock the dolphins would vanish. On this occasion they stayed in close but never again allowed the cameraman while in the water to get on the same side of the boat as themselves. If John changed sides, they switched to the other. It seems clear that trust is a delicate affair; man is still a dangerous, unpredictable creature from their point of view, and you can only go so far. . .

As I dolphin-swam among the curving forms I closed by eyes, just hearing and feeling the ocean. My mind screen registered something like canoes with latticed patterns of green. All of a sudden it came to me: that word in Bob's dream. I removed my mouthpiece and yelled it into the ocean, "Teeepoooheee."

At that moment a dolphin released a huge plume of air from its blowhole just like the exhaust from a scuba diver. My hood may have prevented my hearing any sound it may have made so I swam down and gulped at the swirling screen of bubbles — an improvised response gesture such as the food exchange rituals we shared with people in the islands.

That very instant all the dolphins gathered into a tight formation, a phalanx with a leader at the centre. Beneath Jan and me they swirled around in a clockwise turn, spiralled powerfully towards the surface and vanished out.

As my mask cleared the water, I saw them all poised in midair — some three dozen dolphins in perfect line abreast. Off they sped, the whole row surging north towards Whangaruru in a series of superb leaps. When I climbed aboard *Interlock* every person on board had seen that gesture. (The film captures it perfectly.) And everyone knew it was a final gesture; we would not see the dolphins again that day.

I recalled the words of Waipu Pita: in the old culture when the dolphin leaps in a special way, that is a sign. . .

"Tepuhi", I have learnt, is an especially easy word to pronounce underwater. It has an energy all of its own.

Two nights later, as the film crew were preparing to leave, Bernie the sound man played to us the tape he made that day, when surrounded by dolphins. We heard their blowholes and the music of the catamaran approaching, voices, whale sounds, Bob Feigel whistling. And then we heard whistles close to the microphone.

"Just a minute," said Jan. "Did those whistles come from the dolphins' blowholes?"

John the cameraman said, without any surprise, "Yes." He thought this was quite a normal thing for dolphins to do.

And then, when the film crew left, I had time to follow up my hunch that we'd met Bentfin and his group before. . . There it was: Anniversary Day 1977, the whistling dolphins.

Why didn't we do them the courtesy of remembering them, Bentfin and his group, responding intelligently in a manner consistent with our previous contact: the message tape; complete silence; then Bob's whistle calls? We might then have recorded their responses and taken another step into the unknown.

Our belief models are still too inflexible to allow the dolphins memories better than our own. Will we be given another chance?

Footnote: Jason titled the film "The First Move". He had picked up a phrase I used in an interview:

"We're the manipulators. We have to make the first move. . ."

Tepuhi

When the film was televised — 3 July 1978 — we started to receive some exciting feedback. But the letter we got from Sam McHarg prompted us to sail fifty miles north to meet him. What Sam has to say is extraordinary but we found him to be a no-nonsense headmaster, a Rotarian and a man for whom the sea has been a lifetime passion.

Here is what Sam wrote:

"For over thirty-five years I have spent most of my spare time sailing boats. During that time I have had many happy experiences with dolphins, two scary experiences with orca (Tasman Bay) and one very interesting meeting with a half-grown humpback whale (Tasman Bay 1948).

"For some years I have thought that by whistling at dolphins I could sort of make contact. Many of my friends tap their heads, and look upon me as one might a person who talks to trees.

"November 1978 I was helping to deliver a yacht from Auckland to Kerikeri. It was fine and dead calm. We were about one half-mile west of Hen Island (all of thirty miles south of the Poor Knights), doing four knots under motor. Common dolphins were feeding nearby and broke off to play around our bow. As usual I lay on the bow with my hands above the water doing my whistling act much to the amusement of the gang in the cockpit. After having a very good look at me, one dolphin came right in under my hand and I stroked it. I did this to several. I then called 'Tepuhi' and the dolphins all jumped and crowded in for a stroke! Silence from the cockpit and wide eyes.

"'How did you do that?' I was asked.

"I told them I had given a Maori greeting to the dolphins.

"'Rubbish!' they cried as they called 'Hi there', 'Knickers', 'Muldoon', etc to the dolphins with no reaction.

"I then called loudly 'Tepuhi' again and the whole sea erupted as the dolphins all jumped (for joy?). The crew still wouldn't believe it and kept up their own greeting shouts. No reaction from the dolphins who were swimming on their sides to get a look at us. Three times I shouted 'Tepuhi' and each time the sea erupted. A photo of the crew's faces would have shown open mouths and wide eyes. The dolphins then left us to carry on feeding.

"Good luck with Project Interlock. I think you are really onto something. In the meantime I will keep talking to a creature that I believe has tried to communicate with me."

In the months to come we were to receive a series of letters from Sam — we had found a fellow enthusiast whose dolphin experiences parallel and extend our own.

Spiritual interlock

Journal, 20 August 1978: Our researches suggested that each winter the common dolphins usually withdrew from these coastal waters from late May until early August. They may move further offshore and we have had reported sightings thirty miles out during this period.

I had just returned from a lecture tour and felt a great need to renew our acquaintance. Visiting us at the time were Michael, Paddy and Janice, three Greenpeace people from Auckland, and Terry, a Friend of the Earth, from Christchurch. Although they came to discuss communication aspects of the tragic Manukau *Pseudorca* strandings (report, appendix A), after two days' talk they were eager to meet the dolphins.

The catamaran had not been to sea for some time owing to bad weather and my absence on tour and we were rather worried whether everything would be in working order. To our delight after all the heavy rain *Interlock* was bone dry and the motor ran smoothly.

Just outside the harbour we switched it off and found enough wind to whisk us offshore nicely. We sighted birds towards the Sugarloaf and headed over. Approaching we noticed a chain of dolphins engaged in fish-herding manoeuvres with gannets plunging in their midst. Respectfully we altered course to run north parallel with them and at least a mile distant. We rang the bell only six times, just enough to signal our presence.

To our delight, dolphins surged out of the water and headed towards us, approaching from the starboard quarter. Our first contact for the new season; how would they react when they saw the bow nets? I felt a great surge of emotion as the sleek forms approached our hulls underwater, shooting beneath to surface between our bows where humpback songs were pulsing through the speakers.

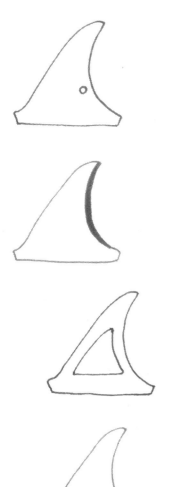

The catamaran was sailing at only three knots and the motor was silent. The attraction that held us cannot be ascribed to bow riding. This was a very gentle, quiet meeting. All on board were affected with a state of blissful calm, taking up positions, one on each bow and three in the nets, offering open hands and dangling feet in trust. To banish a manipulative mental state I had taken just one telephoto as they headed towards us and then stowed my camera.

This was a human group in a thoroughly receptive mood. The dolphins were a youngish group, with no sign of worn dorsals, so were hard to recognise. I did sight one with a white spot near the trailing edge of its dorsal, left side. Some had pale dorsals. One in particular was a very pale grey, almost white with a black fringe to the trailing edge. Another had a pale grey triangle in the centre of its dorsal and another a small white scar the size of an egg on its left side under the dorsal.

Whenever they broached I would call "Tepuhi", the blowhole word. These dolphins were behaving in a special way: swimming on the surface with their backs awash for prolonged periods, or on their sides just beneath the surface, gazing up at us, thronging tightly around the bows interweaving and ducking under one another to avoid collison. Often when they dived they would raise the tail-fin gently and slip under just as we do with our fins.

Then they blew our minds. One dolphin directly in front of us made a distinct, high-pitched sound with its blowhole. Everybody on board heard it. The only sound from our ship was the whale song — it seemed that the dolphins were listening to the tape and making low frequency sounds in air for our benefit. Then it occurred again, right under me on the starboard bow. I watched the blowhole pucker and vibrate. From the way these dolphins were clustering around the bows and turning on their sides it seemed the rondels were being scrutinised. Another blowhole sound, like someone blowing raspberries.

Our first contact for months, seemingly strangers to us, yet these dolphins appeared to know the boat and what it was about. There was no mistrust of the net. One dolphin out ahead slapped down flat on the surface several times and another made several leaps. There followed a distinctive turning, surging, up-and-down movement which seems to signal departure. The main part of the fish-herding group was miles to the north where gannets circled overhead. In a flash they left us. Time had been distorted; what seemed an hour was an intensive twelve minutes of sheer joy.

On the ship an aura of great happiness surrounded us all and it remained for the rest of the day. As Terry remarked, "I hardly knew you people before," indicating Michael, Janice and Paddy, "but I do now."

During the first part of the interlock Terry had been steering. The dolphins were coming around the stern too, slapping their tails on the surface near him. Wishing they would come he had even articulated his urging, "C'mon give us a share", as in football.

We called this the spiritual interlock; it demonstrated to us the value of a highly ethical approach to dolphins: just signalling our presence on the outskirts of their "village" was all we need do. In these circumstances a small band separated from the main group to meet us on a highly communicative level and the behaviours we were able to observe were of a very different nature from the usual bow-riding high jinks dolphins display around a vessel moving at speed. It also showed us that an inflexible, methodical approach could very well be counter-productive if we were to learn the subtleties of dolphin behaviour. For the future of such studies this objective/subjective polarity entails the greatest enigma of all.

Footnote: During the winter of 1980 the withdrawal pattern changed: *Delphinus* remained in the Poor Knights area throughout the winter months. We received a report and photos of individuals that responded to physical contact from the bow of a charterboat.

Another recurrence?

Journal, 17 November 1978: Today we may have again met the dolphins who were present the first time the dolphin suit was tested, *exactly one year ago*. Karla woke us with a cup of tea and the radio to listen to the marine forecast. It was going to be a boat day. We took a while to get moving as we had been up until 2 am projecting transparencies with Quentin Bennett, on a visit from Napier.

We were stunned by the incredible quality of Quentin's slides — among the most exquisite underwater pictures we have seen. Quentin has been diving from the earliest days and we share passions for marine life and being in the ocean. Always a pioneer of new techniques in underwater photography, optics and equipment, Quentin introduced the decompression meter and constant volume Unisuit to the New Zealand diving world. His boyish zest and quiet sincerity, his love of body surfing and concern for the coastal environment of Hawkes Bay all endear him to us. I was never more delighted than to learn that Quentin is equally interested in dolphins and dives with them at every opportunity.

So over breakfast we asked his plans. We would like to go out on the catamaran if he could fit it in. Although he had to drive to Rotorua that night he wasn't going to miss a day at sea. We had a few chores like going to the shop for weekend supplies and fuel so it was eleven before we found ourselves on the ocean.

We sailed east towards the Knights and as the wind shifted, altered course until we were to the north, off Matapouri. By now we had adapted to sailing, allowing the wind to determine our course rather than pursue a fixed goal.

We sipped tea with the warm sun shining on us and the rippling blue ocean all around. Suddenly Jan felt a surge of elation. A very positive feeling that something good was going to happen. She had been apprehensive about getting into the dolphin suit again after a winter break and wondered if she could cope. But that moment she felt sure it was going to be fine and never had another qualm. At first she hesitated to mention her feelings to us. What if nothing happened? But at length she did say to Quentin and me, "I feel positive something good is going to happen today. Perhaps it's because Quentin is with us."

Shortly after I spotted gannets diving, trained the binoculars on them and yelled "Whales". There were quite a few, well spread out and they seemed to be feeding. They were bringing their heads well out of the water, then splashing down, sweeping around in a circle on their sides with one huge flipper rising high above the water. They may have been rounding up plankton or small fry. We trailed them quietly observing their actions until they drew too far ahead. Just as we altered course towards the Knights a whale surfaced astern giving us quite a surprise.

By now the day was well advanced but Quentin decided he was enjoying himself far too much on the ocean to worry about driving to Rotorua — so we just kept going. We sighted a huge sunfish. I'd seen a fin a few minutes before so there may have been two in the area.

I was gazing around the horizon and had centred on some birds working. Jan was steering. Suddenly she turned her head to the right. We both saw it, toward the Pinnacles, and exclaimed together. A dolphin had leapt high out of the water, its white belly flashing and sparkling so clearly there was no doubt. And yet it was such a long way off — some five miles upwind. We motored over.

We didn't see dolphins for a long while but headed towards a flock of gannets that formed fragmentary groups diving down, breaking off and moving on, as when they are with fast moving dolphins. Not till quite close did we sight them. We rang the bell. Four broke away from the hunt to frolic around the boat. Two gave an amazing demonstration of love making. One turned upside down, resembling a small yacht, its white belly flashing as it sped past, its mate on top. Joined belly to belly

92

they rolled and manoeuvred in joyful display. Jan and I grabbed each other in a mock demonstration of the human equivalent.

Quentin was already in his suit. "Would you like to get in while we get ready? If they stay around we'll swap over."

One of us would have to mind the boat. We lowered the sails so we wouldn't move too fast once divers were in the water. The dolphins were up ahead. We motored towards them ringing the bell. When they rejoined us this time there were more of them and they showed great interest.

Jan had the tiller and the dolphins kept going back and playing around the inflatable and at the stern. Then they would rush up to the men on the bows. I turned the motor off. The tape was playing and they were poised quite still in the water all around the bows in the listening stance.

Quentin was in the water hanging onto the net. Then he swam out and away from the boat. The dolphins showed not the least surprise or fear. They stayed around him playing together near the stern. Quentin dived and dolphin-swam. They continued to circle and frolic. Clearly it was interlock so I joined him. Again it was instant acceptance.

Meanwhile Jan was taking longer than usual to find all the bits and pieces of her suit and wondering if the dolphins would still be there. Something told her, "You must get in and show them the suit."

Once those thoughts crossed her mind she hurried as fast as she could. With the sails down and the stern platform lowered causing drag, the catamaran was barely moving — fine for those in the water.

Quentin and I got out raving, even though the water was a murky green with a springtime plankton bloom and Quentin had found it strenuous snorkelling in the Unisuit as it still had some air trapped in it, restraining his descents.

With the murk it meant the dolphins had to come very close for visual contact. In such conditions they could readily have echo-located the diver without his seeing them at all.

But these dolphins were extremely friendly: rapidly familiar with the boat, moving slowly and examining everything in detail from bow to stern and around the inflatable. We looked for identifiable markings but they had perfect dorsal fins. One had a tiny nick near the top. *Yet we had a feeling we had seen them before*. I even mentioned that they could be the same ones we'd met last year, the day one had bonded with Jan in the dolphin suit for four hours. That day it had been a small group of dolphins too, and four of them had broken away from the main group to play, finally one staying beside her while others resumed their fishing.

It was now Jan's turn. While Quentin and I were out the dolphins had moved on. We motored up ringing the bell again. A number broke away and played on the bows. We turned off the motor. Jan slid down the stern ramp thinking she would have to swim up to the bows to be with the dolphins. To her delight as she entered the sea there was no need to swim anywhere.

From the bows the dolphins came to meet her. She had no time to consider whether she was in good shape or not. She had thoughts only for the dolphins. Six of them circling so close. She dived and dolphin-curved. A familiar pattern recurred. Whenever she went below the dolphins would mill around, but closer than ever before.

She just couldn't believe her eyes. She felt a warmth all over, just as when with someone you love or a very close friend. Her attention was drawn to one in particular who came the nearest of all. There was no vertical side scar nor any other blemish but she felt intuitively it could be Sideband, the same one that befriended her last year. The size seemed about the same, a big, powerful dolphin. Superficial scars may heal completely and are not reliable for longterm identification.

She recalled how, when we first started getting in the water with dolphins, they used to dart away and then come rocketing back at high speed looking at us on the way past. How things had changed! These dolphins were so close and swimming so slowly with no sign of nervousness. They were like the tamest of pets.

Initially Jan dived frequently. As she left the surface she might not know where they were but then they would suddenly come into view, sweeping all around. She could easily have touched the special one but something restrained her hand. She was afraid it might spoil the whole interlock, breaking the spell.

"One day I'll know when I can do that — stretch out my hand and touch a wild dolphin. There will be a right moment for that."

As she tired she lay on the surface watching them weave beneath her. But then the dolphins came closer to her while on the surface than ever before. She had only to dive a few feet to be right beside them. She didn't even have to clear her ears.

Next dive she really concentrated on this one dolphin. As it circled she revolved, admiring it continuously. The other dolphins withdrew. There was only Jan and the special one. Eventually she had to return to the boat from sheer exhaustion. The dolphin rejoined its companions.

Quentin, who had swum with dolphins before, was deeply impressed.

"Those dolphins came closer than the tame ones in Napier Marineland. In captivity they were very suspicious of me."

Jan: "Yes, and these are wild dolphins. They don't have to stay around us at all. They don't even have to come near us."

By this time the day was getting very late but I desperately wanted to get a few photos of fin patterns. The dolphins were feeding intensively now but when we approached several obliged by coming to our bows.

On the home run we had a very late lunch/tea as it was 6 pm, chatting and enjoying sailing into the setting sun. Quentin decided to go below and sleep as he had a six-hour drive ahead of him. About two miles out from Tutukaka something caught Jan's eye as she tended the jib. A dolphin swimming alone on the inside of the port hull. We wondered how long it had accompanied us, miles from its companions — most unusual.

The first thing we did on reaching home was look up the fin identification file (normally kept on board). To our utter amazement we found that it was on this very same day one year before that we had met a small group of dolphins and one had bonded with Jan for four hours!

94

So the dates coincided. That put a whole new light on things. We chewed it over asking ourselves dozens of questions. Why? Why? Why?

Why had Jan been so sure something was going to happen? Why had we both independently noticed that dolphin leap from so far away? Jan asked, "Why that feeling that I simply *must* get in with those dolphins in the suit? And why the feeling that I knew those dolphins?"

We could only guess, which is sad. We don't even recognise our friends in the sea that we met a year ago unless they bear some disfigurement. But Jan intuited they were the same ones from the whole pattern of their actions, their super friendliness, total lack of fear and the close approaches. Then we recalled how they had spent so much time around the inflatable. They kept coming back to play near it — not a typical behaviour. The previous year it was the inflatable we'd been using. Sideband had stayed beside it every time Jan boarded it for a rest. On that occasion we were not aboard the catamaran but the charter vessel *Marco Polo*, with the inflatable in tow.

We reprimanded ourselves for not having the identification file on board. Then we might have known at once that this was the same day and perhaps managed to establish whether it was the same dolphins from a year back.

A week later my transparencies returned from the processors. Several fin patterns matched closely with those from last year's 17 November encounter and the "touching day" group (18 November).

It now appears as if "recurrences", as I call them, have occurred on the anniversaries of our two most important communication experiments: the message tape and the dolphin suit; acoustic and body-language channels.

While the cynic may justifiably say that such conclusions are conjectural, the converse could as readily be true. And the implications of such intent in the context of all that science has now learnt about dolphin capacities, are food for deep consideration.

Both experiments elicited responses quite out of the ordinary in the history of human/dolphin relationships. The dolphin brain has the storage potential to remember and respond to something at an interval of twelve lunar cycles. Within the limitations of body language what better way to reaffirm the communication than celebrate its anniversary? And stumbling over our own incredulity we have twice failed to respond with full recognition.

The enigma we face in exploring interspecies communication has already been foreseen. As I was writing a friend showed me the works of Indian Sufi mystic, Pir Vilayat Inayat Khan.

"The day we are faced with the problem of communicating with beings on other planets, we shall be forced into thinking in terms of our identity as planetarians, beyond our individual identity. Then we will realize that our language, the tool of our individual thinking, stands in the way of our intuition. The only language that will enable us to communicate will be intuition. Similarly, when communicating with beings on planes other than the physical, we shall have to overcome our consciousness of ourselves as created beings (cf. Jan forgetting herself

2.1.78) in order to communicate at the only level that links all beings: the divine consciousness.''*

Elsewhere Khan defines this as ''omega consciousness'' which starts with experiencing what it is like to be another person, finally reaching a collective level of consciousness linking all beings — planetary consciousness.

*Physics and the Alchemy of Consciousness, Pir Vilayat Inayat Khan, 1979.

PART THREE

Dolphin Approaches to Humankind

"The cetaceans in many subtle ways have shown us their willingness and their initiative to help: their co-operativeness is real and ancient. It is time for us to respond to them with our best knowledge and our best efforts."

— Dr John Lilly

6

The ambassadors

SHORTLY AFTER Quentin Bennett's return to Napier that same month, a lone dolphin, a *Tursiops*, arrived off Westshore beach close by the airport. With spectacular tail standing leaps it drew attention to itself and would hover around a marker buoy in the bay. When boats approached it delighted in frolicking on their bows. By 4 December, its antics had reached the notice of the local press and a small circle of dolphin enthusiasts began to devote their time to observing its movements. Bottlenose dolphins are uncommon in this area.

To complement our own attempts to initiate meetings with wild dolphins I had been researching the written record of dolphin approaches to humankind. I thought the story began with the famous Pelorus Jack and Opo epics in New Zealand but then I learnt of a similar episode at Hippo in North Africa in A.D. 109 (See page 115).

In modern times I had found accounts of Nina in Spain, Charlie in Scotland and Donald in Wales and England. I'd been avidly following reports of Donald who played intricate games with British divers for six years. When Dr Horace Dobbs wrote a book, *Follow a Wild Dolphin*, about Donald I was enthralled. Two scientists wrote papers on aspects of Donald's behaviour which I added to our DINT file. I labelled these episodes "dolphin initiated interlocks" and then coined the acronym DINTs (see next chapter).

And now something was happening in New Zealand for the third time in recent history. How wonderful that it was in Napier where Quentin would follow the developments and keep Project Interlock informed. How odd that this dolphin had chosen Napier, the only place in New Zealand where captive dolphins are on public exhibition, to make its approach.

Events at Napier were still budding when Quentin was surprised to receive a letter from me written on 22 December which read as follows:

We've just concluded two amazing days of involvement with a lone *Delphinus*, who came into Ngunguru River. Now, as I cast my mind back over the events since last Monday morning, I can see it as a series of happenings or a pattern of things that we learnt about dolphins and human behaviour toward them.

Terry and Ali Goodall, a young Christchurch couple smitten with the Northland bug, have been having their third holiday up here, this time staying over in the geodesic dome. Terry was with us the day we first met *Delphinus* this season — the day we call the "spiritual interlock" because of the energy level it reached.

Ever since then Terry has been totally overwhelmed with dolphins — he arrived up here with a hydrophone and speaker linked to a tape recorder that he'd put together.

Unfortunately throughout their stay the sea had not been favourable to interlock experiments — he came at the end of a long, calm spell of weather to enter one when our wind generator has been screaming.

On Monday morning around ten I was down in the summer garden playing around with an irrigation system, when Jan stepped into the glade: "There's a dolphin in the river."

Mrs Johnson, who lives on the bend opposite the first mangroves in the Ngunguru estuary, had driven up to tell us it had been there since 9 am, just cruising around on the incoming tide.

"This *can't* be a coincidence," said Terry, arriving up the hill at the barn just as I got there and told him the news. "I've just come to collect my diving gear. Ali and I were going for a mangrove dive."

Most of our diving gear is stored aboard ship but we managed to hunt out one old wetsuit and the new sets of fins, masks and snorkels which Allan G. Mitchell donated to us.

Out in the river we saw a black fin being followed gently by two boys in a dinghy. From the description we suspected it was a small *Tursiops* — especially since this species has been observed in situations like this. To my surprise Jan yelled across the water that it was *Delphinus*. She was first to establish visual contact underwater. Out amidst a line of boats and moorings she dived under and the two met at six feet range. We were staggered to find a common dolphin, creature of the open sea, cruising in an estuary.

On the river edge a group of children were calling, "Here dolphin, here dolphin," their hands outstretched. The dolphin moved towards the children. We couldn't believe our eyes when it swam through the shallows right up to the children and grounded. It didn't appear to be in the least afraid. Afterwards Jan said it seemed as if the dolphin had a mission to accomplish. Children were milling about straining to pat and stroke the sleek form. Sang one little girl with shining eyes, "I've never touched a dolphin before."

The total trust and passive self-surrender were quite uncanny. Somehow this affected the beach dogs. They were barkless and spellbound by the whole interlock as the children lavished their affection on the shining sea creature. I was so interested in watching this spontaneous child/dolphin interaction that I didn't involve myself for some time. I took some pictures and then approached.

Jan was warning the kids not to put their hands near its blowhole. Gently they splashed water over the glistening skin and she told them to avoid getting any near the blowhole when it was breathing. Faces alight with pleasure they were wide open to any suggestion and very ready to learn. I began to whistle to it. The dolphin replied, with inexpert wheezings through the blowhole. Quite obviously it was a young dolphin attempting to respond to my whistles with airborne sounds, a feat quite beyond its learned capacity (unlike the oldster who replied to Bob

Feigel). I would have liked to explore the avenue at greater length but there were others to share the visitor with and it revelled in the attention, showing no fear of being stranded with the falling tide — seemingly confident that we would give aid.

Concerned the dolphin might get hurt as the tide receded I eased it into deeper water. As I turned to walk ashore the dolphin rolled on its back playfully displaying its white belly.

The second time the dolphin came ashore a little further upstream. We were attentive because we knew by now it didn't mind being touched. We examined it carefully. A beautiful creature with not a blemish but for one small half-inch scratch on its back just in front of the dorsal. A perfect dorsal all black with a tiny nick in the trailing edge near the tip. We decided we could take the liberty of rolling it over to see what sex it was — something we have never been able to determine in all our encounters. A young female — the anal genital opening much closer to the tail-fin than I expected, flanked by the two mammary slits. To determine her length I stretched out alongside her on the sand. We matched: 5 feet 6 inches. She seemed to respond to this manoeuvre with pleasure — perhaps a nicer way to encounter man than meeting a forest of legs.

The tide was falling faster and we decided she should return to her element. There was a considerable distance of shallow sandy plain with only two feet of water covering it. As I guided her out I felt a rising panic — a sympathetic response to her predicament, unable to determine which way to head to deeper water and the tide receding every moment. But then I could raise my eyes above water and use my knowledge of the landmarks — the physical features of Ngunguru estuary — to guide me. We reached deep water, I released her and we swam along together for a time.

Out in the racing mainstream Terry met her with his underwater camera. Despite the sandstorm he managed to capture a close-up portrait and then passed his camera out to gambol with her. After several exchanges of body language the dolphin came wafting down current towards him. He lay on the surface both arms extended, palms up, fingers outstretched. Then to Terry's astonishment, "She *touched* me, turned my hand over with a gentle muzzle, rested on my wrist watch and slowly rocked her head laterally five or six times — tickatickatickatick — ten seconds touching."

As the tide receded further she began to hunt at a point where the river courses through a rocky race — a spot where mullet would be easy targets for an acoustic creature. I decided to stay with her until I knew the outcome — would she return to sea or advance back up into the estuary? When I left at 5 pm she had disappeared beyond the river entrance. I felt assured she had returned to the sea with the tide.

As I learnt later this was not so. She must have returned with the incoming night tide, and was sighted at both 8 pm and 11 pm cruising among the moored boats. . . That night we reviewed the day's discoveries ecstatically. Terry and Ali both wrote us accounts of their experiences. We decided to call her Elsa after a mutual friend with certain affinities.

How unusual for a *Delphinus* to come inshore like this — seemingly far more trusting than Opo had been. Was Elsa on a mission, to show us the problems that beset a dolphin when it visits our world?

Sometimes the question is asked, "If dolphins are intelligent why don't they come and tell us?"

I could see there is a lot for man to learn before we could enjoy Opo-style contacts more often. Fortunately she chose a very quiet Monday: an outboard approaching her would, in such confined waters, be very dangerous. The noise would be like an alarm clock going off inside her head and would disrupt her sonar navigation.

Some people could cause her distress by following too closely in boats, shepherding her into the shallows and then failing to realize her need for aid if the tide were falling. Children were willing to learn but, if untutored, could have injured the delicate blowhole or caused her to choke. Elsa had to be shaded or bathed with water to avoid over-heating or sunburn. Had the dogs become agitated she might have been bitten. Perhaps it was some sound she emitted above our hearing, but the dogs were quite bemused. Clearly the splashing of feet through the shallows was a disturbing sonic event for her and her head swung from side to side possibly trying to get a fix on the sound source.

I thought it over and it came to me that the public, who would dearly love to experience more Opo-type encounters, need to be educated about the basic physiology and needs of a dolphin which puts itself at our mercy and delight.

Next day we set out for the catamaran early hoping to encounter Elsa at sea. But a grim-faced Mrs Johnson met us at the foot of the driveway — Elsa had returned to their landing and she was in a bad way. The sight of her immaculate form so sorely stricken gave us all a jolt.

In the early hours of the morning, it seems, she must have been stranded among sharp, oyster-covered rocks near the river mouth. Her left flank was deeply lacerated with oval-shaped gouges right through the skin to muscle level. Sea lice had attacked the wounds. Beneath her chest linear scratches showed where she had struggled over a sharp surface. We found her being tended by the Johnson family and friends.

Fisheries biologist Lew Ritchie had called in on his way to work and was in town trying to arrange for advice and assistance. Jan and Terry and I put on wetsuits and took over. We arranged for her to be shaded and held clear of the rocks in such a way that she could breathe without any effort while completely at rest — from what we learnt from the people on the beach she was in a state of shock and exhaustion which our sympathy and physical intervention might alleviate.

A former nurse, Jan could feel the heart-beat under her hand and knew when she was calming down and when she became agitated. As people came wading up to look, her heart would speed up and she would start wagging her head back and forth in a searching manner trying to find from where the thing was approaching. As people left and everything was silent she calmed right down. Her breath smelt very clean and sweet with only a faint fish odour.

Mrs Johnson and another lady sat on the rock near her throughout, offering tacit help. Her daughter held an umbrella over Elsa to keep the sun off. Karla was standing with us and Brady, James and Mark were trying to catch live sprats to see if Elsa might eat some. They had also made a huge pile of sandwiches for everyone. A lady had brought some dead sprats that had been caught the night before but Elsa wasn't interested. A kindly gesture all the same. The motel manager across the road offered hot showers when we had finished. People, very concerned, kept coming and going and all wanted to hear Elsa's story. We must have told it many times.

While it was Jan's turn to hold Elsa she kept talking to her, telling her that we were going to take her back to sea in a boat to her mates — not to be afraid — we would never harm her intentionally even though at times it may seem we are stupid — telling her how beautiful she was and so on. She became very calm during this period.

Elsa Smith arrived to meet her namesake. A strange thing happened. Elsa was bending down with her hand just hanging in the water beside dolphin-Elsa's head when the dolphin deliberately rubbed her hand several times.

It was nearly three hours before Lew arrived with a veterinarian and we discussed possible courses of action. The sea was rough offshore — a northerly sweeping down the coast. He would bring his boat down from Matapouri. We would lift her aboard and take her out as far as the rough seas allowed in hope of restoring her to her mates. Otherwise, in this estuary she would starve or destroy herself.

During our long periods of personal involvement we all gained a great deal of intimate knowledge about her. But the biggest shock for me was the moment I heard Lew's boat off the river entrance. With the roar of his stern drive the thought flashed through my mind, "This will be Lew."

At that moment there was an explosion — a loud bang from Elsa. I was just in time to see her do it again — she had retracted the sphincter of her blowhole revealing delicate membranes and muscles deep within. A fold in the skin was inflated like a cherry — it bulged. Then with a deliberate crack she burst it. Just as you would comfort a child I had just explained to her what was going to happen. This loud response, the first such sound she made in two days' acquaintance, seemed a clear acknowledgement that the distant whine of Lew's motor meant something to her too.

When the vessel arrived we steered Elsa out to the knee-depth hull. Alongside I explained our next actions and she made another volley of cracking sounds with her blowhole. Terry got the hydrophone and tape recorder in action. Just before we lifted her aboard a series of high-pitched underwater vocalisations were recorded. Then, without the least struggle, totally relaxed, she allowed us to lift her aboard onto a foam rubber squab. We covered her with wet sacks, soothing her with our voices all the while as the vessel carried us down the river and headed straight out to sea. When the waves became violent enough to jolt the hull sharply I told Lew I thought it best to stop and release her lest she suffer internal damage from the boat's action. As the vet gave her a shot of antibiotics in her back near the dorsal fin, she didn't even flinch. We waited for any shock reaction before lifting her over the side. She let out a series of deep sobs from her blowhole and bobbed her head. Then she was calm. Her suffering and self-control stirred us deeply.

Without the slightest jolt we eased her over the side into moderate following seas. She swam on the surface with no difficulty. We hovered by as she made a series of circles, seeming to orientate herelf. Then she set out into head seas, on a northerly course.

About a mile ahead Terry glimpsed a flock of gannets wheeling. There was a chance she might locate her companions out there beneath the diving birds. We all hoped intensely she would meet up with them — so vulnerable to shark attack by herself. The seas were very rough — poor Terry became ill, we were drenched with spray. Lew headed for the nearest haven — Tutukaka.

Ever since we've been yearning for a good ocean day so we can go out in the catamaran and see whether, joy of joys, we may discover Elsa safe and sound with her kind.

Quentin meets Horace

Meanwhile down in Napier that December, Quentin Bennett was spending every moment he could spare from his optometry practice out in the bay getting to know the new ambassador. The special leaps and friskings ceased once the dolphin achieved friendly companionship. A male *Tursiops* about ten feet in length, Frank Robson named him Horace after Dr Horace Dobbs whose book about Donald had impressed dolphin-lovers around the world. Quentin noticed the dolphin didn't fool around with his inflatable as he would with solid hulls. In the water he was very suspicious of hands and arms, until they had been playing a while. So Quentin avoided reaching out for him, leaving any contact to Horace.

"I feel he can usually recognise me," he wrote, "when I'm aboard a boat. Certainly so if I've just been with him in the water. Twice when I've got out and removed my mask he has swum alongside, looked up at the boat and then shot off. He wishes to be playing actively the whole time and gets bored quickly."

Every time Quentin went out into the bay he met the dolphin in the same small area (until 21 February). Usually, because of his work, it was in the early morning or late evening. Entering the water in his wet-suit he would dive to the bottom clicking a metal clicker such as you find in Christmas stockings, and making motorbike noises with his mouth. When Horace arrived he would give him a chance to scrutinize him thoroughly with his sonar while submerged. Then they would play the wildest antics: only a very flexible, fit diver could match Quentin in this respect. Chasing, turning, swimming upside down, corkscrewing and haring around, jack-knifing under, rising rapidly out of the water, dolphin and diver strove to outdo each other in boisterous mimicry. Quentin would spend as much time as possible underwater and the dolphin tried to impede his return to the inflatable when he tired. Each play session ended with Quentin's utter exhaustion.

More and more friendly trickery entered their gamesplay. One afternoon Quentin took Perry Davy, a young boy, out to meet the dolphin. As they became chilled Quentin suggested they should return to the boat. Horace approached Perry and led him gradually to change his course until he finally had the boy swimming in exactly the wrong direction.

As summer advanced Horace enjoyed escorting yachts and fishing-boats leaving Napier. He frolicked with any small craft that came near him. By 19 January he had begun to accompany yachts up the channel into the inner boat harbour. Frequently, as a yacht was entering the channel Horace nudged the rudder and altered its course back to sea. Other yachtsmen found their rudders strangely immobilised. He would await small boats at the jetty. Just as they were preparing to tie up he swam over and shoved with his beak to push them off course.

In Napier's main harbour Horace was a favourite with the construction divers and fishermen. He would steal the divers' flippers and flick floating onions around with his beak. He accepted live fish tossed to him from fishing-boats and would take a fish from a trawl net, playing with it before swallowing.

In the course of our research we were delighted to receive a letter and photo telling of a meeting with Horace at sea. Although it belongs later in the story, I will present it here:

"Our dolphin experience happened on May 20," wrote Pat Wellgreen. "Horace was known to follow people out to sea, and so we were overjoyed when he chose to accompany our thirty-five-foot trimaran. While we were motoring out of the channel he kept rubbing himself against the rudder. As we got further out into Hawke Bay, he became more used to us, and came up alongside. Someone suggested that we use the blunt end of the boat-hook to splash in the water to attract his attention. Horace thought this was okay and he had a rub against it. We played with him and the boat-hook for ages. He then decided to do a few flips for us. It was fantastic. Much better than Marineland! He seemed to take a perverse delight in splashing us all.

"We had hoped to do some fishing, but Horace's fishing was much better. He chased a large kahawai round the boat, between the outriggers, as if he was a cat after a mouse. Eventually he caught it and dragged it backwards by holding its tail in his mouth. When it was quite dead, he swallowed it head first. All the while we were running round and round the boat yelling and clapping.

"Horace stayed with us most of the day. However, just as we were heading for home, he saw a fizzboat and went over to say 'hi' to them.

"That day, we were told, quite a crowd had assembled at the sailing club, ready for a demonstration of Horace. It was a shame that so many people missed out, but we had such fun with Horace that we couldn't feel too sorry. Best of luck with your project."

Then came a letter from Quentin in which he remarked on a peculiarity he had noticed in Horace's play: mirror-image mimicry, which suggests a subtle level of abstract thought. The pattern first began to emerge on 26 December when Quentin tried to teach the dolphin to leap over his inflatable, a game Donald used to play in Britain. Swimming rapidly up from the bottom to the side of his inflatable Quentin slithered aboard, strode across and dived headlong in again. But to his dismay, Horace did not follow. In a dinghy tethered behind, Quentin's small daughters, Annika and Camilla, were convulsed with laughter at the dolphin's antics as he totally fooled their father.

"Horace was right behind me so I couldn't see what was happening. As I went over the boat he turned *upside down* and slid under it, in effect, mirroring my whole act. Because of the usual Napier murk I hadn't the least idea as to what was going on but the children could see it from the dinghy.

"Every week we are hearing more stories about Horace's games and antics. One thing that appears increasingly is this mirroring of what people do. It is mostly with yachtsmen that he plays and quite often he gives unknowing sailors serious frights by banging on the bottom of their boats when they don't expect him. Of course he is always pushing up centreboards and interfering with rudders. Apparently if he pushes up a centreboard and the sailor slams it down, Horace slams it back up. If it is pushed down slowly, he thrusts it back up slowly. . .

"I had a friend out following the national Flying Dutchman champs from a little put-put boat. Horace started playing around so he steered his boat on a weaving course. Horace adopted a weaving course too, mirror image.

"The other day he alarmed a young girl in a yacht who was not very experienced and rather worried at his antics with the centreboard. He came up beside her and she threw water on his face, 'Go away!' He turned face down and flicked water back at her with his flukes.

"Apparently he has tipped a small yacht right over in the inner harbour. It must have pricked his conscience a little as he came right over to the unfortunate sailor and checked that he was all right, and the chap was able to touch him. The Archbishop of New Zealand, Paul Reeves, has had the centreboard of his Sunburst sailing dinghy split by an over-zealous Horace."

By the end of January Quentin was often touching Horace briefly. The dolphin would spend part of his time playing around in the main harbour where the working divers enjoyed his company. On 7 March underwater blasting operations began, to deepen the port. Each time the chief diver telephoned a warning and former dolphin trainer Frank Robson would entice Horace out of the danger area with his boat, into the safety of the inner harbour.

Our excitement reached Opo level when Quentin wrote to us of his 8 March adventure. (Strangely it was 8 March 1956 when Opo, New Zealand's previous dolphin ambassador, died.) This day Quentin set out in Frank Robson's boat to get the first underwater pictures of Horace. Up till then, although an ardent photographer, Quentin had not attempted photography at any meeting. They found Horace near a trawler fooling with a large flatfish. After shooting two rolls of highspeed film, Quentin decided that was enough — time for their usual play session.

"I played the games of my life. We put our noses together. Horace's beak against my face mask for ten seconds at a time. He towed me around in various ways — me holding his dorsal fin, me holding his chin; me holding his pectoral fin, he holding my hand in his teeth.

We played more complicated manoeuvres: he sliding his body along my fins, me doing similarly to him. The usual barrel rolls and somersaults. Body vertical in the water, head up. Head down. Face to face: shake heads and him screaming around me making the motorbike noises that I do to him at times.

"It was something the like of which I've never heard before. Something that makes me feel very honoured to have been part of. I was very careful not to hurt him — it worries me holding his fins.

"Quite often when playing one sees that he has an erection. At these times he is quite aggressive in a sporting, challenging manner. He will try to lead you from the boat and trick you. Yesterday, after I put the camera away, it was something totally different, almost like a ballet; mutual feeling and respect were certainly part of the episode. No erection."*

Quentin is a busy person and not a wordy letter-writer so I was amazed to hear from him just three days later. Graeme Thomson and Roger Bishop from Wairoa had arrived wanting to meet Horace. They searched all his usual spots out in the bay and then headed back to the inner harbour — where he had been all the time. Hoping for clearer water they led him out but it was still very murky: less than one foot visibility, which makes it difficult to play underwater with a dolphin.

He would come up underneath the divers gently pulling first one flipper, then the other, turning the diver in a circle, and manoeuvring his legs apart.

"I had a while with him," wrote Quentin, "warming him up. He is careful and needs quite a bit of play before he gets involved. He and I got quite involved. I held him several times and finally he came under me and lifted me out of the water astride him and gave me a ride! I was in front of his dorsal, arms raised above my head in sheer exhilaration. We were all incredulous. Then he gave me a tow, holding his dorsal fin. The murk made it difficult to see what we were doing and we were afraid we might accidentally kick him in the eye with a fin, and put him off humans for a while. I was cold and had to get out."

Quentin was just about to leave on a journey to Sweden when late in the afternoon of 28 April he made a last visit to Horace with his wife Tina and some friends. By this stage Horace had established court in the inner harbour centred around the yacht *Tiny Dancer*, where he met a regular set of human friends.

"We all had a great swim with Horace: about half a dozen people with him at the same time. I had perhaps a dozen or more tows, mostly along the bottom. Visibility was about twelve inches and there were three boats around the whole time. At one stage I jack-knife dived. Horace and I collided beak to mask. It shook me and I was quite stunned — almost knocked out. (Except for this collision which I am certain was a mistake, he never once hit me, although he did hit others, rather shaking them up. This intrigues me, as I always played rather rough and energetic games with him.)

*Quentin says, "Erections were common in our early days, but after the end of December, perhaps January, were not evident. Perhaps he had found out that I was straight!"

107

"I don't think my rides are anything special — just that my type of water-play really gets Horace going at high speed, buzzing in head on and jumping out of the water. We have familiar routines and the murk doesn't matter so much. Other people in the water get frightened at this and think he is aggressive. I feel he is just boisterous and I give it back to him — unless it has been me that has been the boisterous one and he is 'giving it back to me.'

"Then I got a surprise. Tina has never swum with Horace before. She hopped in and he came up from behind in the nil visibility water. As she was still facing the boat he could not have approached from the front. Gently he nudged her in the small of the back. Instantly she turned, as no doubt he expected, and he took her right hand in his mouth.

"Now Tina is rather chary of animals (she is a superb diver) and no animal, not even a pet belonging to her closest friend, would be permitted to take her hand in its mouth. Yet she happily lets this so called 'wild animal' do it without thinking, on their first ever meeting, in filthy water. Why did Horace wish her to turn and take her hand? Did he understand the human significance of this manoeuvre? It was something simple, meaningful to any human being from child to academic, and something special.

"At every meeting with Horace humour seems to have had a part. I wonder what intellectual level this capacity would indicate to a psychologist?

"There is a young couple, Rosamond and Allan Rowe who go down to the inner harbour with their two children almost every afternoon after work to meet Horace. You should write to Ros. She keeps records of each interlock — a lovely, natural girl with an incredible feeling and affection for Horace. He has given her three rides recently."

And with that letter Quentin had to leave New Zealand.

Rosamond Rowe

On Quentin's suggestion I wrote to Ros and Allan Rowe and an extensive correspondence developed. Eventually I flew to Napier to meet them. Here is a letter I received from Ros later:

"I hardly know where to begin regarding my friendship with Horace. Our relationship — meaning my husband, our two children, Selwyn and Odette and our elderly friend, Miss Bingham — has been on a simple level and is a rather personal thing but we have in the course of our interspecies 'love affair' made some rather startling observations of his responses to us.

"First, I will answer your questions about my background in relation to the success I have had with Horace. I am a deeply committed Christian and my attitude to Horace has been influenced by this fact; I do not find my beliefs a handicap — rather I feel the relationship has been enhanced by them, as Horace does seem to have a kind of spiritual awareness. You may find this passage from the Scriptures relevant:

> Even birds and animals have much they could teach you, ask the creatures of the earth and sea for their wisdom. All of them know that the Lord's hand made them. It is God who directs the lives of his creatures; every man's life is in his power. — Job 12:7 — 10.

108

"As regards my experience as a swimmer or diver; well, I can swim a few yards if necessary and there my qualification ends. As the sufferer from a middle-ear disease, I am not really supposed to go in the water, but I feel safe and happy bobbing around on the surface in my wetsuit. It seems to be no handicap to my enjoyment of Horace or his acceptance of me.

"As regards previous experience with animals, I have always been surrounded by them, both wild and domestic, and sometimes wish I could just take off to the hills to commune with all other living things.

"I was interested in Jan's comment that although she had never touched a dolphin before, the feeling was familiar. I felt the same. Then I remembered I *had touched* a dolphin! It was autumn about twenty years ago, when I was a small girl and my mother and I were walking along Clifton beach, near Cape Kidnappers. We came upon a small dolphin stranded well up on the sand — about five feet long. A dusky I think.

"We were with friends who were not at all fussy about touching such an object, so my mother and I struggled for a very long time before we succeeded in carrying the poor creature into the water where it displayed its gratitude by performing a dance beyond the breakers before darting off.

"When we heard in the news media of the arrival of Horace in December of 1978 our family spent all the Christmas holidays trying to meet up with him. It was not until around 18 January that we first met him on the sea's edge off Westshore beach, and played in the breakers with him.

"Early in our friendship (18 February) my husband Allan swam with him several times out in deep water in the bay and the two enjoyed games of chase and hide and seek with seaweed. Horace would come up to him with a piece of bubble kelp in his beak. When Allan grasped one end Horace tugged until it snapped. He then dived to some depth and released it, returning to challenge Allan for the other half. This continued until only a shred remained. By this time the first half had floated up and the game resumed.

"Horace must have learned to associate Allan's voice with these games and when he started coming up the channel into the inner harbour, whenever Allan called him from the shore he would dart off and return with a piece of seaweed."

For five months the Rowe family devoted their lives to following the movements of Horace and from 20 March to 26 May Ros kept a log of all sightings and interlocks with him.

Over the sixty-eight-day period they recorded thirty-nine sightings of the dolphin of which two-thirds were in the vicinity of *Tiny Dancer* in the inner harbour; the rest in the river channel (6), the bay (4), and the main harbour (5). Human/dolphin in-water exchanges occurred on twenty-two occasions. They noticed that when Horace was actively feeding in the river he did not want company and would indicate this with rapid tail slaps if approached.

On average Horace stayed up to three days at a time and the average of absent days was about the same, with the longest stay seven days and the longest absence ten. Before one lengthy absence there had been a severe gale.

While there were other people interacting with the dolphin, Quentin Bennett and the Rowe family appear to be the most intensive from an in-water interlock viewpoint. Ros Rowe's letters highlight their most exciting encounters. The letter continues:

Feet Upon a Rock*

"One incident which is clear in my mind, and always will be, took place on Wednesday, 28 March. This was before we had purchased our wetsuits and rowboat and I was forced to stay within my depth because of my silly, giddy head. Horace was playing with the rudder of his favourite yacht, *Tiny Dancer*, moored thirty metres from the sailing club beach in the inner harbour. The temptation to get out to him was very great so I threw caution to the winds and got an acquaintance to tow me out to the yacht with his catamaran.

"Once there, I clung precariously to *Tiny Dancer*'s rudder and watched enchanted as Horace swam around very close to me. At this stage I knew him only as a fin and I was only a voice to him, which had called his name wistfully from the shore. After a while the effort of clinging to the slippery rudder became exhausting, so I called Allan to swim out and help me ashore. Once he reached my side I felt able to relax my grip a little, so I stretched my stiff and weary legs down to prepare for the trip to shore. To my surprise and utter relief I felt a solid rock beneath my feet. I was able to have a breather.

"I said to Allan, 'What a clot I am. All this time I've been hanging on for dear life and there's been a rock to stand on.'

"'No there isn't, you dope,' was his amused reply.

"'Well, what do you think I'm standing on then?' I retorted.

"I stretched my legs down again to prove my point and was astonished to find there was nothing solid there. I had been standing on Horace!

"After a spell on shore I saw he had followed us into the shallows so I raced in again. This time as he glided past I stretched out my hand and touched him for the first time.

"The feeling of awe that Horace had supported me when in need, and stayed stockstill when to have slipped from under me would possibly have spelt trouble, giddy as I was, deepened next morning. Writing it up in my diary I felt moved to abandon the task for a moment and pick up my well-thumbed Bible. I opened it at random and my eye fell on a verse from Psalm 40: 'He set me safely on a rock and made me secure.'

Stroking

"The 14 April encounter was special because it was the first time Horace presented himself to me to be petted from a boat. I felt my previous physical handling of him was with his acquiescence whereas this time he was actually *inviting* me to touch him.

*Title of an autobiography by Rosamond Rowe (Caveman Press).

"We went down to *Tiny Dancer*'s mooring in the inner harbour to see if our friend were still present. And there he was — bumping the yacht's rudder, so we eagerly launched our little boat and the four Rowes hopped aboard to go and ask Horace if he wanted our company.

"As soon as we started rowing he left his yacht and came alongside us. I rolled up my sleeve and cautiously extended my hand to see if he would resume this morning's game (when she had clicked her fingers in the water and Horace repeatedly nuzzled her hand, both gently and boisterously). He inspected my hand and let his body slide past it. Then he lay passively just below the surface allowing me to stroke every part of his body and then at times raised his head right out while I cupped his beak in my hand or stroked the top of his head.

"It was very moving for me and I shed tears all over him. He would occasionally swim away from the boat and return upside down inviting me to rub his underside.

"Once as I was turning my head to speak to the kids he came up smartly and nipped one finger hard. It hurt quite a bit and I told him I didn't think much of that trick. Next he came back with his mouth open in a wicked grin, seeming to dare me to trust him by putting my hand in his mouth. So I did. I received several more nips but none as sharp as the first.

"My parents were on the shore so we brought them out to watch as Horace presented himself for more caresses. It is funny how, after a particularly rewarding communication with Horace, I have dolphins leaping through my dreams all night long.

First ride

"The first time I was given a ride by Horace was well timed in a very special way. Earlier that day (23 April) I had heard the distressing news that the beloved companion of my childhood, my horse Giselle, had died. Feeling rather flat, we went down at four-thirty as usual to look for our friend. There he was and in a very trusting mood. He allowed both Allan and Miss Bingham to touch him. I decided to experiment with singing to him as I had been wanting to try it for some time but felt a little foolish in public. I sang "You are my sunshine" and Horace seemed enthralled (which says little for his appreciation of the arts) and he lolled placidly beside the boat, his pinhole of an ear above the surface, to listen.

"Then I climbed out of our little rowboat into the water with him. He immediately swam beneath me so, on Allan's suggestion, I spread my legs as if straddling the back of a horse. Horace swam beneath me, then rose up gently until I was astride him. I was not sure where I was sitting until Horace came up to blow and then I discovered I was between his blowhole and fin. I was borne carefully and majestically through the water, completely overwhelmed by the experience. The ride ended when he gently swam free. He played around a bit more before repeating the procedure several more times. A surf ski whizzed past and Horace shot off like a rocket to pace the man on the ski.

"To our amazement Horace left the ski by the Iron Pot and headed back to us. I leapt out of the boat again and was joined by a different

Horace — this time the party got a bit rough. I was nipped on the leg, butted in the behind and herded in tight circles. The water was churning and boiling and I was just flotsam completely at the mercy of our huge friend. At one point he leapt out of the water and entered again, his large tail within inches of me. A boy arrived in a dinghy and Horace darted over, repeatedly slapping his tail on the surface.

"Strangely enough he did not resent Allan's presence in our boat. I looked enquiringly at Allan knowing he would tell me to get out if he thought things were getting out of hand. Then I decided to wait and see what developed. Horace remained excited and I was starting to tire, so I landed.

"A short while later Horace turned up again, just behind the boat. I got in again, as much as anything to try and end the interlude on a quiet note. Fortunately Horace seemed to feel the same and he calmly greeted me before slipping away to inspect *Tiny Dancer*'s rudder. I swam ashore.

Miss Bingham possessed

"Our friend Miss Bingham who is seventy-two enjoys meeting Horace and we had always thought the dolphin respected her advanced years, treating her with a special gentleness. However on 8 May he exploded this myth in no uncertain fashion.

"On this evening he turned up in the inner harbour after an absence of ten days. Miss Bingham excitedly jumped in to swim with him and by the time I had done the same she was being tossed around pretty roughly by Horace. He was sexually aroused and not responsive to her attempts to settle him down. So she reluctantly left the water. I decided to stay and try to quieten him and was successful for only a short time before I too was being buffeted around."

Miss Bingham sent us her own account in which she suggests that her helplessness wearing a buoyant wetsuit with no lead weights may have been a factor in the episode, besides the long absence of their friend.

"My excitement was intense and Horace must have picked it up as the prods with his beak became more and more insistent. He was determined to make this ridiculous creature play: the prods and butts became harder and the lifts more spectacular. In spite of laughing and enjoying it I knew I had to get out. Allan was laughing so hard and trying to take a photo he did not realize my calm request for help was really a shriek of near-desperation. After one last terrific jab in the ribs I was able to grab the boat and scramble onto the rocks with, so they told me, Horace following hopefully.

"Ros swore it was a clear case of attempted rape and Allan said, 'Well, you did have your wetsuit flap trailing provocatively behind you.' In my haste I had forgotten to buckle it up before getting into the water.

"In any case my ribs were sore for months afterwards. Some days later I met him again, with my lead weights on, and he behaved like a perfect gentleman."

In her letter Ros Rowe concludes the incident with the comment: "Horace has been contrite ever since. In fact in all the times we have played with him he has acted that way only twice — the other occasion was on the evening of my first ride. Probably my excitement in having this experience was communicated to him.

"On 21 May we enjoyed a lovely interlude with our friend, from our boat. We met him in the part of the inner harbour called the Iron Pot. He was in an extremely placid mood and showed every sign of delight as we rowed into the area. He quickly swam over to us and there he stayed a very long time. He lay beside our boat and lapped up our caresses and words of endearment. Selwyn, our eight-year-old son loves to stroke Horace but sometimes misjudges his distance and places his hand a little close to the sensitive areas of the eye and blowhole.

"Horace never seems to mind and on this occasion appeared to want Selwyn's attentions, squeezing his eye shut in an exaggerated fashion and staying beside our son instead of moving away as one would expect."

The following night the Rowe family had their last intensive interlock with Horace. He gave Ros numerous fin tows, coming up from below, nudging her gently and nipping her hand affectionately. When she got out he seemed to want her to return and gurgled like a human baby when she did. Then he took her for the longest tow ever — so far out she let go and swam back.

When Miss Bingham got in, he would approach her gently from behind, put his beak into the small of her back and push her quietly across the surface.

There followed only two more in-water sessions, on 23 and 26 May. On the final encounter in retrospect Horace seemed nervy and different. There was little physical contact apart from nudging Ros's hand several times. And from that date nobody saw Horace again.

Miss Bingham thinks she saw him at dusk on 7 June feeding about thirty metres from the coast where she lives, a few hundred metres from the main harbour. That night an enormous blast shook the houses in the vicinity of the wharves. This time nobody had given a warning for Horace to be enticed to safety before the charges were detonated.

Three days later there was a report from the yacht *Trinity* of a huge fish floating on the water a mile out beyond the pier heads. But Horace's fate is not known. He may yet turn up among the bottlenose dolphins to the north where his species is more common. Or could it be the diesel spill in the boat harbour on his 28 April visit? Oil on the lungs leads to slow death. . .

In the history of lone dolphins approaching human settlement, one thing is clear: it is a highly dangerous mission.

7

Children of the Gods:
a history of the DINTs

IN HIS TREATISE "On the Intelligence of Animals", Plutarch (A.D. 66) wrote that the dolphin has a gift longed for by the greatest philosophers — unselfish friendship. "It has no need of any man, yet is the friend of all men and has often given them great aid."

For three years Jan and I conducted the Project Interlock experiments to see what would happen if we set out to meet dolphins in the wild every week of the year. This we considered a research programme but gradually we have come to feel we are the experiment and they, the observers. We have been showing the dolphins aspects of human behaviour. Our attempts to mimic them have led to quite unexpected responses. But have you ever paused to consider how strange it really is that these large brain creatures frolic on the bows of boats, an utterly vulnerable position that has often led to capture or death? There is something implicit in such surrender that sends a shudder up my spine. Something beyond us.

Enough stories survive from the past to suggest dolphins have been observing human behaviour for many centuries. It is quite likely that, if the history of DINTs (dolphin initiated interlocks) was set down in its entirety, the serious researcher could gain some surprising new insights. The more recent episodes are as yet unpublished and have come to light from our own enquiries.

In his book *The Dolphin: Cousin to Man* (Penguin), Robert Stenuit gives an excellent review of the many DINTs that occurred in antiquity, plus three more recent incidents in the U.S. in 1945, 1949, 1960. While dolphins were regarded as messengers of the gods human attitudes towards them were benign. In such a culture, as with the Maoris* in New Zealand, dolphin friendships might be expected to flourish.

From a civilisation centred on harmony with natural forces symbolised as gods, Europe shifted to a creed based on human supremacy, dominion over nature and exploitation of all resources for the benefit of man.

For many centuries any communication with animals was linked with witchcraft. Dolphin meat was served in Parisian restaurants during the

*See Waipu Pita's anecdote, chapter 5.

114

Age of Reason. . . Thus, from around A.D. 109 until the twentieth century very little in the way of dolphin/human encounter entered the western written record. This does not mean none occurred. We know that in non-western cultures symbiotic fishing relationships flourished. But in the west, for a variety of cultural reasons, the climate was not favourable for interlock.

In the Roman period around A.D. 109 Pliny the Younger writes of the Tunisian sea town of Hippo where a dolphin befriended a boy swimming offshore, bearing him back to the beach. Next day the dolphin returned but the boy fled. For some days the dolphin leapt high above the water and frisked about until the young men of Hippo lost their fears and played with it. A deep friendship developed with the boy who established first contact.

Eventually its fame attracted crowds of visitors to Hippo and the dolphin was officially honoured. But resentment at the disruption to city life developed and it was secretly put to death.

After the classical period I can find no further accounts of DINTs in the western world until the strange episode of Pelorus Jack, well described in Anthony Alpers' book *Dolphins*. He escorted the ferry steamer through a narrow strait in New Zealand for some twenty-four years (1888—1912 approx.). But this guiding behaviour really belongs in my next chapter on dolphin assistance to mariners, as no in-water encounter took place.

There are close parallels between the Hippo story and the next two DINTs in the published record: Opo in New Zealand in 1955 and Nina in Spain about 1972. In all three cases the dolphins approached bathers on a public beach, triggering a mass response bordering on social upheaval. In all three cases the dolphins were officially honoured: the Hippo visitor was anointed by a proconsul; at Opononi and La Corogna statues were erected. And in all three it seems the dolphins were covertly despatched as a result of resentment they aroused. Then the pattern of DINTs alters. . .

The story of Opo always fascinated me but I must admit that until I met wild dolphins myself it remained more of a legend.

That summer of 1955/56 when a young female dolphin arrived at Opononi in New Zealand's Hokianga Harbour, she made headlines throughout the world. For the first time in modern history a wild dolphin approached people at the sea's edge and drew holiday crowds of some 14,000 to the remote village. Hokianga was the landing place in about A.D. 925 of Kupe, the Maori explorer.

Opo's popularity grew until she became a major tourist attraction and had to be protected by a special Act of Parliament. The very day after it was passed, 8 March 1956, she was found dead, probably from a dynamite explosion. The dolphin was buried with the full ceremonial rites of a Maori tangi.

Opo was a bottlenose dolphin, *Tursiops truncatus*. When she first arrived she would follow yachts around the harbour. Gradually she grew more trusting and approached the beach. That did it. In no time she was the delight of the summer children, adept at games of water ball, and slipping between the legs of her favourites to give them rides on her back. Adults were equally affected by the aura of gentleness around the dolphin and would plunge into the sea fully clad just to touch her satin velvet skin. Opo never accepted gifts of dead fish.

A documentary film made at the time shows that to some adults the dolphin was a beach donkey on which they were intent on giving their offspring a ride. Opo clearly expressed a dislike for such manipulativeness with sideswipes of her tail at offending shins. But to the children she was sweetness itself. I have now met several people who experienced Opo as children and were profoundly affected by it for the rest of their lives.

In his book *Dolphins*, Cousteau gives an account of a similar happening on the opposite side of the globe, at La Corogna in northern Spain. He is vague about the date but I estimate that Nina appeared around 1972. By this time skindiving had developed as a sport and this bottlenose first approached clam diver Luis Salleres, observing him at work beneath his boat. Luis petted the dolphin and she responded with pleasure. They became firm friends.

One day she rescued a visiting diver Jose Vasquez, overcome with cramp. The moment Jose waved for help to Salleres' boat the dolphin came close to him, remaining absolutely still while he put his arms around her for support.

One of Cousteau's diving team, Jacques Renoir, spent a week scubadiving with Nina and filming her. Each time she would approach on the surface and swim down the anchor line to meet Jacques on the bottom at forty feet. Seeing her, Jacques would extend his hand and Nina immediately rubbed it with her genital area. Gamesplay sessions would last some thirty to forty-five minutes and there was always a time when she became very active, leaping into the air and then returning to frolic with the diver. All those divers who met Nina were deeply affected by her manner.

Cousteau describes the process of Nina's becoming a national heroine. After she appeared on television playing with Franco's grandchildren, tourists flocked to La Corogna. She made a fuss of every boat that approached her. She mixed freely with bathers on the beach, allowing them to pet her and giving some rides on her back. As many as 2000 people thronged into the water to touch her.

Nina would never accept any gifts of food. Each day around noon she would vanish for about an hour, possibly to feed. After five months of human companionship her corpse was found on the beach — human agency was suspected.

Between Opo and Nina there was a low key DINT in Scotland from 1960 to 1967 involving another female *Tursiops* called Charlie who frequented an area of the coast around Elie, Fife and later, Northumberland. This dolphin was friendly towards divers and would approach boats and rub against them. On no occasion would Charlie accept dead fish offered her.

Donald in Britain
In March 1972 a male bottlenose dolphin began to observe biologists installing apparatus on the seabed near a marine laboratory on the Isle

of Man. For the next six years history's best documented and longest term human/dolphin exchange ensued. For the initial four years Donald's movements and socializing were traced by Dr Horace Dobbs. Christine Lockyer of the British Whale Research Unit wrote an academic account up to December 1976 and Dr Nicholas Webb covered the final two years.

During this time the dolphin made a southward journey along some 300 miles of British coastline, from the Isle of Man to Wales, and then Cornwall. Along this course he adopted a series of home territories for varying lengths of time leaving in his wake reports of sociable behaviour which, viewed overall, exhibit a remarkable development in variety and complexity.

During an unexplained absence in 1975, when explosives were being used in Port St Mary, and before Donald arrived on the Welsh coast, I suspect he may have visited the east coast of Ireland where some yachtsmen reported an episode with a friendly dolphin to whom they played classical music. (John Denzler in *Yachting Monthly*, August 1978.)

The small harbours, boat havens and coves in which Donald stayed show similarities, in that boating and fishing activities were intensive, with moored small craft, diving and swimming activities usually present. The bays were mostly around ten metres deep or less, often with a rocky shore and sandy bottom. He had a fascination for wooden dinghies and mooring buoys and would usually establish his presence around one or other, leaping over dinghies, lifting, tugging and circling buoys so that his whereabouts were soon known to the locals.

If overcrowded in these "special areas" he would become quite upset and apparently defensive. Donald enjoyed yacht races, small craft and canoes. He would push them around, peer over gunwales at occupants, bite paddles, splash and capsize. The more excited people became the greater his activity. He showed little interest in ball games and refused all offers of food but accepted petting and stroking, when he would sometimes become sexually aroused. Donald allowed himself to be measured and clearly recognised certain divers as individuals from voice or appearance.

Pulsed sounds interested him and he made a speciality of causing boat propellers to cavitate by exhaling close to the blades, so altering the noise pitch. The rattle of anchor chains also aroused his curiosity.

Dobbs' book *Follow a Wild Dolphin* serves to flesh out the academic papers by Lockyer and Webb. On one occasion Dobbs lost his brand-new underwater camera. Searching in the murk he feels a playful nudge — Donald. After repeated nudges he is induced to follow the dolphin until it stands on its head, flexing its great body like an arrow — pointing at the lost camera.

On another occasion Donald rescued a diver in distress, supporting him gently on the surface, helping to tow him to the boat, and remaining alongside until he recovered. Yet just before this the dolphin had completely upset a diver-training session involving simulated rescue situations.

One day in Port St Mary, in October 1974, Donald, quite spontaneously took Horace Dobbs' thirteen-year-old son Ashley for a ride around the harbour, depositing the delighted youngster in front of his father.

While Dobbs was making the film *Ride a Wild Dolphin* (June 1976) he was towed behind a boat on an aquaplane. Donald appeared as soon as the tow started:

"When I refused to let go he bit my arm progressively harder until I had to release the handle. Then he grabbed the board in his mouth and enjoyed a tow behind the boat."

Dobbs' book gives detailed accounts of the subtle ways Donald would change a situation to gain his own ends. In later months the towing game developed to the stage where Donald would tow another swimmer after the boat until level with the aquaplane, while the boat followed a zigzag course (Webb, July 1977).

In 1977 while on the Cornish coast Donald drew attention to his presence increasingly by towing yachts. At this stage Dr Nicholas Webb takes up the story, describing in detail* how the dolphin picked up the thirty-five-pound anchor of a seven-ton schooner and towed the vessel 100 yards in a semicircle. The largest boat was a ten-ton catamaran which he hauled for nearly half a mile at speeds up to two knots. He would also tow divers on a rope with a rubber ring over his beak, returning to the diver if he let go, enabling him to take the rope again for another tow (September 1977).

Dr Webb wrote another scientific paper** about Donald's sexual behaviour to women and his carrying of women and children which he terms "possession". Anybody studying this aspect would find parallels in the behaviour of the male *Tursiops* DINT in New Zealand in 1978/79.

As far as is known, the first person whom Donald ever contacted physically was a wetsuit-clad woman diver Maura Mitchell in the Isle of Man phase, 1972. Dobbs' book gives numerous instances of the lengthy and tender relationship between these two, with croonings and cuddles at each meeting, during which the dolphin shut its eyes.

When he met women subsequently they were often bathers, not clad in neoprene. Women usually behave very gently with dolphins and on a more receptive level than the diver-photographer eagerly posing his friends. Just as Nina became sexually aroused when petted, so would Donald (and other "dinting" dolphins, Sandy and Horace). At these times boisterous responses sometimes alarmed new acquaintances. With such people it seems Donald did not repeat the behaviour.

Gentle mouthing of limbs was Donald's body language channel for establishing mutual trust (as with other DINTs and captive orca and dolphin). But in cases where a bather was not prepared for this, resistance occasionally led to scratched legs.

Down in Cornwall in his sixth year of DINT, Donald gave rides to

*"Boat Towing by a Bottlenose Dolphin:"
Dr Nicholas Webb, *Carnivore* Vol.1 Pt.1, January 1978.

**"Women and Children Abducted by a Wild but Sociable Adult Male Bottlenose Dolphin:" Dr Nicholas Webb, *Carnivore* Vol.1 Pt.2, May 1978.

118

people more and more frequently: men, women and children, with little or no preparation. Fear was sometimes aroused and such incidents were described as "possession by the dolphin". On other occasions such events were regarded with delight. In this respect I see an ambiguity: Donald's PR problem could be seen as a communication gap between the people he met. He could *not* assume a pooled fund of experience transmission and a continuity in those he approached. When people initiated play activities his responses overjoyed them but when the initiator was Donald there was sometimes an ambivalence towards his intentions.

Thus, while in all his human encounters the dolphin was exceptionally benign, at times he did give alarm. This apparent inconsistency may be resolved if each episode is examined in the context of Donald's previous experiences and compared with other dinting dolphins. Such a study is urgently needed and would require flexibility of thought and avoidance of the anthropocentrism of conventional scientific method.

For herein lies the key to understanding human/dolphin relationships and the problems involved in meeting an alien mind.

Donald's mission to man was not easy. He suffered a gunshot wound to the head, a gash from an outboard skeg, a stranding, and explosive charges within his home range. He was last sighted in Falmouth, February 1978 just before a huge storm.

After reading everything on record about Donald it occurs to me that much of his complex behaviour served to draw attention to his presence, and elicit companionship; it demonstrates surprising manipulative capacities, reason and memory. At times the dolphin may have been frustrated at the lack of creativity in those he met, who were often more intent on observing or recording him on film than responding. An overall picture of his behaviour shows a development from person to person and place to place. With new acquaintances his games were often brief. With familiar divers he played for long periods and resented being ignored.

Dictionaries define intelligence as "the capacity to meet situations especially if new or unforeseen by a rapid and effective adjustment of behaviour" or "alert, quick of mind, having intellect, endowed with the faculty of reason, communicative". Regardless of academic arguments, to man in the sea there can really be no question as to the capacities of dolphins. So many diver anecdotes reflect this acceptance of their high degree of understanding and even mind-to-mind contact.

The two following anecdotes are from first-person accounts in *Diver* magazine:

Tom Treloar was diving on a reef in Prussia Cove at the southern tip of Cornwall. Visibility was poor and he got separated from his buddy, Bill Weddle. He decided to circle the reef to locate Bill. Suddenly he felt very uneasy.

Looking about he saw a shape glide by on the verge of vision. Bluish grey and as big as a bus. He fought back panic and continued to search for Bill. Then he got the urge to look behind him. A metre away, looking over his left shoulder, was Donald. Surprise and joy took place of fear. Donald had a friendly mien and passed slowly and gently within feet of Tom, who followed, only to lose him. Donald returned, nodding his head like an excited dog.

Tom stretched out his hand and touched the beak. He examined all the scars on his body: a propeller cut, a bullet hole. . . They swam side by side, Donald eyeing him, as Tom thought, in a protective manner. Then suddenly, with a flick of his powerful tail, he sped out of sight. There in front of Tom was the anchor chain. Donald had brought him back to the boat. Then a trail of bubbles began heading towards the anchor line. The dolphin led Bill back too.

To many divers, encounters with Donald became the greatest day in their undersea lives. In May 1977 when Les Kodituwakku surfaced from a dive near Falmouth he'd lost his scuba tank-boot. But those on the dive boat were frolicking with a dolphin. His buddy, Malcolm Mister, offered to help search for the boot.

"Forget it," Les shrugged. "Let's play with the dolphin." As though he had heard the conversation the dolphin disappeared below the surface and next moment reappeared with the lost tank-boot around his beak. He practically dropped it in Malcolm's hands as if to say, "Let's get on with the game."

Sandy

San Salvador Island is at the southeast end of the Bahamas chain, 385 miles east-southeast of Miami. Twelve miles long by five wide the island has one motel and a charterboat fleet. It is a first-class skindiving resort. In twenty feet of water off Long Bay stands a monument to Columbus, as at this point, historians believe, the voyager first landed.

During the later stages of Donald's travels in England I heard of Sandy, another lone dolphin behaving similarly at San Salvador. For a time there were two DINTs in progress on either side of the Atlantic and both dolphins withdrew within a few weeks of each other.

I drew up a special questionnaire and sent it to divers with experience of Sandy. In response, divemaster Chris McLaughlin sent a superb set of transparencies and wrote this letter to me:

"I am always interested in information about human contact with dolphins in the wild, whether one or more dolphins are involved. I will try to describe Sandy and his involvement with divers on San Salvador Island. I first heard of big-game boats seeing a friendly dolphin playing in their bow wake in early 1976. The contacts became more frequent and on a few occasions he approached dive boats during that summer. Of course we stopped the boat and everyone jumped in the water. Sandy left immediately but would sometimes come back and swim with the boat for a while.

"In October of 1976 we anchored at Sandy Point dive site where he would hang out. He approached the divers underwater for about twenty minutes, but very much like a shark. He would stay thirty or more feet away and retreat when divers followed. From October until December Sandy remained in this general area and came closer and closer to divers underwater or snorkelers on the surface. It was not until February of 1977 that I saw him allow anyone to actually touch him. Most of the time we went to Sandy Point he was there. He derived his name from this: 'Sandy'.

120

"No one knew if he was a male or a female at this stage. By June of 1977 it was quite obvious as he would get an erection and rub it against the diver's side and back. From June 1977 until 3 March 1978 when he disappeared, he was extremely friendly, playful, intelligent, warm and wonderful. We had an average of fifty people a week share in the experience of hugging and posing with this one lone dolphin. Almost everyone got to hold him at least once.

"I would estimate his age at four to nine years judging from photographs of other *Stenella plagiodon*. He was approximately six feet long and probably 160 to 220 pounds. He was never taken out of the water and weighed nor was he measured with a tape. It's easy to judge his size from photographs with people. To my knowledge he never ate anything offered him and we tried everything.

"During his very friendly phase (ten months) he would usually single out one person to play with; that could be a diving guest or a divemaster depending on his mood. Until they got out of the water he would follow them continuously and rub and nudge them, looking for recognition.

"He would model for photographers and bite down on an octopus mouthpiece if it was offered. In other words, he was a big ham. The strobe flash never seemed to bother him at all. He created such an atmosphere of excitement at the hotel amongst the guests that no one cared about the diving on the 'wall', which is excellent. Everyone wanted only one thing, to see Sandy for the first time, or to go back and see him again.

"From November 1977 until March 1978 when he left, he began travelling up and down the lee side of the island and you could never be sure where he'd turn up.

"I made six night dives during which he showed up. Nothing is more exciting on a night dive than to be seventy feet deep concentrating on a photograph when a six-foot dolphin drops by and nudges you for attention. I had people who were so scared they climbed up the side of the boat instead of the ladder! Sandy had that streak of mischievousness so common in captive dolphins, not to mention in many people. If people got tired of petting him and swam off down the reef, he would open his mouth and hold them by the snorkel or mask until they renewed their attentions, which they always did.

"He has been photographed by most of the prominent still photographers in the United States and on 16mm and 35mm movie footage by Al Giddings, Smokey Roberts and Jack McKenney. The January 1978 edition of *Skindiver* featured him on the front cover as did the April 1979 *National Geographic*. He was never tagged, blood sampled, or run through testing for hearing or sight. Everybody got to know him so personally that those ideas were never carried out."

By the time Sandy had spent eighteen months at the diving resort his fame attracted divers from the United States by the plane-load. The tropical deepwater location meant that this DINT was especially a diver/dolphin saga, with optimal conditions of clear, warm water and year-round good weather.

In all some 2500 divers met Sandy. One underwater photo shows eleven photographers in the background each armed with a sophisticated S.L.R. camera and strobe. In such situations Sandy was hard put to find a playful contact.

Writes Timothy O'Keefe, a visitor to the diving resort:

"On arrival at Sandy Point our skipper put the engines in neutral and revved them to make more noise. Suddenly a cigar-shaped shadow was off our bow. There was a spray of water followed by a quick roll of grey triangular dorsal fin. Sandy!

"Dave, already in full wetsuit, jumped into the water to greet his buddy. Of all the divemasters on San Salvador, Dave seems to have established a special relationship. Dave grabbed Sandy's dorsal and was towed around the boat. He let go, then grabbed Sandy's long thin beak and prised it apart to show us his teeth. Next Dave stuck his head through the jaws imitating a liontamer. Finally he picked up Sandy's head and tossed him. Sandy responded by swimming around in front and slapping his tail inches from Dave's face, showering him. So Dave grabbed Sandy's tail only to find himself quickly dragged down and under. Dave spluttered back to the surface.

"When I'd finished my film Dave climbed back aboard and we both donned scuba. I jumped in the water, Dave handed me my camera and strobe and down we floated. Sandy was busy harassing the other divers. He's quickly learned where our weak points are. He tugged the mask of one diver, causing it to flood. Then he went over and pulled on the regulator hose of another diver. Neither action was done with any great force. He was using just enough strength to flood a mask, not rip it off, as he easily could have done.

"Another of Sandy's favourite tricks was to swim away from a boat as though leaving. Concerned that he was tired of them, divers would quickly follow, swimming hard to keep up. After Sandy had lured them far enough to make it an uncomfortably long swim back, he returned to the boat to try to entice the next group away.

"It's almost as if Sandy's antics were part of a carefully rehearsed game. Yet he is the one who's devised all the tricks — without coaching from anyone. . .

"I'd been keeping my distance to film Dave and Sandy. Evidently Sandy decided I'd ignored him for too long. He came straight up to my camera and stopped just inches away, almost as if posing. I stayed motionless to film, not swimming. Sandy decided I was no fun. He reached down and gave my left leg a solid thump with his nose. When I still refused to swim he gave me another. I reached out and stroked his side. He stayed there as I caressed him, running the flat of my hand along his firmly muscled, rubbery skin.

"Soon Sandy headed upward for air. I looked down at Dave, framed him in my camera and waited for Sandy to return. When he didn't, I lowered the camera, only to get a nudge in the shoulder. Sandy was back, playfully seeking more attention. It was then I took hold of his dorsal and feeling like some god out of Greek mythology, went for my ride. It wasn't as fast as I'd visualized — we moved slowly through the water while I hung off to one side so my camera gear and belt buckles wouldn't scratch the dolphin. The ever present smile was only inches from my mask. I was entranced."

122

Pat Selby, a woman diver, wrote to us sending pictures and impressions:

"Sandy was such a special experience in my life. I cannot imagine anything to equal it. I first met Sandy in December of 1976. He appeared at Sandy Point, leading the boat — when I went over the side with my camera however, he disappeared. When the boat started up again he led it for a few miles and then withdrew. It was several months later that he approached snorkelers and they were able to touch him.

"In July of 1977 I took Al Giddings down to meet Sandy. He has many excellent pictures and was enthralled with him. Dr Sylvia Earle, Al and myself went back in September 1977 and Sylvia's children came down also. Sandy loved children and would give them a ride, with a gentle hand on his dorsal fin.

"There are experiences too numerous to mention but I can point out certain characteristics. First of all, Sandy had a remarkable sense of humour. He was not averse to removing your face mask when you weren't looking. He loved to rub against fins and rubber wetsuits. Very often he could be heard before seen underwater. His staccato echo-locating clicks were very clear. Interesting enough, a few people could not hear him. If I did not pay enough attention to him he did not hesitate to pull my hair or tap my head with his beak. Photographer Chris Adair could free dive to 110 feet accompanied by Sandy. The dolphin loved this human who wasn't cheating with bubbles spouting from his mouth. Chris and Sandy had a very close relationship.

"Sandy had several prominent scars, one on his dorsal fin and shortly before he disappeared he was caught in the prop on the dive boat just above the tail fluke. He had healed well from that wound however and I last saw him January of 1978. In March he disappeared while a research vessel was on the island. Whether he was taken by a collector, fell prey to a shark or just simply went off to find a mate, no one knows."

The Monkey Mia dolphins — a group DINT

On the opposite side of the globe from the Bahamas, about midway along the strangely bleak western coastline of Australia there is a vast bay swarming with marine life named by English buccaneer William Dampier: Shark Bay. It was here that Dutchman Dirck Hartog landed on 25 October 1616 and nailed a pewter plate to a post; the northern tip of Dirck Hartog Island, Cape Inscription. Eighty miles into the bay thrusts Peron Peninsula. On its sheltered eastern coast, at the end of 160 kilometres of rough road, is Monkey Mia caravan park. "Mia" is Aboriginal for "home".

And there for more than a decade the most unusual of all human/dolphin friendships has been quietly unfolding. Were such events to occur anywhere other than in this remote corner of the globe publicity and human pressure would probably have overwhelmed the dolphins long ago. The rugged Australian outback takes care of that.

At Monkey Mia up to a dozen wild dolphins visit the beach by the caravan park, mothers and babies in kneedeep water accepting fish with an audible squeak and transforming people of all ages into glowing children again. This is the oldest DINT on our records. These dolphins break so much of the pattern: they accept gifts of dead fish; they maintain a social grouping; they accept human contact but refuse to allow swimmers to touch them, and especially, they avoid people wearing diving gear.

One of the first to write about the Monkey Mia dolphins was underwater explorer Ben Cropp in 1978. Cruising off the West Australian coast in *Beva* in a cold thirty-knot southwesterly he sought the shelter of Monkey Mia. As he approached the anchorage there were bottlenose dolphins on his bow but when he slowed to anchor they left and sped straight for the beach. Right up in the shallows they were begging for a feed from several fishermen cleaning their catch. One fisherman waded in, handed a fish to a waiting dolphin and gave him a scratch on the back. The dolphin stayed there as if wanting more. Five dolphins lingered in the shallows, fins slicing the water amidst the boats at the edge of the beach. With cameras and some fresh fish, Ben and his friend Lynn Patterson approached them.

Lynn waded out with a couple of fish. The dolphins swept straight in and one nudged her leg as she dropped a fish into its waiting jaws. Then Lynn slipped her hand under the dolphin's jaw and kissed its forehead. It exhaled a blast of spray in her face. It swallowed the fish in her other hand and circled back to her. This time Lynn held the fish in her teeth and let the dolphin gently pluck it from her mouth. As a former owner of a dolphinarium, Ben could scarcely believe his eyes.

"With captive dolphins it takes up to six months of intensive training and lots of kindness and attention to achieve what Lynn had done. The Monkey Mia dolphins are in the wild with the open ocean right behind them. Yet they choose to meet and trust the people who come here."

Next we heard from Interlock friend Ian Briggs who visited the area that same year:

"At present," Ian wrote, "the resident colony consists of nine adults and three young. They hang around in the Monkey Mia vicinity throughout the year except during the November to February period when they leave, presumably for breeding purposes. Even during this period they make a day visit every couple of weeks."

As far as Ian could tell the exact origin of this human/dolphin exchange is a little uncertain. It goes back some years and involves people who were not in contact with each other. It seems a young girl on holiday began to feed some dolphins around the fishing jetty many years ago. (Accounts vary from 1966 to 1972.) Eventually she lured the dolphins into the beach and regularly fed them. One dolphin became extremely friendly. "Old Charlie" the fishermen called him, although he may have been a female. This dolphin became a legend in Shark Bay and would let children sit on him as their parents snapped photos.

Charlie would turn up at the end of the 150-metre jetty at precisely 7.15 am and round up the bony herring, nosing them towards the fishermen. Keeping them closely packed while the men jag-fished, he would only pick off the injured herring that broke loose. If by chance he himself were jagged he would come in and almost beach himself while the hook was removed. Then at 8.30 am, practically on the dot, Old Charlie would scatter the herring in all directions and that would be the end of baitfishing for the day. Nobody thought anything of it — it was just the accepted thing that Charlie rounded up the bony herring each morning for everybody's bait.

Then, as with so many legendary dolphins, somebody shot Charlie, possibly a holiday-maker resenting his presence near a net. But since then other dolphins have continued to visit the beach by the remote caravan park.

In 1976 Hazel and Wilfred Mason became proprietors of the park and from them we have received a series of letters, photos and tape recordings, even a visit from their son Noel.

They first wrote on 1 March 1979:

"We'll try to give you a little of our history and what we know of our friends the dolphins. We moved to this area three years ago from Perth to take over a very rundown small caravan park in a sheltered bay. We arrived in January and occasionally a dolphin and baby came in very close to the beach.

"We were amazed to find we could feed it but were soon advised by the locals that this was quite normal — ever since 'Old Charlie' was tamed. And we started to piece the story together. So many people now say *they* taught the dolphins to come in and feed. Personally we think it would take longer than one short holiday period to achieve this. Possibly it was the joint effort of quite a few before they became as tame as they are at the moment.

"As our first-year progressed we found that the dolphin and baby came in more and more as we kept feeding the mother. At this stage the baby was never allowed closer than fifty yards from the beach but one day Hazel was down there swimming when the mother brought her baby in. For three-quarters of an hour Hazel had the pleasure of swimming up and down the beach with the mother keeping the baby near to her. After that the baby seemed to be allowed to come in much closer, so perhaps Hazel was being introduced.

"As that first season progressed there were more and more dolphins coming in but mainly mothers with babies (which makes us wonder if perhaps Charlie might have been a mother who had lost her baby). At one stage that year we fed eleven. We only supply a small portion of their daily requirements and would never consider more because they must not become dependant on us for food.

"After three years the babies, who were small when we arrived, are now weaned and taking fish from us. It will be interesting to see if they return in this coming year or whether they will go their own way, perhaps to return when they have babies of their own in later years. We wonder if this may be just a nursery area. Will the mothers who have now weaned their babies withdraw and other mothers with young babies arrive?

"I hope this gives you some idea of the 'set up' here. The best of luck with your project."

We next received a letter dated 27 April 1979 from a globetravelling yoga teacher, Chi-uh Gawain from San Francisco. Chi-uh heard of the dolphins while in Perth and made the 500-mile journey up to Monkey Mia to spend a week with them. While there she read our correspondence with the Masons and kindly offered us her experiences. Subsequently Chi-uh visited us at Ngunguru, came to sea on R.V. *Interlock* and then paid another visit to Monkey Mia, which is described in a letter at the end of this chapter.

She wrote: "It is wonderful to be here and watch the dolphins turning smoothly just offshore. They whistle through their blowholes to attract attention. When anyone wades into the water they come up to greet him with heads just out of the water and will open mouths if a fish is offered. If they are offered a fish they like they will accept it from anyone. They seldom eat whiting, mullet or pieces of fish, preferring bony herring.

"If they don't want the fish they swim away and come past two or three times within touching distance. If you try to touch them they often swim quickly out of reach, but sometimes will glide slowly under your hand to be stroked — especially if they know you or have just accepted a fish. I don't think they take them because they are hungry. They are in good condition and always look full.

"People say, 'What can I do with the dolphins?' and all they can think of is to offer them a fish. They don't always eat the fish but treat it all as a game and go off dropping it underwater. I have only once seen a dolphin swallow a fish that I offered, but then Hazel had selected one they especially like.

"When I first came they didn't know me at all but five came to greet me, all accepted fish and two let me touch them, one coming back several times to glide under my hand. But when I go swimming among them they ignore me or at the most make fast circles around me at three to five metres distance. Sometimes they come close to Hazel and Wilf and cavort around them, but nobody, not even the Mason family, can touch them while swimming and *they won't tolerate anybody near them using face masks*. [Verified by several others; perhaps divers at some time have been too aggressive in seeking rides.]

"They are especially attentive to children. Provided they stand still in water up to their knees people can touch and pat them. They have come in every day, sometimes seven dolphins, but always at least three. Usually in the morning — sometimes before sunrise and at other times not till 10 am. They leave in the afternoon but have often been seen near the jetty at night. If the weather blows up they usually stay clear. Fishermen clean their nets in the morning and feed the dolphins fish they don't require — this may account for the morning visits.

"They did seem to hang around a little closer the day I stood waist deep and whistled the same little tune for about twenty minutes — I'm *not* a good whistler, but when I tried it again today they were not interested. I have the impression the dolphins don't want us to have any *purpose* in our relations with them. And especially no tricks or pretence. (Scientists please note.) Just be ourselves and they themselves and meet as friends."

One day some children came up from the beach to tell Wilf that Speckledy Belly, the oldest of the group, had a hook in her mouth:

."She had a big snapper hook jagged in the side of her mouth and a long wire trace hanging out. I felt I had to do something so I grabbed a pair of pliers and called Speckledy Belly in. She came right in on the sand and lay there, quiet and trusting while I struggled to remove the hook. It took me a good thirty seconds twisting with the pliers and she never moved. I had the feeling she knew exactly what I was going to do. When the hook came out she shook her head, swallowed a couple of fish I gave her, and moved out, wriggling backwards into deeper water."

Beautiful is a mother who brought her suckling baby to meet the humans. She would still suckle, lying on her side while in their company.

Holeyfin is the most trusting and friendly of the dolphins. Holey it was that Lynn Patterson held and kissed at first meeting. Holey has a hole in her dorsal fin, possibly from a bullet. The Masons are extremely concerned to get special legislation passed so that these dolphins can be protected. They feel a fulltime custodian is needed to keep an eye not on the dolphins, but the public: teaching them how to treat the dolphins, what to feed them, and what not to throw to them. Many deaths in captivity are caused by foreign objects being thrown to the dolphins. Speedboats need to be kept out of the crucial area and all netting banned.

Publicity has recently begun to focus on the Monkey Mia dolphins with television and news media, postcards and travel brochures. Already two of the babies have been found dead with a slash across the head, most likely from an outboard propeller. In 1977 a new dolphin swam up to Hazel making an unusual sound.

"She was definitely crying," Hazel says. "I tried to feed her but she wouldn't hold the fish in her mouth. I tried several ways but she could not swallow anything."

A few days later they found her dead on the beach. A bullet had passed through the jaw, shattering the hinge. Unable to feed, there was no way the dolphin could have survived. Treated so harshly by a human it still sought other humans for help.

Hazel believes the dolphins become more demonstrative when the holiday period brings larger audiences. "They are the biggest hams. The more people on shore, the bigger the show. If cameras are pointed at them they stick their heads out and grin, often four dolphins in a line."

When the dolphins returned for the 1980 season the Masons were able to answer some of their previous questions: not only did Holeyfin bring in her new baby, but also her previous offspring, Nicky, now weaned. "Normally they keep their babies well out but she let it come right in between our legs. I (Hazel) was talking to a chap when Little Joy, as we have named the new babe, swam to and fro between us. We were in chest-deep water swimming — eight people and five dolphins cavorting together.

"Yesterday Wilf and I went in with face masks. Crooked Fin and her baby were around but would not stay while we wore masks. So far (8 March) this season we've had five here most days: Holeyfin, Little Joy, and Nicky, Crooked Fin and her baby.

Dolphins, Orca and Whales

The story of a developing
interlock with humans,
told in words and pictures

Plate 1: The first step towards interspecies communication is establishing mutual accept-ance and trust. In five years of study our longest, most intimate dolphin encounters have been when we presented them with the greatest range of interesting behaviours — as on Nudelock Day when these two photographs were taken in sequence. The tiniest dolphin was suckling its mother. Between human mother and child, body language and sound are primary communication channels. We decided to test them with dolphins.

Plate 2: As forms of expression music and play can span language barriers
R.V. *Interlock* is a Polynesian catamaran equipped to bring dolphins
musicians and gamesplayers togethe

Plate 3: Our favourite meeting ground is in the vicinity of a giant sea cave at the Poor Knights Islands, off the New Zealand coast. Observing the response of dolphins to music we wondered what would happen if we allied it with body language and mimicry. *Credit: Carter Haven*

Plates 4/5: Rikoriko Cave is a huge sound shell and safe anchorage. Within it we practise swimming in rhythm to music. My fascination with dolphins began in 1972 when I first met a group of bottlenose dolphins, *Tursiops truncatus* in this cave. In pairs they inspected me closely

Plate 6: The dolphin suit enables us to enter the dolphin body and dance through the water using their appendages. In this way more complex exchanges of mimicry are possible.

Plate 7: A bridge: with interlock symbols on hull and mainsail, sound transmitters in each bow and intimate water access fore and aft the catamaran creates interest for dolphins and helps establish mutual trust before we enter their space.

Plate 8: Our initial interlocks were with common dolphins, *Delphinu delphis,* one of the shyer species. They often feed offshore on baitfish i symbiosis with gannets. When they see us or hear our bell the dolphin may leap out and come over to frolic in the field of music between our bow:

Plate 9: The first time Jan joined them wearing the dolphin suit one dolphin, Sideband, bonded with her for over four hours. Twelve months later to the day, Jan met him again.

Plate 10: Not reflections: three *Delphinus* couples demonstrate the joy of love-making to Jill Gray near Mayor Island. Mother and baby, thirteen months later. *Credits: Jill Gray*

Plate 11: *Delphinus* dolphins have a distinctive black/white hourglass pattern on their sides. Dorsal fin often has a white area variable in shape. *Bottom right,* This dolphin has approached several diving groups at the Poor Knights and permitted direct contact. *Credit: Grant Couchman*

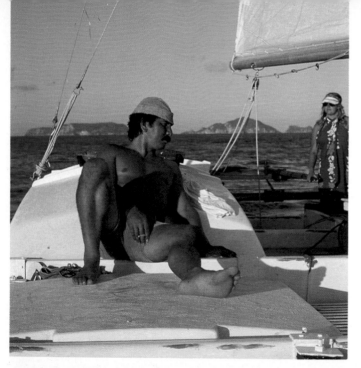

Plate 12: We learnt that for Maori people like Witi McMath there is a tradition of communication with dolphins along our stretch of New Zealand coastline. At special places where ocean and forest meet, as in this cave, tohungas or priests would commune with them.

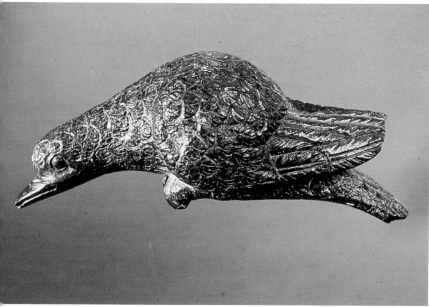

late 13: A solitary petrel often flies with a group of bottlenose dolphins.
ur observation tallies with Maori tradition. Regarding it as a bird of omen
riests formerly chanted invocations to Tukaiaia as an intermediary with the
olphins.

  According to Waikato Maori tradition, Korotangi or "the bird of stone" is
eputed to have reached New Zealand shores aboard *Tainui*, one of the
ouble canoes in which they migrated here, "guided by whales." In this
ght the sculpture could be seen as a stylisation embodying both petrel and
olphin. *Credit: National Museum, Wellington*

Plate 14: Bob Feigel told us he once had a dream in which he saw ou catamaran surrounded by dolphins. One communicated a word to me "Tepuhi". A Maori elder told me this means the flowing out of the breat from the dolphin's blowhole — an onomatopoeic word, which one day repeated to dolphins . . .

Plate 15: Bob Feigel's first encounter with dolphins occurred just as our study began. On a launch near the Poor Knights Islands he experienced something like an acoustic holograph, a moment before a dolphin leapt from the sea beside him. Research suggests the dolphin's sonar equipment provides a three-dimensional acoustic hologram of its surroundings. My photo from a car crossing Auckland harbour bridge at night approximates his impression. Movement incorporates the time dimension. With graphics and stained glass, artists Hal Chapman and Barry Fenn translated Feigel's experience into a window.

Plate 16: Learning of the Maori tradition, our attention shifted from th
offshore dolphins to their more coastal cousins, the big bottlenos
dolphins, *Tursiops truncatus.* This winter day we anchored in a sheltere
bay on the Tutukaka coast and awaited dolphins. Between rainshowers, Ja
tested an electric towpedo while wearing the dolphin sui

Plate 17: Four dolphins arrived and accompanied us home right into the harbour, fulfilling all our wishes. From such meetings we began to recognise them as individuals. *Credit: Bottom right, Colin Lee*

Plate 18: Then came that momentous day when four human gamesplayers met a large tribe of bottlenose dolphins: Nudelock Day, when the catamaran seemed to sail itself, and beneath a clear summer sea the dolphins glided towards us lying in the bow hammocks. *Credit: Dr Tony Ayling*

Plate 19: On this day Jan joined them in the dolphin suit and later, with
Avril, in the nude. *Credit: painting by Avril Ayling*

Plate 20: Among the dolphins on Nudelock Day were a number of individuals from previous meetings who seem to have signalled to us when we were slow to recognise them. At the outset a certain dolphin came very close, hovering between our bows where Tony Ayling skimmed the surface in the hammock, his camera just beneath. Nicks in the dorsal fin and the figure eight pattern on its side enable us to recognise it: Simo
Credit: Dr Tony Ayling

Plate 21: After a lunch break we met what we thought was a second group
of dolphins. But our pictures told us otherwise: Simo was there, trying to
attract our attention; *top photo,* Simo with companion above.

   Lower photo, While his usual companion defaecates right in front of the
lens, Simo trails seaweed around his tail, his fins, his jaw . . . Simo, we
were to learn, has quite a history of friendly approaches to people,
brandishing bits of seaweed.

Plate 22: Triplenick impressed us with the mimetic displays and clos
attention. Among the dolphins this day was Busy Bee who once wa
rescued from a box net. Damaged by a rope the base of his dorsal look
like a protruding thumb. *Credit: Robin Solomc*
As with the common dolphins, our nude bodies, the dolphin suit, mus
from our bows and the boat rig all served to heighten interest in us, and i
the end it was we who had to break contac

Plate 23: Next day fisheries scientist Mike Bradstock entered this same area on a trawler. He took a sequence of six pictures of dolphins leaping just as we'd seen the day before, in patterns that recall our bow and sail symbols.

Plate 24: Our dolphin experiments have brought us in contact with an increasing circle of people who have had similar encounters. *Top,* Quentin Bennett (*left*) and Meda McKenzie; *bottom,* Morgan Wiese (*left*) and Ros and Allan Rowe have all played with wild dolphins and shared their experiences with us.

Plate 25: Jan always writes up her own record of each interlock, then we compare notes. I find nature "arranges" things at times.

Dolphins Approach Humans: DINTs

Plate 26: In 1955 a lone female bottlenose came to Opononi, a village in New Zealand's far north, and frolicked all summer with people at the sea's edge. When Opo died she was buried with full Maori ceremonial rites. Today a statue stands in her memory on the shores of Hokianga harbour.

Sculptor: Russell Clark

Plate 27: For six years (1972-1978) a male bottlenose called Donald played with people in small coves and estuaries along the British coastline. At Coverack Cove in Cornwall Donald hovered among the fishing-boats while villagers were holding a thanksgiving ceremony to the ocean.

At Falmouth he had a special friendship with a fisherman's dog and once rescued it from the water. *Credit: Dr Nicholas Webb*

Plate 30: Near the Bahaman diving resort on San Salvador Island a youn
male spotted dolphin, *Stenella plagiodon* spent about 18 months (1976-1978
playing with diving tourists. As a sign of mutual trust Sandy would gent
accept a hand in his mout

late 31: Among his favourites was Chris Adair who often free-dived with
im to depths of over 100 feet. The pair swimming together symbolise the
otential for a human/dolphin symbiosis, a partnership of equals based on
iutual respect and unconditional love. *Credit: all photos, Pat Selby*

Plate 32: Early in 1978 both Sandy and Donald, on either side of the Atlantic, withdrew. In New Zealand some months later Horace began his games and Elsa, a common dolphin, came to Ngunguru estuary. When children called to her she swam up onto the beach to their hands. Out in the river she rested her beak on Terry Goodall's wrist and rocked to the ticking of his watch. *Credit: Terry Goodall*

Plate 33: In January 1981 the New Zealand city of Whangarei was delighted when a bottlenose and then two common dolphins travelled miles up their tidal river to spend separate days in the busy town basin. By the *Bounty* replica swimmers joined the dolphins and soon became the focus of their activity.

Plates 34/35: The strangest human/dolphin friendship has been happening
for several years on a remote stretch of West Australian coastline. At
Monkey Mia caravan park up to a dozen bottlenose dolphins have been
approaching people on the beach and accepting gifts of dead fish. In no
other case have visiting dolphins done this, but to the Monkey Mia dolphins
it may be a game, a ritual which both species understand. Clearly the fish
are not a source of sustenance as the bay abounds in fishlife and the
dolphins often drop their "gifts" nearby.

    Every day the dolphins come to the beach, bringing their young and
suckling them at the feet of the bathers. Children are the dolphins'
favourites and adults are transformed into children again.

Plate 36: The Monkey Mian story began many years ago when Old Charlie
began rounding up sprats each morning at the end of the jetty while
fishermen jag-hooked for bait. Regularly after an hour he would dismiss the
fish school. Eventually somebody shot Old Charlie, but not before he had
introduced others of his species to the locals. *Credit: all photos, Ian Briggs*

Plate 37: Off Cape Brett, Bay of Islands, a rare albino common dolphin has
approached boats. *Credit: Nigel Croft*
   At Sandy Bay, a popular surfing beach in Northland, New Zealand, a lone
surfer shares the waves with three bottlenose dolphins which surfed with
him. *Credit: Malcolm Pullman*

Interlock Around the World

Plate 38: The day I dived with Jim Hudnall at Lanai we met the Hawaiia
spinner dolphins, *Stenella longirostris.* This was a group familiar to Jin
Just as we find in New Zealand, a distinctively marked individual Jim call
Tatters has been coming closest to him and his various boats for year:
Tatters, *top centre. Credit: Jim Hudnall, Maui Whale Research Institut*
Bottom, A photo from the film "Dolphin", a Michael Wiese Production. O
Lilly Bank in the Bahamas a member of the film crew exchanges bod
language with spotted dolphins attracted to their schooner by underwate
music, confirming our own findings that dolphins respond to playful approache:

Plate 39: Off Valdes Peninsula in Patagonia dusky dolphins, *Lagenorhynchus obscurus* herd baitfish into a tightly packed meatball during feeding activities. *Credits: Dr Ricardo Mandojana*

Friendly Whales

Plates 40/41: On 3 February 1979 three orca glided over the morning calm near the Aldermen Islands, New Zealand. Gary Dods and his father, aboard the launch *Hirawanu,* were amazed as they advanced closer and closer, just beneath the surface. Gary began to click off photos. With his eighth shot a large female rested her head on the stern platform of their launch. A rare event but many boatowners would have fled in terror. *Credits: Gary Dods*

Plate 42: With his waterphone and thermal suit Jim Nollman exchanges musical notes with a group of orca off Hanson Island, British Columbia. For several years Jim has returned each August and met the same group. Nearby Dr Paul Spong has built his orca research station. *Credits: Peter Thomas*
Old Tom, a male orca whose skeleton is preserved in a small museum at Eden, New South Wales, where early this century he used to assist aboriginal whaling crews by braking the harpoon line with his jaws. Note the effect of an abscess in the upper jaw. *Credit: Ramari Stewart*

Plate 43: Gundi Day reacts joyously as she rubs the head of a Bryde's whale which sought human contact in the Galapagos, January 1978.
Credit: David Day and Marine Mamma! News

    Friendly grey whale, San Ignacio lagoon, Mexico. *Credit: James Hudnall, Maui Whale Research Institute.*

    Notchy: for three consecutive years Jim Hudnall has met this same distinctively marked humpback whale in the waters of Maui, Hawaii. Notchy now lets people touch him. His movements have been traced to Alaska and islands off the Mexican coast.
Credit: James Hudnall, Leish Wilks, Maui Whale Research Institute

Plate 44: Dr Ricardo Mandojana first dived with the southern right whales of
Patagonia in 1975. Off the windswept Valdes Peninsula, "the huge black
head floated motionless, semi-submerged a few metres from our tiny
inflatable . . . I grabbed my camera and eased myself below the cold
Patagonian sea . . .
". . . as I swam near one of its paddle-like flippers the whale retracted this
limb. It carefully stuck the fin close to its side as if to avoid hitting me . . .'

Plate 45: ". . . I stroked her side and back gently with my bare hands. The skin felt like very smooth, slippery rubber. I was surprised to feel a distinct quiver under my hand, like the tremors of a horse when patted close to the muzzle . . ." *Credits: Dr Ricardo Mandojana*

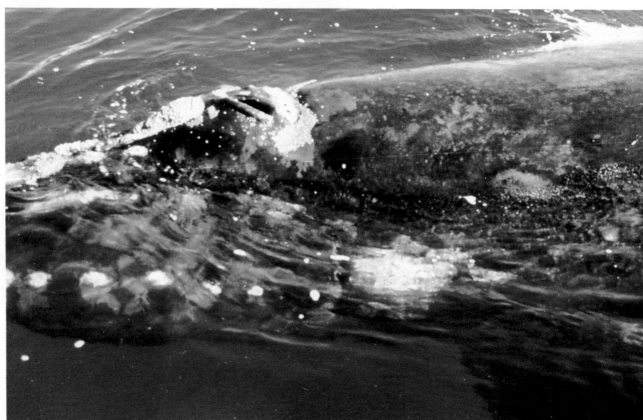

Plates 46/47: A friendly right whale approached the fishing vessel *Pirimai* of the Kaikoura coast, New Zealand in spring 1980. Three fishermen entered the water with the whale. It was very gentle when moving near them

ight alongside it arched through the water lifting Peter Kelliher clear of the
ea. All the crew were convinced the whale made a deliberate attempt to
ommunicate with them. *Credits: Barry Harding*

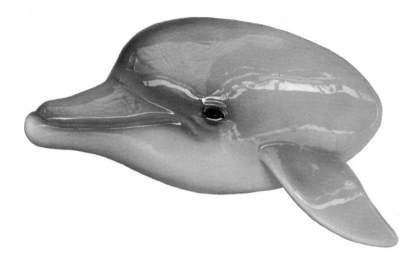

Dolphin bust by Ingrid Orbom

"Twice now we have had the experience of telling the dolphin who was not eating a particular fish to 'bring it back and change it' and the dolphin picked it up and dropped it at our feet. After four years of talking to them every time we feed them we wonder if they understand — as a dog would. They certainly make noises as if trying to talk to us when feeding.

"We've had a very interesting visitor by the name of Jacques Mayol who has been interested in dolphins for many years and has an emblem on his T-shirt so close to yours it isn't funny. He is very keen to meet you. Jacques established the world record for free diving: 100 metres in three minutes forty seconds two years ago when he was fifty years old. He has learnt things from dolphins that help in his diving. I hope you meet him as he is a real dolphin lover." (Jacques uses yoga techniques to control autonomic body responses on deep descents.)

Chi-uh Gawain was back at Monkey Mia in August 1980 and wrote to me on 31 August:

"It is such a treat to be here, to be able to walk out to the beach and wade into the water greeted by two or three dolphins swimming up to my knees and lifting their heads out of the water to be petted. And watching them frolic with one another. They are spending much more time here every day than they did when I was here for a week sixteen months ago. I don't know if that's just seasonal, or whether they are becoming more and more friendly as the years go by. This time I'm privileged to spend twelve days here, and am keeping a detailed journal of my experiences with the dolphins.

"There are twelve dolphins that I can call by name and recognize by their appearance and personalities, and as many as fifteen were counted here all at once on the one day, about two weeks before I came.

"Seven dolphins are real pets, and come regularly to take fish from anyone's hand and allow themselves to be touched — plus of course the new baby, now eight months old, who is here every day with its mother, but mother doesn't allow it to be touched, nudging it away if it comes close to shore.

"The dolphins keep away from swimmers and if anyone puts on a face mask, they leave! I don't know if any amount of build up of trust will ever change this. But it is really marvellous to be so affectionately greeted when I stand just kneedeep in the water. They will even rub against my knee, and let me stroke all along their sides, swim away and come back for more. All this daily, from dolphins who then swim off to the open sea, and who have never been captive or trained."

Footnote: Chi-uh has written and published a book on these dolphins, titled *The Dolphins' Gift*, Whatever Publishing Co., San Francisco, 1981.

8

Dolphins aid mariners

SCIENTISTS NOW know more about the dolphin brain than that of man. Ever since the studies by Dr Peter Morgane* of Worcester Foundation, Massachusetts and his associates, science is agreed that it has a complexity on a par with that of *Homo sapiens*. But they don't yet understand what it is all for: does the huge storage capacity of this organ (greater than our own) endow it with an advanced intelligence or is it just for navigation?

In captivity dolphins are now performing complex behaviours bordering on language but they cannot communicate much to man that we accept as intellect. Meanwhile, thousands are slaughtered each year as if of no account.

I must admit than when I first read Bernard Moitessier's dolphin episode in *The Long Way* I could not believe it as utterly as I do now. Over the five years that we have been studying dolphins in the wild we are becoming more and more amazed, as our understanding grows, at their ability where they are free to take the initiative.

In the course of our work we had heard, half believingly, stories of yachtsmen being assisted by dolphins. But from the time I read Moitessier we opened a new file: "Yachtsmen's Experiences with Dolphins." Project Interlock now has a growing collection of anecdotes which reinforce each other and suggest strongly that ancient Greek and Maori traditions were correct: if a mariner regards dolphins highly enough to take notice of their body language they *may* save his life. What these anecdotes have to say about the intelligence of cetaceans I will leave to the reader to decide.

Heading east on his global solo voyage aboard *Joshua*, Bernard Moitessier was thirty-two miles from Stewart Island on 27 December 1968. Ahead were dangerous, outlying reefs. Suddenly the sky became overcast, the wind holding a steady force 5 from the west.

"I hear familiar whistlings and hurry out, as always when dolphins are around. I don't think I've ever seen so many at once. The water is white with their splashing, furrowed in all directions by the knives of their dorsal fins. There must be close to a hundred. . .

"A tight line of twenty-five dolphins swimming abreast goes from stern to stem on the starboard side, in three breaths, then the whole

*Morgane's "The Whale Brain: the Anatomical Basis of Intelligence." *Mind in the Waters*. Scribner, 1974.

group veers right and rushes off at right angles, all the fins cutting the water together and in the same breath taken on the fly.

"I watch, wonderstruck. More than ten times they repeat the same thing. . . I have never seen such a perfect ballet. And each time, it is to the right that they rush off, whipping the sea white for thirty yards. They are obeying a precise command, that is for sure. I can't tell if it is always the same group of twenty or twenty-five, there are too many dolphins to keep track. They seem nervous; I do not understand. The others seem nervous too, splashing along in zigzags, beating the water with their tails, instead of playing with the bow, the way they usually do. The entire sea rings with their whistling.

"Another passes from stern to stem, with the same abrupt, graceful turn to the right. What are they playing at today? I have never seen this. . . Why are they nervous?

"Something pulls me, something pushes me. I look at the compass. *Joshua* is running downwind at seven knots *straight for Stewart Island*, hidden in the stratus. The steady west wind had shifted around to the south without my realizing it. The course change was not apparent because of the quiet sea, without any swell, on which *Joshua* neither rolled nor tossed."

His course corrected, the dolphins accompanied the yacht in the usual playful manner. Moitessier describes their behaviour in detail:

"And then something wonderful happens: a big black and white dolphin jumps ten or twelve feet in the air in a fantastic somersault, with two complete rolls. And he lands flat, tail forward. Three times he does this double roll, bursting with a tremendous joy, as if he were shouting to me and all the other dolphins: 'The man understood that we were trying to tell him to sail to the right. . .you understood. . .you understood. . .keep on like that, it's all clear ahead!'"

At one point he was tempted to steer for the hidden reefs to see what the dolphins would do — to test them as a scientist might, but something held him back.

"It would be easy. . .but the sea is still full of their friendly whistling: I can't risk spoiling what they have already given me." (From *The Long Way*, by Bernard Moitessier. Adlard Coles, 1969.)

After two hours all the dolphins but two, suddenly left. The remaining pair stayed on either side of his bow until dusk — a full five hours' escort. . .

In 1976 American geologist, Dr Richard Watson wrote the following letter to Project Jonah:

"I had an experience with dolphins this summer which I would like to share. During August we were returning to St Pete, Florida, aboard my forty-six-foot sailboat, engineless and silent, and had the opportunity to sail through the eye of tropical storm Dottie about two weeks after a near miss with Hurricane Belle.

"We were about 100 miles off Jacksonville when the storm popped up off Lauderdale. We were in the dangerous semicircle and unable to sail to windward in the heavy winds to escape the storm so we decided to reach downwind under bare poles, surfing for twelve hours, and try to get through the eye and into the navigable semicircle before the storm got too strong.

"A few hours before we reached the eye, and after maybe fifteen hours of outrageously heavy weather, we were approached by about fifty dolphins, *Tursiops truncatus*. They exhibited behaviour that I have heard about once before — in Moitessier's book about sailing around the world. They shot in unison up our port side and then simultaneously made a hard left turn. This was repeated maybe ten to twelve times. I dove below after checking the wind direction and with the help of Bowditch (H09) checked out the course to the eye of the storm. The dolphins were correctly telling me the course within ten degrees.

"As soon as we took their advice and altered course about ninety degrees, they left. Once we were in the eye, entered on N.E. corner, I was below trying to sleep and get some much needed rest, when I heard the dolphins talking their heads off. I went up on deck and maybe 100 dolphins were lolling (not playing) along with us next to the cockpit and looking up at us such as I had never seen before. Betsy was sure that she recognized one by a chewed up dorsal fin. They stayed with us for a long time, going at our very slow speed under full sail in the eye.

"As we were leaving the eye on the relatively safe S.W. corner, the dolphins tried to get us to turn back into the eye. Of course we knew we had to get out of there sooner or later and the sooner the better. Within five minutes we were in gale force winds again, but weaker than on the other side and were able to sail very fast with a storm jib. Within about six hours we were out of the storm with an experience which none of us will ever forget."

In 1978 four South African fishermen were rescued by dolphins. Kobus Stander, his young son Barend, Wessel Mathee of Parow, and Mac Macgregor of Maitland, were snook fishing off Dassen Island on Sunday 28 May, when a heavy fog engulfed them.

"I have never experienced such heavy fog. We could not see more than two metres away from the boat. We were all more than a little scared," Kobus said. They hoisted anchor and began moving slowly toward what they thought was the shore. After about twenty minutes they realized they were lost.

Macgregor was in front of the boat trying to peer through the fog. Suddenly about four dolphins surrounded the boat.

"They began nudging the boat towards the left, and Mr Macgregor was convinced that the dolphins were trying to steer us in a certain direction," said Kobus. "I had just swung the boat to the left when we heard waves breaking, and through the gap in the fog I could see the rocks. We would have hit if we had not turned. Another three minutes and we would have had it. This convinced us, so we let the dolphins lead us. Two of them stayed on each side of the boat, bumping on the side when they wanted us to go in a certain direction. We were sailing blind, but by then we had full faith in our helpers."

When they reached calm water the dolphins changed their swimming patterns.

"They all began swimming round the boat, as though they wanted us to go no further. They would not let us go in any direction, blocking our way. I decided to drop anchor, and this seemed to satisfy them. They swam around us for a while, jumped and frolicked as though they were happy, then disappeared."

After a while the sun dispersed the fog — and to their surprise they saw they were in the sheltered bay at Ysterfontein from where they had originally set out.

"It was a miracle. We could not believe our eyes. How do you explain it? It was a great relief and I will always be grateful to those four dolphins."

The dolphins were with them for about ninety minutes, which means initially, they had been sailing in the wrong direction.

Guided by radar Roger Kempthorne was taking his fishing vessel towards a fog-shrouded passage at the Three Kings Islands in New Zealand's far north. Not happy to trust the machine entirely, he gave the wheel to his deckhand and went up onto the bow to keep a lookout.

A group of smallish eight-foot bottlenose dolphins came frolicking around the bow. Gradually they were replaced by a diminishing number of larger and larger dolphins until there appeared a solitary, very large creature heavily scarred and obviously of some age. This dolphin made a gesture something like a "bowing aside" and another species of cetacean, possibly a pilot whale some twelve feet in length, took its place. It was much clumsier in its movements but made a series of ungainly leaps.

Meanwhile the vessel had passed through the danger zone unscathed.

In early 1980 in heavy following seas and out of sight of land, fisherman Lin St Pierre was alone, heading for shelter at Houhora, off the northeastern coast of New Zealand. The weather was deteriorating, his boat was very decrepit and he was anxious for his safety. He was most concerned as to when he should turn west and head inshore for Houhora Harbour. The land is very low lying in this region, the only feature being Mt Camel.

Dolphins appeared on his bow. From certain gestures they made he felt they were trying to indicate the direction he should head. For half an hour he struggled with indecision. When he finally resolved to accept their guidance he felt that he had little choice that offered any greater hope. For some time he followed the dolphins. The moment he sighted Mt Camel and saw he was on course for Houhora Harbour, the dolphins made a leaping gesture and vanished.

Newspaper headlines "Dolphins Saved Us!" led me to contact well-known yacht designer Rob Woollacott of Auckland for his story. With Brian Haslip he was participating in the 1980 round North Island yacht race when a tropical storm struck. Rob wrote to me:

"At 0930 on 13 February 1980 one and a quarter miles off Houhora beach we were joined by a school of eight or nine dolphins. Our position at this stage was precarious as our thirty-two-foot yacht *Isalei* was dismasted and rudderless.

"We were proceeding under motor with a series of jury rudders made of floorboards which kept on breaking because we did not have time to construct anything substantial. Also the ten to fifteen-foot breaking seas were causing bad propeller cavitation and periodical shaft whip which necessitated throttling right back to prevent damage to the shaft. Weather conditions were bad with a forty-knot plus onshore easterly, driving rain and low cloud cutting visibility to a quarter-mile.

"After some time I felt the dolphins were trying to help us as every time we had to stop they became agitated — slapping their heads or tails on the water alongside the cockpit and then racing off towards the sea. While we were mobile they would stay in the wave ahead of us. Subconsciously I started following them and found the going easier through the seas. A couple of times they appeared to break up seas which were going to break on us. Just having them around was a great psychological lift. By 1200 we were in less dangerous seas and at 1300 two fishing-boats appeared out of the murk and took us in tow. As soon as the tow rope was attached the dolphins all disappeared.

"Once in shelter we learnt that the fishing boats had *not* been looking for us in response to our radio calls for assistance but in fact were running for shelter and did not even know we were out there. The dolphins had stayed with us for three-and-a-half hours and appeared to have led us eighteen kilometres to the fishing-boats.

"The dolphins we encountered were the big bottlenose species, eight to ten feet and mottled grey — they appeared to have a few scars and looked quite old."

Don Anderson might have lost his yacht and all his family were it not for a dolphin warning. This is what he wrote to me:

"I left Whangarei Town Basin on 19 January 1979 at 0625 hours on a Piver Nimble trimaran named *Manu-Moana* with my wife Karen and son and daughter. We had been in Whangarei Harbour for about a week having our clutch fixed. We motored from the harbour for about two hours and the sea was like glass. We were going up to Tutukaka to meet some friends.

"The wind came up fresh and just north of Bream Island we were heading into N.N.E. winds and lumpy seas. After a couple of hours the wind dropped to nothing. We started to motor but the clutch began to play up, so Tutukaka was out. After rolling around for more than two-and-a-half hours, the wind came up again right on the nose, so we decided to head south for Kawau Island. It was a long night — arriving off Kawau at 0400 hours.

"By now with no wind and a slipping clutch we were idling along at three to four knots. It was pitch black and I decided to head towards the beacon on Kawau, then turn, keeping Maori Rock on my starboard side. Karen was up in the pulpit trying to spot it. At this stage the motor decided to cut out, a fuel blockage.

"With the tide on the flood we were drifting towards the northern end of Kawau in the North Channel — and it's all rocks there. I had to dash below and after disconnecting and blowing down the tank I restarted the motor. During this time Karen was standing by with the anchor. Still no sign of Maori Rock. Then there was a large splash on our starboard side — which caused me to swing the boat to port until I saw, with great relief, it was a dolphin, so I came back on course. That dolphin stayed on my starboard side for quite some time then disappeared. On looking back, I could see Maori Rock only about a cable away *on the starboard quarter*. It was really amazing.

"I often wonder if the dolphin stays in this location or if it was there by chance? After reading about the remarkable things dolphins are capable of and do, they deserve all the protection we can give them. My daughter cried when she read what the Japanese do to them.

"All the best in your project."

One day at Tutukaka a visiting solo yachtsman, Alan Fouts from Louisiana, told us of an experience he had had when dolphins gave him a warning. Afterwards I had the urge to track Alan down and get his story verbatim. I traced him to Mauritius and he obliged with a narrative of two dolphin warnings in the same area two years apart! His letter reached me on 18 February 1980:

"Greetings from Mauritius, cyclone capital of the South Indian Ocean. *Navajo* is well moored in Grand Bay awaiting the arrival of the third cyclone to visit Mauritius this season. The first was a real ripper with winds to 150 mph. *Navajo* suffered some damage but was lucky not to wind up on the beach or rocks. I'm sorry to be so long in replying to your request about dolphin warnings. I have thought often of you and Jan and the rest of the mellow people on your hilltop. . .

"On the night of 20 August 1977 and in the following early morning hours I was more than a bit nervous as I approached the entrance to Torres Strait, north of Australia. Eastern Fields, Portlock and Lagoon reefs and East Cay, barely break the surface and are strewn as obstacles at the Bligh Entrance to Great N.E. Channel. There are strong and shifty currents due to the large tidal difference between the Gulfs of Papua and Carpentaria. Also the mighty Fly River empties into the Gulf of Papua bearing huge trees torn from its banks. In clear weather one might be confident — but rain and low cloud had mostly hidden the stars and sun for the three days since leaving Port Moresby. A twenty to thirty-knot S.E. breeze urged me forward in the short choppy seas of the Papua Gulf and the waves broke strangely in whirls of current.

"At the entrance to Torres Strait in the Gulf of Papua lies Bramble Cay — a few hundred yards of sand and scrub on a mile of reef with a light. Once you locate Bramble Cay the rest is relatively easy. Should you fail to locate Bramble Cay and pass on west or south you enter a maze of reefs. Not a pleasant prospect in my present situation of wind, rain, sea and total darkness, broken by explosions of blue green phosphorescent light. Accordingly I set a time limit within which, if I failed to locate Bramble Cay, I would have to turn about and tack east against a fresh wind and steep seas. It was around 3 am: that low point, the ebb in human metabolism.

"Time had just about run out and several times I nearly tacked ship as waves broke suddenly in a welter of light and foam. Time nearly up and no sign of Bramble Cay light. Time to put *Aniara*'s helm over and bash to windward. One last sweep of the horizon with rain-soaked binoculars. Was that the loom of a lighthouse off a bit to port? There it is again! Fifteen seconds can be an eternity on a dark night foaming on towards possible coral reefs. But there it is again and on time! Group flashing, two every fifteen seconds.

"I didn't see the lights every flash — far from it. Sometimes *Aniara* was on the crest and other times in the trough at the appointed instant as I counted aloud to myself alone in the cockpit. But it *was* there and that distant loom gave me the confidence to sail on, sure I was on the right track amongst all the surrounding reefs. After about a half an hour of sailing towards this regular double loom every fifteen seconds, spying it when I could amidst the spray and rain, counting all the while — checking and checking — my mind suddenly did a double take: resolution of an optical illusion. Not the distant loom of Bramble Cay light, but a close, rapidly approaching, school of dolphins leaping regularly in unison; twice, then pause for fifteen seconds. They approached, passed close to port and continued on their way straight on, seemingly oblivious to *Aniara*.

"I then had a brief moment of panic as I realized that I had sailed half an hour past my deadline on the strength of a 'signal' that was definitely not Bramble Cay light! True, it was in what I considered the most likely direction. A further careful survey of the horizon ahead revealed a tiny point of light dead ahead just visible as *Aniara* rode the crest at the top of a wave. It flashed twice — two points of electronic light then darkness for an eternity of fifteen seconds. Two points of light again.

"I can tell you I was very relieved and elated and subsequently sailed past Bramble Cay at 0630 that morning on my way into Torres Strait and on for a pleasant forty-day sail to Port Louis, Mauritius.

"The phosphorescence from the dolphins was well timed and orchestrated. The quality and colour of the light was very different from the strobe on Bramble Cay but the timing was *exactly the same*. Those dolphins really helped me out that night. Perhaps they were simply imitating the rhythm of the light for their own amusement. I believe they felt my predicament and responded in a remarkably intelligent way."

Coincidentally, they were of use to Alan again at that same spot two years later, on 28 September 1979, after Alan had met us in New Zealand and related the first incident to us.

"I was on a fifty-eight-day solo, nonstop voyage between Fiji and Mauritius. Fifteen days out of Lautoka — having averaged an amazing 178 miles a day — I was making the approach to Bramble Cay under much better conditions. Plenty of star sights and a good moon made me confident of sighting Bramble Cay light sometime in the early hours of morning.

"For some reason — probably because I hadn't slept for a while — I was asleep below when I was awakened by the sound of dolphins about the boat, whistling and clicking and carrying on. Upon coming on deck to talk to them, there was Bramble Cay light, dead ahead perhaps twelve miles distant. Whether I would have continued to sleep and so

136

perhaps had intimate contact with Bramble Cay, I don't know. It was nice of them to awaken me!

"I see from my log I was visited by dolphins seventeen times during those fifty-eight days at sea. Mostly in the Timor Sea and South Indian Ocean. An average of six to eight dolphins per school encountered, although there was one lone dolphin in Torres Strait and once there were over twenty. They ranged in size from three to seven feet and seemed at least three different types.

"The wind howls outside as rain spatters horizontally everywhere. The latest forecast predicts the centre will cross just south of Mauritius before noon tomorrow. It's 2340 now.

"I hope you can use some of this in any form you like for your book. It sounds interesting and I look forward to reading it. Sorry I've taken so long to write you! I admire you for your efforts in the furtherance of human/dolphin interlock. Keep up the good work, the planet needs men like you."

This is perhaps the most amazing account on our file to date. We hope that other mariners with experience of this nature will feel encouraged to send them to us at Project Interlock, Box 20, Whangarei, New Zealand. While there will, undoubtedly, be more stories as yet unrecorded, I am also mindful that such experiences may become more common once mariners develop more interest in dolphins.

How often has a warning gone unheeded? There is an illuminating paragraph in that remarkable book *Papillon*, by Henri Charriere, published in 1970 by Hart-Davis, London. It makes a thought-provoking footnote to this chapter.

With six men in a sixteen-foot open boat out from Trinidad, Papillon takes up the story:

"Three days passed with nothing much happening, apart from our twice meeting with schools of dolphins. They made our blood run cold, because one band of eight started playing with the boat. First they'd run under it longways and come up just in front — sometimes one of them would touch us. But what really made us quake was the next caper. Three dolphins in a triangle, one in front and then two abreast, would race straight for our bows, tearing through the water. When they were within a hair's breath of us they would dive and then come up on the right and the left of the boat. Although we had a good breeze and we were running right before it they went still faster than we did. The game lasted for hours: it was ghastly. The slightest mistake on their part and they would have tipped us over. The three newcomers (crew) said nothing, but you should have seen their miserable faces!"

In the middle of the night of their fourth day, a great storm hit them and all night through they fought to survive, baling furiously for seven hours.

PART FOUR

With Larger Minds

"These magnificent beings may teach us that we have too long accepted a view of non-human life which denies other creatures feelings, imagination, consciousness and even a right to exist. They may show us that in our rush to justify our exploration of other life-forms we have become blinded to their incredible essence, and so have we become incomparably lonely."

— Dr John E. Nelson

9

Meeting with bottlenose dolphins

I WANT TO take the narrative from our journals back to a point just after the making of the film "The First Move": February 1978. Until that month, in all our dolphin expeditions, we had not once interlocked with the big bottlenose dolphins, *Tursiops truncatus*. Strange, considering it was these dolphins that set our whole project in motion, the day we danced with a huge gathering of them back in 1975 (as described at the outset). And there was that unrelated event when they met me alone in Rikoriko Cave, before I was interested in dolphins.

Subsequently we had once seen bottlenose dolphins when returning from a sea trip in the fast runabout days; three big fins right at the harbour entrance. We stopped and I leapt in but it was murky and the dolphins showed no interest.

Our journals record that the bottlenose meeting which changed the whole pattern of interlocks, occurred two days after we took our Maori friend, Witi McMath to sea. To me in retrospect, it is important to mention this link because of the contribution his knowledge made to the evolution of our thinking about dolphins; so many seminal ideas that are easy to forget, but which later bore fruit, came from this source.

It was Witi who directed us to Waipu Pita, the Maori elder, and from Witi I learnt the historical context of our research: the coastline on which we operate has a pre-European history of very intimate human/dolphin relationships which, with western influence, have gradually wound down during this century. To the Maori people the Pelorus Jack, Opo and Horace episodes were a carry-over of traditional relationships into modern times.

From Witi I learnt that the Ngatiwai, the people of the sea, formerly lived also on the offshore islands including the Poor Knights, Great Barrier and their stronghold, Little Barrier. He told me that if their people on the Barrier were in need, a dolphin would arrive in Matapouri Bay and give the message.

At the time I found Witi's story difficult to credit although I knew this was just a cultural problem for me — like a bushman encountering television.

As things unfolded with the bottlenose dolphins, I came to understand we were once again raising the veil of ignorance that has separated humans and dolphins in this part of the globe for only a relatively short time — and that it would take organic growth of our own belief patterns

141

before the bond could re-establish. It would take that Maori reverence for all living things of the forest and the ocean and a deep seated response to the Earth as our nurturing mother, and that activator, the sky: Papa and Rangi, Yin and Yang. Only when we felt truly connected to it all, could we have intimations of the old bond that linked cetaceans and people.

"What is water, Te Rina?" I asked a Maori environmentalist in Napier.

"Water is our mother's milk, Wade. It flows from her breast to the sea. Waiora, water of life. And if we poison our mother's milk, we most surely will die."

So often I have found in Maori tradition these simple, powerful statements of ecological principle. Whereas these statements once sustained a whole way of life, modern society now pays mere lipservice to the science of ecology, spinning environmental impact reports in lieu of prayer wheels, before going on — uncaring.

"Look what they are doing to our mother," said Te Rina, as she drove me to Napier airport across Ahuriri estuary. A dragline was ripping up the streambed to load trucks with gravel. "They are tearing open her belly and killing all her babies. There will be no fish in the sea." Then she told me that, to her, the visit of Horace to Napier was a warning. And she was appalled that the dolphin should receive such an unsuitable name!

Witi comes to sea

Journal, 14 February 1978: Today Witi came to sea with us and I saw the Poor Knights and our whole project through Maori eyes.

"My first time to leave Tutukaka by sea," Witi told me as I steered through the entrance. He loved the Polynesian catamaran, so close to the water, so intimate. He stooped and washed his forearms and face with the sea. "Makes me feel like a kid again," he grinned.

Out around the Sugarloaf and Pinnacles we motored over the summer calm, to approach the Poor Knights beneath the massive rocky bridge of Archway Island, all for Witi's enjoyment. Heaving to in South Harbour I whisked him off in the inflatable, around into Shaft Cave. The immensity staggered him, gazing up at the vast rectangular slot that pierces the very centre of the island, with its rim of trees far above and shafts of sunlight playing like searchlight beams on the dark waters of the cave. Then Witi began to chant. Powerful Maori words that echoed and sparkled with ancient wizardry, sending my mind into a timeless space when carved canoes probed these caves.

A short distance further on we entered the tunnel, paddling silently while Witi gasped: black diamonds slipping by in the blue-black depths — about forty stingrays plankton-feeding in the tunnel currents. Again Witi chanted, to my delight and awe, the echoes ringing to notes that hadn't stirred there for almost two centuries — it was as if the echoing voices were Witi's ancestors. Suddenly all the stingrays surged up to the surface, fluttering to and fro just beneath us as if in response to this chant.

Through Blue Mao Arch we zoomed to the sheltered western corner

142

of Labrid Channel, where trees almost reach the ocean edge. We skirted the shores of Aorangi until a concealed portal opened in the cliffs. Again we paddled in silently. As we entered the interior harbour Witi was in ecstasy. At the first chance he slipped into the water and landed on a kelpy rock, half awash. For a moment his powerful figure seemed to commune privately with that enchanted place. Then I guided the inflatable into a low cavern that opens off the internal harbour, delicately manoeuvring until we were in the farthest recess.

I had only recently discovered this space — most magical of all the Poor Knights' temples. At the end, the cave roof suddenly soars skywards and the rock walls sweep up in parallel towards a lofty forest ridge. At the base of a funnel we clung to the rocks trying to steady the inflatable on the surges. Witi felt that such a place would have been a tapu ground where island-dwelling tohungas (priests) once came to commune with natural forces: an intimate meeting-ground of sky and sea, earth and air.

We went back to the catamaran, hove to nearby, for my cameras. As we returned to the island I had a certain foreboding. Just then, from the slope above the portal a puff of dust grew into a small landslide — rocks fell into the water at the very entrance. In sixteen years out there I have never witnessed a rock fall. As we paddled in, dust from the slide petalled the surface.

Witi steadied the boat as I trained my camera within the temple. A green space: even the rocks glow verdantly. With each ruck and wrinkle the edge is slightly translucent — a greenstone world. Above us the fronds of ferns hang like jade feathers all the way up the funicular slope to where pohutukawas stand on the high ridge, their trunks and branches silhouetted and leaves sparkling in the sunlight. The ocean gurgling around us and the songs of forest birds overhead.

On our homeward voyage, Witi imparted a wealth of Maori tradition which I have never been able to find in any of the books. This area of sacred knowledge was not often vouchsafed to the missionary scribes.

I asked Witi if it would be possible to commune with dolphins in a space like that. Witi said you would have to be obsessed with the subject. Then you start noticing signs like the stingrays and the landslide. Things happening on another level of reality. You then carry right on through. He said he had only seen two places like that cave before in his life. A stairway to heaven. In places like that a priest would practise his divining rites.

We sailed home talking of lucid dreams, eating and sipping tea while the ocean changed colour from gold to silver and silver-grey, reaching our mooring just on dark. Somehow that day I felt very close to the dolphins, yet none had appeared. But two days later. . .

The day of the sea hawk — Tukaiaia
16 February 1978: "That looks just like Tu, the bird Waipu Pita told me flies with the dolphins," I was telling Robin Solomon, a Maori friend, as a dark bird flew up towards our stern and banked sharply, just as I finished my sentence. Graham Mosen looked back as I spoke: just then he saw a dolphin breach in our wake.

"There they are," shouted Robin. And so it began, our first interlock with the big dolphins — *Tursiops truncatus*. Three of them, cruising south along the coast, right at the harbour entrance. We changed course to follow, but they were difficult to establish a bond with.

Everybody was so excited, whistling and calling to them, that we kept it up for miles past the sensible "give up" point. I was curious to know what would happen if we kept on going. We could just keep their fins in view about two hundred yards ahead, breaching in close sequence — a tall, thin white-tipped fin with a tear at the base of the trailing edge like a protruding thumb. Then a short, stumpy ragged one and a perfect black scimitar usually appearing in that order, white tip being the boldest of the trio. Occasionally they would breach off our starboard bow or drop back to within 100 feet of us, but no closer. All the while, the black bird was swooping about, now above us, now out to the east, over the the west, ahead, astern — and always leading our eyes back to the dolphins so we could use the bird as an indicator whenever we lost contact. Funny — ever since I met Waipu Pita his story about the bird had worried me. Everything else the elder told us had proven true. But we had *never* seen a black bird with *Delphinus*. . .

Then it happened — when we were past all hoping the dolphins came to us and took up position in between the bows, two at first, huge muscular forms that suddenly made the bows of the cat seem fragile and small. The finely sculptured tail pumping up and down and the long, lithe trunk. They turned, nosed towards us, fixed us with their eyes and nodded their heads.

When I asked one to turn on its side, two responded in unison. The one with the perfect dorsal had a nick in the left lobe of its tail: Nicktail. The human response was ecstatic: a constant high voltage euphoria enveloped the seven of us that smoky northeast morning. The music tape ran out. Jan restarted it. When the tape came on the dolphins slowed visibly in front of the bows.

Twice they came in and took up positions on our bows. We wanted them to go on forever but then, they may have had other concerns. Robin saw Nicktail "flicker flacker" its tail, then dive down steeply.

"That's it," Robin said, "they're off!"

We did not see them for some time; then they surfaced well ahead. I jumped into my suit to try meeting them in the water. I leapt into the inflatable and Graham and Tony zoomed me ahead of the cat. Directly in the path of the dolphins I tumbled in wearing the dolphin fin. A dolphin passed beneath me. I tried it again. The dolphin passed and then suddenly dived straight down at least 100 feet before disappearing into the blue. That was it. Interlock over. No sorrow. It felt so complete.

We were about eight miles down the coast, off Pataua. We set sail for the Knights. With us all the way came Tukaiaia.* People joked, "Look, there's your bird — leading us to the dolphins." Would he, I wondered, accompany us to the pelagic dolphins further off shore? "Maybe it's the dolphins on our sail," thought Jan.

It was about three o'clock when I slipped below for a nap. "Here

*Also called Korotangi, the bird of stone. Carving in National Museum, Wellington.

they are," someone called.

I snapped out of it at once to find the ship alive with excitement. We'd met them — *Delphinus* — both dolphin species on the same day! About forty dolphins close to the Poor Knights, an active hunting group pursued by about a dozen sooty shearwaters — but not a single gannet. Fast-moving rushes, complex groupings, leaps, tail thwunks, that funny twisting movement in small groups of about three. Jan slipped into her suit and so did all the others — never so many keen gamesplayers at the ready.

The dolphins rode our bows while the ship spun around and took a reverse course, downwind. People in the bow hammocks, trailing over the sides, hanging on to the stern ramp; for five minutes humans and dolphins exchanged glances but it couldn't last: the day was late, a strong southeast wind had arisen and it was too rough for interlock games.

Graham said he felt confused and uneasy at the sea conditions. Just to prove a point we still tried to establish contact. Tantalisingly the dolphins kept half a mile ahead — we followed. It dawned on several of us, independently, that they were leading us towards Tutukaka — for a time invisible in the haze swaddling the coast, but eventually visible. We got home just as a thunderstorm struck.

Footnote: Some time later I met a neighbour with a dolphin story. Bill Shanks was crewing on the fishing-boat *Busy Bee* when it was servicing a huge experimental trap net up at Whale Bay. One morning they found a big dolphin in the net. To release it necessitated hauling the dolphin on board, but it did not resist in the least. They steamed three miles out, soothing it and pouring water over its skin. When set free it leapt clear of the water and vanished.

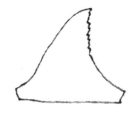

Next day as the *Busy Bee* left Tutukaka Harbour two dolphins met them off the entrance with a series of superb leaps. One of them they recognised as the dolphin they had liberated the day before: a nick made by a rope in the rear base of the dorsal fin.

I showed Bill our first bottlenose pictures. That was how we came to name that big dolphin Busy Bee.

After publishing a description of this dolphin (*Dive* April 1979), we received a report from skindiver Alan Morrison. He had seen Busy Bee at Great Barrier Island:

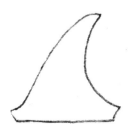

"In the evening of 10 January 1979 at the entrance to the small cove on the north side of Rakitu Island off Great Barrier, members of our diving club met three large dolphins. The two big ones were apparently copulating. We snorkled with them for half an hour. One of the large dolphins had the top of his dorsal missing. Another appears to be your Busy Bee dolphin and the smaller of the trio has a nick from the tail and a small spot on its dorsal."

A short while later — on 22 January — we sighted these same dolphins on our stretch of coast, fifty miles to the north. So much for Witi's story of the messengers. . .

Subsequently the vessel *Busy Bee* was wrecked. The bell was given to R.V. *Interlock*. This is the bell we ring whenever we meet dolphins. A link.

Follow home day

On Sunday 7 May we set out aboard *Interlock* to shoot a few rolls of film for a new proposal. We'd been wanting the resources to document each interlock development since the first film was made. This winter's day the dolphins followed us home, right into Tutukaka Harbour — our first full interlock with the large bottlenose dolphins that inhabit coastal waters.

Our Journal: Today we had a hunch we were going to meet the big dolphins again. On board were Brady and Karla and Ramari Stewart (Dusty), a part-Maori girl who is unusually gifted in communicating with animals and came to offer us her help with the project.

We headed down the coast towards a point called Goat Island, where there would be good shelter from the blustery southerly, and where Dusty had seen bottlenose dolphins two months earlier. She had an uncanny assurance she would meet them again in the same area, although they range far and wide along the coast.

Also on board was an exciting new piece of equipment, kindly loaned to us by a wellwisher: an electric "towpedo" which can tow a diver at one-and-a-half knots. The device is powered by a twenty-four-volt motor and two twelve-volt batteries in series. We wanted to try it out while wearing the dolphin suit, to see what aquabatic benefits there would be in having an effortless source of speed.

We had a pleasant sail down the coast tacking into the southerly squalls with nice turns of speed. In recent months the family has learnt to handle the catamaran without any expert assistance, and we are all finding that coastal sailing in winter gives us much more practice than our easy summertime jaunts out to the Poor Knights.

Just as we dropped anchor off the lee shore, a dark cloud mass appeared on the horizon. Jan struggled into the dolphin suit and I managed to shoot a roll of her setting out with the towpedo before the sun disappeared. She was sitting on the diving platform with a coat over the dolphin suit, sipping a hot cup of tea, when Dusty said in a quiet voice, "You'd better get into the water — we've got visitors."

Around the point, heading into the bay, came four dorsal fins. The bottlenose dolphins cruised slowly past us and began lolling about in the centre of the bay a short distance from our anchorage. Close to our position two skindivers were hunting for crayfish from a small runabout. The dolphins weren't coming any nearer, so Jan wriggled her dolphin body into the inflatable and with my still and movie cameras aboard, Brady drove us over to them. They were magnificent: three huge sleek creatures larger than our boat, and one teenager. We played with them for a while as they swept around our bow, turning aside to look at us and whisking under the hull. Once trust was established Jan slipped in, wearing the dolphin suit and fins. We had never before established contact with the bottlenose dolphins in this way, but with *Delphinus* the suit has created new levels of interlock.

The water in the bay was discoloured by the Ngunguru river-mouth and Jan could see very little but she dived down several times weaving the dolphin-kick. All of a sudden she saw the four dolphins very close

146

beneath her, all swimming on their sides and scanning her closely as she curved along like a dolphin. They didn't come to the surface with her; they only swam near when she dived down.

While Jan dived with them I juggled my cameras to snatch short bursts of film and Brady manoeuvred the boat with special care not to run over his mother. When she became exhausted, we decided to return to the catamaran, where Dusty and Karla were burning to meet the dolphins. We swapped crews, leaving Jan and Brady to ready the vessel for sea and join us out in the bay with the dolphins.

With a fresh roll of film, I took sequences of Dusty up in the bow of the inflatable reaching over to the dolphins all around her while Karla scribbled notes on their fin patterns and behaviour. The smaller one had a perfectly formed dorsal fin with no damage to it. The three others were large and bore many scars and scratches and nicks on their dorsals. I photographed them for our records. One was a pale grey with a large white scar behind its blowhole.

A fishing dory with three men and a boy cruised up and anchored nearby. The child danced with excitement when the dolphins played around their bow and circled between both craft. Then the dolphins left us. We looked around. The catamaran was moving out across the bay. Brady had the cetacean message tape playing through the bow speakers and the human/dolphin insignia came sparkling over the waves towards us. The dolphins took up positions on the bows. Jan lay in the bow net, gliding only inches above the surface while I steered the inflatable on a parallel course and filmed the pretty scene: the yellow hulls, white sails adorned with leaping dolphins, and the dolphins themselves escorting us on our homeward journey.

Winter days are all too short and the late light made the dark coast menacing. We felt sure that the dolphins' hovering actions warned us of the danger as we rounded the submerged tip of Ngunguru reef. We were sorry to be leaving them.

Sailing towards Tutukaka Harbour mouth Jan said, "Wouldn't it be good if they came into the harbour with us!" And then, "Oh no, they won't — it's much too polluted." Dusty said later she was thinking the same.

It was rush hour when we cruised through the entrance — charter boats and runabouts were all heading home at the day's end. On the cliff tops near the motels groups of people were taking an evening stroll. Suddenly they heard yells and screams of delight from below. There was a catamaran, just lowering its sails, and around it four dolphins were playing, right inside the harbour.

There remained one thing I was itching to do. The day would be complete if I could try the towpedo out with the dolphins. I danced into my gear, dolphin fin on my back and leapt over. Jan almost fell on me, passing down the heavy orange machine. With the propeller whirling at top speed it hauled me under and I curved around in the twilit harbour, amazed to find schools of kahawai, snapper and parore, stunned in their tracks as I zoomed into view. Then I met the dolphins. They must have heard the whining motor long before and when they saw me, all four turned on their backs, white undersides towards me so they were highly visible in the dark water. In this position they spiralled around in a tight circle.

Veering the towpedo as hard as I could, I followed them around and we all sped off across the harbour. But they were much faster and I followed while the catamaran and inflatable trailed me for safety's sake — there were boats everywhere. The dolphins put on a star turn for the boats crowded with tourists, but ignored those with nobody on deck. Quietly they skirted the harbour shores and left through a narrow gap in the rocky entrance, keeping us clear of the busy main channel.

Out around the steep headland we followed and they began to play on our bows in the setting sun. Graven on my mind-screen are the silhouettes of dolphin fins on beaten copper. Then the dolphins made a gesture we have seen before from *Delphinus* at the end of an interlock: all four in line, they leapt together and slid under in perfect unison. They reappeared and repeated the same manoeuvre. When we got to our moorings there was just sufficient light to secure the ship.

The very next day I had to face a gruelling courtcase in which I was sued for $14,000 over a diving accident. The dolphin episode gave me such a charge of enthusiasm that I arrived in court still floating on a cloud. While thinking about dolphins I'd had an inspiration that led to our winning the case. . .

Nudelock

22 January 1979: Tony and Avril Ayling, up here for a science congress, delayed their departure by a day to come to sea with us. Both having completed doctorates in undersea ecology, they were just on the point of leaving for Australia, where they would begin a programme of Barrier Reef research with Dr Walt Starck, aboard *El Torito*.

It meant a lot to me to show these two sea people the kinds of things that have been happening to Jan and me when we meet dolphins with our *Interlock* set-up and receive an evaluation of our study methods from two trained scientists.

Tony was involved in the initial interlock back in April 1975, when we danced with *Tursiops* for an hour. This is described in my first chapter. Since then, although we have had many intensive meetings with *Delphinus*, we have not had an interlock with a large group of *Tursiops* like that — until today. I went over in my mind the *Tursiops* meetings we had experienced: Busy Bee, Stumpfin and Nicktail in February 1978; then in May, the four encountered near Goat Island that followed us into Tutukaka Harbour.

On 8 September 1978, Tony Ayling saw a group of *Tursiops* playing courtship games and copulating vigorously in Nursery Cove at the Poor Knights Islands. Tony found it very hard to concentrate on his longterm fish behaviour observations.

A dolphin would swoop above the bubble kelp *Carpopyllum flexuosum* forest that fringes the Sand Garden, dive into the top of the fronds, grab a piece in its beak, break it off, swim with it for a while and then drop it. He saw the seaweed game several times on two separate dives. This links up nicely with what happened today.

This morning at 11.45 Tony thought he saw dolphins leaping a long way to the south. We kept on the same tack and they came to us — all over the ocean, bottlenose dolphins leaping. A tanker heading north along the coast had dolphins shooting from its bow wave. Like torpedoes, several every minute would spurt from the crest of the huge standing wave on the tanker's bulbous forefoot. Just then Eric Wellington, with the charter boat *Southeast*, came alongside us from astern with dolphins on his bow. As he drew away, dolphins were leaping astern of him and in front of us. Then gradually they came to and all round us, some thwacking the water with their tails.

Avril and Tony got into the bow hammocks for an initial short contact. There were many young dolphins at this stage. The dolphins went to Eric and the tanker and then returned, but there were no young ones with them now.

This time interlock really began. Tony thought it was not going to happen, but I said I felt confident it would gradually intensify. With just a gentle southwest breeze we let the boat steer itself. There were three in the net with masks on. Frenetic activity began around the bows.

"You can see them coming from away off," yelled Tony lying in the net, his head submerged. The water was clear, over one hundred feet visibility. The message tape was playing Pink Floyd sped up, and then songs of the humpback whales.

Avril overbalanced and fell in front of the net; so clung there. Brady slowed the boat more and Jan and Tony joined Avril in the water. Tony shot a whole roll of film with his Nikonos and fisheye lens.

Jan noticed a dolphin with its dorsal damaged at the base. "Wade, I think Busy Bee is here!"

Just as I looked over to the port bow a fin thrust into view — it seemed almost deliberate, and with it was a companion with a short stumpy fin. We got out our fin identification file and compared them. It was Busy Bee and its companion Stumpfin who we had met and photographed a year before — on 16 February 1978. Recognising them was like seeing old friends.

Jan got out and put on her dolphin suit. Tony suited up too. Avril stayed at the bow to maintain contact. She exclaimed that one opened its mouth, showing its teeth as it passed, but not aggressively. Another would hang vertically in the water, rising slowly as a diver does for a breath. She called it Triplenick.

Jan and Tony re-entered in their wetsuits, the three of them dragging through the water clinging to the bow net, with dolphins converging from all sides and up underneath them from behind, to inspect the humans dangling from the orange net. The dolphin movements got slower and slower, until some were almost motionless around the bows.

Triplenick became excited, dashing about as all three divers swam away from the catamaran. Jan saw a dolphin with a piece of fishing line hanging from its tail. Three times she yelled "Tepuhi" as the dolphins moved slowly around them close to the surface. She noticed one to the left look directly towards her and let out a huge volley of bubbles like the exhaust from a scuba regulator. It really seemed to mimic her action, but not the sound.

Each time they dived, the dolphins dived also and swept in close, head on, or they would come up behind and curve around in front, only a few feet away. Whenever they came from behind they came closest,

Tony said later, "Closer than I've ever experienced before: two feet from my body, six inches from my hand."

And Jan, "They were huge, such massive, strong forms moving in front of my eyes. I've been so used to swimming with the smaller pelagic dolphins, *Delphinus*. These *Tursiops* were giants in comparison."

Triplenick kept paying Jan, in the dolphin suit, a lot of attention. It would sweep around her, exaggerating the dolphin-swim and tossing its head playfully like an exuberant puppy. When she dived it came in head on, and as she finned horizontally, swam beside her, eyeing her intently. When she rose for a breath, to her amazement it stood vertically in the water and rose up to the surface regarding her as it went. It was so comical she actually laughed. She had the urge to throw her arms around it in a hug. The gesture was repeated several times.

She found later that Tony and Avril saw the same gesture but didn't identify it with Triplenick, although this dolphin appears in several of Tony's pictures. Twice Tony watched a dolphin hang motionless upright in the water just below the surface to sink very slowly, tail first to about fifteen feet, emitting a small trickle of bubbles. On one occasion it made a slow, yawning gesture. Another dolphin approached him horizontally and hung motionless ten feet away just looking at him. In fifteen encounters with *Tursiops* he had never seen such behaviours.

Jan moved closer to the other divers to see what responses they were having. A large dolphin dived towards her and turned broadside on. Passing six feet away, it very slowly opened its mouth twice, open and shut, open and shut. She could see its sharp teeth but this did not appear to her a threat gesture. For the first time she was able to recognise one dolphin as a male. She was ten feet below when he swam past her, up-ended and descended with his underside towards her. Clearly she saw the two in-line slits — no mammaries.

Twenty feet away she saw Avril and Tony together, with Triplenick circling them, then rushing over to her and back around the others, still doing the exaggerated dolphin-swim and tossing its head. She was reminded of a high spirited teenager. Then she heard the message tape playing. She was near the starboard hull. Whale sounds were floating out and she noticed three dolphins quite close to the hull in a stalled position, just hanging there with their flippers drooping, slightly hunched as if listening to the sounds.

During this time I was operating the hydrophone and the message tape, shooting movie and still, and assisting Brady with the ship. Although bursting to get in with the dolphins, it seemed most important that the two biologists should have the fullest possible experience of our set-up before they went overseas. The message tape was conveying an analogue expression of the frequency we use, paralleled with low frequency whale sounds.

I heard a dolphin make a blowhole sound in air just as it breached by the bow and surged off at right angles — a loose "raspberry" sound. Gradually the number of dolphins around the catamaran diminished until only six remained, including Triplenick. Two sets of three.

I wanted to film them at close quarters but the cat was drifting south and the dolphins stayed put. As Jan swam to the boat it may have seemed

150

as if she was leaving — she was feeling seasick and tired. Perhaps they sensed this. We were all hungry and in need of a break. Towards the end of this interlock two dolphins came curving in on their sides and then one made a series of vigorous tail slaps. I replied. We had been together continuously one and a half hours, our longest interlock ever.

We lunched, drew fin and tail identifications and sailed on a northerly tack parallel to the coast. Just as we turned east we saw a pair of dolphins leap high out of the water forming a neat pattern, like our sail symbol.

They did this three times about 500 yards away. Then at 2.45 several dolphins joined the boat. One of them was Triplenick. This easily recognisable dolphin made three approaches to the starboard bow and then headed off, at right angles, to the southeast. I took photos of the fin. Then, following in that direction, because it seemed like a gesture, we saw lots of dolphins approaching.

The second interlock began at five past three and lasted an hour. We were about three miles off Tutukaka, in line with the Pinnacles. This time Jan, Avril and Tony were nude. There were about fifty dolphins including several youngsters, one so tiny it must have been recently born. About eighteen inches long, it still had vertical stripes (birth folds) on its sides. Its mother and another dolphin kept it between them.

This time I just had to get in. The ocean was warm and deep blue. A hundred feet clear. I dived down with my twenty-four-millimetre lens, dolphin-kicking, and found I could get thirty dolphins in my viewfinder at a time. Using High Speed Ektachrome I took some shots at 1/125 f5.6, then 1/250 f4, in case of excessive movement. Jan and Avril looked exquisite with their long hair flowing in rhythm with their dolphin movements.

Afterwards, Avril sent us a painting she did to celebrate her first dolphin experience — two nude human figures and five nude dolphins. With it she wrote:

"Suddenly there were dolphins all around, big bottlenose dolphins, arriving and flying through the rays of light that shot the deep blue sea as if it were silk. There were perhaps sixty dolphins and we felt beckoned to be in there with them. With our bodies naked and trembling with excitement we repeated their swift movements; effortlessly Jan and I flew with our dolphin-kicks, looking down into the cones of light that swept from our bodies into the darkness below and then around at our partners in this ballet."

Jan felt that the dolphins were scanning her with their sonar at fifteen feet range and then moving in close for visual scrutiny. "I felt so free and everything seemed right. We were in our natural state just as they were."

She counted seventeen then lost track. There were babies of all sizes, then others making up, as it were, the whole village family. She saw one huge old dolphin, very dark with mottled grey blotches — and one peculiar individual with a "punched" snout like a bulldog.

Tony and Avril were curving in unison like dolphins. Jan and I joined them, perhaps the most sublime moment in all our dolphin days. Avril

151

and Tony held hands and caressed to show our touch responses. The dolphins did likewise, rubbing along each other's sides and folding across each other. Trustingly, these dolphins had brought their young to see us and allowed them to come very close.

When three divers were below at once, each was approached in turn, the dolphin heads swivelling to and fro as they scanned the human forms. We are so limited underwater, unable to communicate — completely cut off in spheres of "self".

Jan noticed the tiniest baby swim up under its mother and nuzzle her underside to suckle. Meanwhile another dolphin (aunty?) came up under the baby, gently rubbing it and holding it securely between the mother and itself. Then, as the baby resumed its position beside the mother, it was flanked by the other dolphin, the two adults rubbing their sides against the baby, as if cuddling it. I took a picture of them. I am usually reluctant to use my camera when we meet dolphins, as I feel like a tourist in a village. But, with the second meeting, I felt we were accepted. The dolphin pictures Tony and I got that day are the best I've seen of bottlenose in the open ocean.

Seaweed — Simo: I noticed a dark dolphin with a strand of worn-looking bubble kelp wrapped round its forehead. It came past again on the same level and course with the kelp draped around one flipper. Each time the pattern of approach, course, level and distance were the same. A gesture.

Jan saw this same dolphin earlier with the kelp draped around the dorsal and later, around its caudal peduncle. Tony saw it with the seaweed in its mouth when down deep, and around a tail fluke when near the surface. But *nobody* saw it change the position of the seaweed.

By this time I was alone in the water. Out of the midst of the dolphins came a strange shape. A large bronze whaler shark. My first reaction — is there any danger? I looked at the dolphins cavorting with their young. They showed no fear at all. A calm feeling flowed into me. I took a shot of the shark as it cruised past, eyeing me and swimming to the southeast away from us all.*

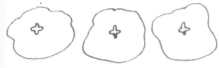

I saw three jellyfish, in line and almost touching, with mandalic orange centres. I shut my eyes in the midst of dolphins. Mandalic hypnogogic images, rich, green unfoldings, like complex plant tissues writhing and transforming. My film was finished. I gave Brady the camera and got a beach ball, tossing it to Tony over the water. But the ball is a surface thing. We need something more submersible, a slow rising buoyant thing like the seaweed — a bit of nylon rope? — to start an exchange game. While Tony and I were tossing the ball we didn't notice, Jan says, a dolphin leap out alongside us.

As I think back over the kaleidoscope of activity that I observed, several significant things emerge. I recall the photo I took of a large dolphin with a white mark on its jaw. At closer range I saw its beak had been deformed as if from impact. It looked like a pug dog.

*I have also seen a large hammerhead shark swimming with common dolphins who showed no concern, but have an anecdote of bottlenose dolphins attacking a mako and killing it in fifteen minutes, tossing its body clear of the water.

152

One dolphin defaecated in front of me. With *Delphinus*, we think this may be a gesture. I swam down through the cloud as it swerved around and watched me. Another two dolphins, six feet apart, released gulps of air from their blowholes simultaneously after I shouted "Tepuhi".

If only I could get a series of pictures or movie sequences of all the special behaviours. In review: Jan noticed that when I entered with the camera the dolphins stayed about ten feet from me. When they came closer it was from behind. Then suddenly a dolphin would swoop past so close it was hard to fit in the wide-angle lens.

In our second interlock the dolphins moved in large groups rather than as individuals and frequently dived deep. Again it was the humans that withdrew from exhaustion. In sum, the day provided the longest period of intensive interlock we have ever experienced. Avril's first and Tony's best out of about fifteen contacts.

For the first time we showed the dolphins both male and female nudes. They saw Tony and Avril caressing. There was the re-meeting with Busy Bee and Stumpfin, the behaviours of Seaweed and Triplenick, the tail-standing breath rises, jaws-open passes, blowhole sounds, bubble-blowing responses, the defaecation gesture, close-from-behind approaches, Triplenick's signal approach to the catamaran, farewell tail-slapping, sonar scrutiny approaches, the mother-child-aunty association, and the shark.

It would be valuable to analyse *all* the pictures Tony and I took underwater, establish all the recognizable body features and attempt to identify as many individuals as possible ready for future meetings.

We got home at five, under sail, just in time for the Aylings to catch the bus on their journey to Australia. Avril was ecstatic. Tony no less.

As an aftermath, we have since learnt that the following day (Tuesday) at 6 pm, *Tursiops* were sighted around the entrance to Tutukaka Harbour, and that from the Monday to Wednesday a large aggregation of *Tursiops* was observed by fisheries scientist Mike Bradstock, while aboard one of the pair trawlers working at 300 feet just north of the Chicks in the exact area we met the dolphins. He said there were lots of squid there which, they suspected, the dolphins were feeding on — possibly at night. The trawl caught a lot of John Dory. Mike sent us a superb sequence of photos he took the day following our interlock, and in the same area where we had met the dolphins. Four shots which show dolphin pairs leaping in variations of the patterns on our sail and our bow symbols. . .

Footnote: Some months later when studying the pictures taken that day we discovered that in photographing the dolphin making the defaecating gesture I had unwittingly recorded the seaweed dangler, its companion. A triumph as by then I was lamenting that I hadn't taken a shot of Seaweed.

From this picture and others, we were able to identify the same pair of dolphins close to the camera at both meetings — as if they had been giving us extra special attention. Photo comparisons also suggest strongly that Seaweed was one of the "Follow Home Day" quartet. And there is little doubt that our Seaweed is the same bottlenose that Val Walter, the lighthouse keeper's wife, had been meeting each summer for the past five years, the dolphin she called Simo (See chapter 10).

Rap-on-the-knuckles day — ESP or not?

Sunday 29 April 1979: Just three of us aboard — Jan, myself and veteran diver, Mac McCaffery — we were heading south along the coast toward the Hen and Chicks Islands when I thought I saw a dolphin leap, but wasn't sure. In a matter of minutes bottlenose dolphins were making the most spectacular leaps off our bows.

It was during a hard gust and the catamaran was screaming along. The rough water and strong winds didn't seem to worry the dolphins in the least. They were magnificent, completely free and at ease in the rough conditions.

Jan yelled to them, "We can't get in the water and play with you out here. It's far too rough. We'll see you in on the coast in the shelter of the land."

Heading straight towards the coast, I decided to play Jan's game and assume that they *did* understand us. Having to handle the boat in rough seas we didn't recognise any dolphins at this stage. We saw them heading north, then they disappeared. We felt a bit silly, actually sailing *away* from where we last saw the dolphins. However, we carried on towards the coast. Mac began to get into his wetsuit and I did likewise. As we entered the lee, out of rough water, we suddenly saw the dolphins pop up just ahead. This was wonderful. We rang the bell and they came towards us.

They swam on the bow for quite some time. I was on the port bow and Mac the starboard. Jan was at the tiller and could see our delight. Mac leapt into the net and shortly after yelled that they had gone.

Jan replied, "No they haven't. They are back here with me."

The stern platform is so low in the water that the dolphins seemed almost on the same level. They were cruising along on their sides looking up at her. She felt a sudden surge of pleasure to have them near again. Two were swimming along beneath the inflatable, upside down. Then Splitfin and Stumpfin surfaced beside her. There were two other smaller dolphins side by side surfacing together. Their fins were identical, with no markings. She glanced behind and saw a dolphin surface. She yelled excitedly to me, "I think it's Busy Bee."

I looked back and at that moment the dolphin surfaced again. Sure enough, it *was* Busy Bee. They played around the boat as we went along. Busy Bee has never come close to anyone in the water in all the time we have seen him but always seems to stay around and expose himself long enough for positive recognition. . .

The conditions were still not good enough for us to leave the boat so Jan said, "We'll see you up at Goat Island." There we knew it would be flat calm in the sheltered little cove. The dolphins vanished and we continued on our way.

Then we noticed a few dolphins close in the shallows on a golden sandy beach. I took a photo when one surfaced. Mac looked down at reefs through clear water and said, "This looks a good place to dive."

I felt it was a bit absurd keeping up this "talking" game with the dolphins. We couldn't very well refuse Mac a dive but at the same time we *had* said we would meet the dolphins at Goat Island. We decided we might be going too far. What if the dolphins didn't turn up at Goat Island? We would look as if we were quite mad. I decided to drop anchor so Mac could have a dive. The dolphins we saw in the shallows had disappeared.

Once we had anchored the wind began to gust. The boat swung too close to the reef for safe diving. Jan felt really unsettled about not keeping her word and continuing to Goat Island. We decided not to stop. Eating lunch we moved along the coast slowly with only the foresail so we could ignore the squalls. We had wasted an hour by the time we got to Goat Island. It was very calm where we anchored. I took Mac inshore in the inflatable and dropped him off for a dive, then, still clad in my wetsuit, climbed to the top of Goat Island, an old pa site or lookout. There I had a panoramic view for many miles. Not a dolphin.

Jan lay on the boat thinking of dolphins but they did not come.

Just as we got home Dave Brind walked up our driveway. He said, "You should have been at Goat Island earlier today. About an hour before your boat arrived in the bay the dolphins came in and were playing and jumping all round in the shallows!" Dave had been on the beach watching them.

That was a great rap on the knuckles for us. If we had not stopped; if we had just kept going without worrying about lunch and taking our time, as we had intended, we would have been there with the dolphins. We had let them down!

It was a lesson for us: either we accept ESP or "visualization" and stick to it, or dismiss it entirely — with communication you can't sit on the fence. We had shifted to another model of reality. Thinking it over, I realized that we really expected the dolphins to stay with us, if they understood Jan's words. But from their point of view that would be absurd — it would only mean they had *followed* us. With their speed what better response than to head off and await our arrival?

Several of these were dolphins we had met before. Would we ever get another chance? Had we lost our sanity?

10

Simo and the keeper's wife

TWENTY MILES east of the forest-clad hill on which we live, a lighthouse winks on the horizon. One day I got the urge to write to the keeper of the Mokohinau light to see if anybody out there was interested in dolphins. To my delight a reply, dated 9 July 1979, arrived from the keeper's wife, Val Walter. This developed into a regular exchange, once we discovered we both knew the same bottlenose dolphin; that Val's Simo was our Seaweed. . .

"I was pleased to receive your letter with regard to sightings of dolphins around the Mokohinaus. Dolphins are my 'special' friends. I mean this in the sense of being interested in them as individuals rather than just as a species.

"During the summer of 1976-77 I had several unusual encounters with one particular dolphin and his companion. Due to a problem with sinus and asthma I am unable to dive but nevertheless I did form a sort of communication with my oceanic friend. As you say we are in one of the best situations for observing these beautiful creatures in their own environment. We have been on this island now for seven years and in the lighthouse service for twenty-one years.

"About late October or early November 1976 I used to spend many afternoons fishing off a point of the island that juts into Edith Passage. One day I noticed two large bottlenose dolphins approaching quite close inshore. I hurriedly pulled in my line so I wouldn't snag them accidentally. Much to my surprise one continued to within a few feet of the rock I was standing on. It was so close I could hear the blow as it exhaled and a curious high-pitched, twittering whistle. I was startled but stood quite still and tried to whistle back through my teeth. I don't know if it heard me or not but I suddenly remembered reading a story when I was young about a Greek boy who whistled up a dolphin that called itself Simo — so I called 'Simo! Simo!' as high pitched as I could, making the 'Si' as much like a whistle, as sibilantly as possible.

"The dolphin turned and approached again to within three feet of my rock, rose up on the surface and shook itself, then dived and swam off toward the other one out in the channel. A few days later I was again fishing at the same time and place when the dolphins suddenly appeared together, about twelve feet from me, seemed to observe me for a few moments, and then swam off about their own business.

156

"This became, over the summer period, a regular occurrence, the dolphins usually appearing about half an hour after I arrived on the rocks. Sometimes I would go down and whistle and call to no avail, then just as I would be ready to leave, around the corner they'd appear. On several occasions I lay or sat on the point and reached out into the water and although the one I call Simo came quite often within arm's reach, I hesitated to make a grab in case I scared it off.

"Then one morning in late January 1977, several bottlenose dolphins appeared in our landing bay and put on quite a spectacular display of leaping, chasing and general play. After lunch my husband Ray launched our small boat off the block and we all went out into the bay and joined the dolphins. At first we thought the outboard might frighten them off but, after circling the boat at a distance for a few moments, they came in close and started rather an alarming game. We had stopped the outboard to listen to their chirrups and whistles as they surfaced. Then they started bumping the bottom of the boat in a sort of game of tag. One after the other about six of them approached rapidly on the surface, dived about two metres from the boat and gave it a sharp bump as they passed beneath. We had a glass box in the boat so we observed them as they passed under us. You can imagine my surprise when one turned, swam slowly up, and stopped. One twinkling brown eye peered back at me through the bottom of the box! I had an almost irresistible urge to hop over the side and join them. Only the fact I was fully clothed stopped me.

"About twenty of them stayed in the bay for the afternoon. We had plenty of time to let the other family take turns with the boat and the children had a wonderful afternoon. At one stage Andrew, one of our young sons, then about seven, was kneeling in the bow of the boat, his hand trailing in the water as we cruised slowly across the bay with dolphins either side.

"Several times he almost touched one. Then the one I call Simo came very slowly alongside and up under Andrew's hand. For a few moments he held its dorsal fin and then, suddenly, it leapt straight out of the water and came down with a mighty splash! We were all drenched and the children almost hysterical with glee. I am sure it was quite deliberate on Simo's part for he veered away, rapidly dived and surfaced alongside the boat with a long trailer of seaweed draped over his beak. Several times he tossed the seaweed toward the boat and caught it again. After three or four hours they tired of our company and went off out to sea.

"The dolphins were here until March 1977, on and off. Sometimes they met our supply ship *Stella* between Fanal Island and Mokohinaus and accompanied her right up to our landing block on her fortnightly trips. We then saw little of them until September — October 1977 when Simo again appeared at my fishing spot.

"By that time we had another assistant-keeper who was a diver — wetsuit and snorkel. One day in December, while he was diving off the landing block, he was suddenly surrounded by five curious dolphins who circled him several times, brushed him and nudged him as he tried to stay close to the bottom. He said they squeaked and whistled almost constantly underwater and the sound in his head became so unbearable he had to surface. We all wondered whether some action on his part caused concern to the dolphins or if he was just very susceptible to their sonar.

"Like Simo these were bottlenose dolphins but on occasions we have had common and bottlenose together in the bay at the same time. This was the case last October when the air force divers swam with them and saw Simo.

"In October 1978, we had a party of twenty air force divers out here on a ten-day underwater mapping expedition and I discussed this experience of mine with several of the divers. I also showed them photos of 'my' dolphin. A couple of days after the conversation a group of about thirty dolphins came into our bay by the landing, and all of the divers had the thrill of swimming and playing with them.

"Three of the divers were certain that one particular dolphin was 'my' friend as it has three very distinctive scars and, from its behaviour, I would say it was the same one."

"Please, say please. . ."

The afternoon of 13 January 1979, Val Walter went down to her favourite fishing spot, a reef that juts into Edith Passage between Burgess Island, where she lived, and the two adjacent islands. (She sent us this narrative on a tape.)

"I was sitting on the end of the reef, pretending to fish, my usual occupation, and whistling 'Amazing Grace'. You asked if I sing to Simo, well I whistle more often than sing. As I whistled I watched the channel toward the north because that's the direction the dolphins generally come from.

"On that day Simo must have come from the south, towards Little Barrier Island, because he surfaced behind me about six feet away. I heard that soft phphew, puffing noise of a dolphin exhaling and turned around. Just then a little breeze picked up the small hand towel I used to wipe my baity hands and whirled it into the water, landing close to Simo.

"I said something like 'blast' or 'bother' and jumped up, grabbed my fishing rod and tried to get the towel. It did go through my mind that Simo might pick it up like he does seaweed and toss it back to me, but he didn't. He backed off very smartly and watched me, from a few feet away, trying to fish up the towel. It floated beyond my reach but was still on top of the water. As it drifted away he moved towards it, but lost interest when it started to sink.

"He came back and reared up out of the water at the end of the reef, looking at me and making funny little noises, like a Pekinese puppy, 'Yip, Yip, Yip!'. I felt he was saying, 'Well, what use was it anyway? What did you want the darned thing for?'

"I laughed at him. As often happens when he's done something to make me laugh he reacted by thrusting his head out of the water and wagging it from side to side — quite comical. But that was the first time he has ever made that funny noise.

158

"Then I noticed he had a couple of companions out in the channel, cruising up and down, as if waiting for him. I felt they wanted to go so I said, 'Well, don't let me keep you here, Simo. Just come and see me next time you're passing.' For all the world you'd swear he understood. He just dived and joined them out in the channel. Then all three leapt clear of the water, one above the other in the most beautiful triple arch, all facing north, and landed back with a mighty splash to swim away to the north.

"Apart from a couple of sightings of bottlenose dolphins from the lighthouse, that's the last time of actually speaking to Simo (tape made late October 1979). Perhaps it seems strange to talk to him just as you would another human being but after meeting him many times I feel he *is* just another being, a friend, and that's the way I address him."

(Nine days later Jan and I met Simo to the north; see page 148.)

The correspondence continued with a letter from Val on 30 September 1979:

"Thank you for the tee-shirt (with the Interlock symbol), a perfect fit. I had been thinking of asking you if I could mount the rondel on a board at my point on the island where I have so often made contact with Simo. I thought if perhaps he is the same dolphin as your Seaweed, he would recognise it. I keep referring to Simo as 'he'. I can't say I've identified him as male — I just feel he is.

"Jan, I was very glad it was you who mentioned telepathy as it is my personal belief this is exactly how dolphins communicate. Again I hesitate to say so, for fear of the 'crackpot' label. It is so very easy to say too much and be misunderstood. After all, a hundred years ago very few people knew anything about radio waves — but they existed all the same, just waiting for use. What other methods exist that we fail to use because we do not understand? There is a very large area of our brain, the use of which is not known, so the potential is there. If only the dolphins could teach us. Everytime I look at Simo I get the feeling we have a lot to learn, and a long way to go.

"Reading Robin Brown's book you sent me, *Lure of the Dolphin*, I was appalled at the apparent arrogance of most officialdom who it seems are only concerned with interspecies communication on the grounds of what dolphins can be 'used' for. A fine state we've come to when we make 'friends' only with the intention of 'using' them to our own ends. What human would accept friendship willingly knowing you intended to 'use' him for your own advantage? Enough said!

"Yours in friendship."

7 November 1979: "I just have to tell you straight away about something really weird that happened between me and the dolphins yesterday afternoon. I know it stretches credibility more than somewhat, but you two will be the only ones who may be able to say if what I am about to tell you is actually fact. I wrote to you Jan, a few days ago saying I wanted to try something with Simo next time he turned up. Well what I had in mind was this — I was hoping I could somehow get a mental picture through to him of you and your boat *Interlock* and get him to do something I requested next time he met your boat.

"Yesterday I was standing on the edge of the 'crater' about 250 feet above the sea, looking towards the mainland and trying like mad to get a firm mental image of R.V. *Interlock*, which of course I've never seen, but I was thinking of the picture in one of your articles of the boat at the Poor Knights. I was thinking that when I next saw Simo I would think hard of the boat and the Interlock rondel and, at the same time, visualize Simo coming on the left-hand bow, staying there a few moments, crossing to the right-hand side, doing three complete right-hand rolls and then a leap away to the right hand of the ship. This would be a simple enough manoeuvre for him and a sequence you would notice and could recognize.

"I had gone over and over this mental picture like playing back a piece of film about a dozen times, when a totally different picture filled my head. The only way I can describe it is that it was similar to coming out of an anaesthetic with a brilliant light being shone in my eyes. The bow of a boat was coming straight toward me or perhaps I was approaching the boat very rapidly. Leaning over the side rail was someone with red hair or maybe they were wearing a woolly hat, an Interlock tee-shirt and the pants of a dark blue or black wetsuit. I got no impression of what sex the person was but just below the waterline on the boat's dark hull was a long orange-red scratch mark. This mental picture was so different from what I was actually trying to think and it was very sudden and brief. I felt shocked by it!

"Almost at the same moment about ten big dolphins came round the point into the crater below me. From that distance I couldn't tell if Simo was among them but I felt sure that's where the 'picture' came from, so maybe he was. I honestly don't know if the mental impression I received is something that's already happened or not. I also really don't know why I'm so perturbed because it's exactly what I was trying to do. I guess it's because I was trying so hard to 'send' and wasn't prepared to 'receive' that I got such a shock.

"The dolphins went across Crater Bay and back twice, then headed out to sea, north towards the Poor Knights. I'm sure I don't know what you will make of this but it's just as it happened to me — maybe I'm 'Rock-Happy' but I don't think so.

"There is a Navy helicopter due here tomorrow so I will ask someone to post this. I feel it's important you receive it quickly, so you are aware when next you meet up with our ocean-going friends."

11 December 1979: "I am sending you my photos to have copied if you wish. No doubt you may identify some of your friends from the fin nicks but Simo is the one with the figure eight scratches along his right side. I noticed last summer the depth of the scratch marks had smoothed over but the other scars were still noticeable.

"I have to finish this in a hurry as I have a chance to get a ride across to Auckland with Dr Simon Cotton for a day's Christmas shopping. I'm taking my tee-shirt in case we meet the dolphins."

160

20 December 1979: "I must write and tell you the really marvellous day Sunday 16 December turned out to be. I took Dr Simon Cotton up on his offer of a trip to Auckland and, although it was blowing a very strong southwesterly when we first set out, none of us regretted it, as you will see. I don't think I told you that Simon and some friends had been out here making an underwater 'Diver Safety' film on a new device for divers to wear on their arms.

"We left at nine-thirty to go to Auckland. It should have taken us about four and one-half hours, but we didn't arrive until six-thirty because we spent four and one-half terrific hours with the dolphins. It was very rough at first, and as we were towing a big inflatable it was pretty heavy going. *Corofin* is an extremely rowdy, smelly (exhaust), fast, thirty-five-foot launch, so I never really expected to see any dolphins. However, I had some hopes and was wearing my Interlock tee-shirt just in case.

"Just off Fanal Island the wind dropped, the sea calmed down, and a large number of *Delphinus* appeared. They stayed well off from the launch, however, and wouldn't let us approach them. I told Simon we were making far too much noise and smoke and asked if we could slow down, which we did; but still the dolphins stayed off, although some of them approached the *Zodiac* which was being towed well astern. After about twenty minutes Simon set off again and we left the dolphins.

"Just off Little Barrier Island I sighted five *Tursiops* to port and again asked Simon to slow down. All this time I was trying like mad to concentrate and 'think' dolphin. This time he slowed straight away and sure enough the dolphins approached, but stayed well off or just came in and looked at the inflatable, so I said, 'For goodness sake, do something interesting!' As it was, the foredeck was bristling with cameras, as everyone except me had a mighty fistful of expensive picture boxes.

"Simon started making a really weird noise like 'Arrgh! Arrgh!' — a sort of a cross between a moan and an old lady admiring infants at a baby show. He insisted this was a call sign of the orcas, and would you know it, but three of the *Tursiops* straightaway came to the bow. Everyone gasped because one of them was the biggest dolphin any of us had seen. It was of a pale grey colour with black-grey patches. Because of the black spot on his head, like a cap, I've nick-named him Pope. Simon just about fell overboard, camera and all. Everyone was crowded on the bow and I suddenly felt very sad because all they did was take pictures.

"I went aft and climbed over the welldeck onto the dive platform and trailed my legs in the water while watching the two dolphins still pacing the inflatable. We were moving fairly slowly as my son Andrew was on the wheel, so all five men could go forward to take pictures. I sat there whistling and wishing the two dolphins following would come closer, when one left the inflatable and disappeared. I thought they were leaving, but suddenly one surfaced right beside me about a foot away from the side of the boat. I realized it was Simo. I was so thrilled I shouted 'Look — it's him!', but no one took any notice of me, so I lay down on the platform, hung on with one hand and reached out.

"The next time he surfaced, he was right under my arm and hand. We touched, and I felt so happy that all thought of trying to communicate any other way, or pass on instructions, or anything like that just left my head. Then I remembered, and said 'Hey look — Simo — look!' and I sat up and patted the Interlock symbol on my tee-shirt. He surfaced and just brushed my foot that still trailed in the water and veered off quickly.

"As I looked up along the boat I saw Simon had put aside his camera and was hanging over the bow, one hand to the bow rail. The big grey dolphin was beneath him, but shortly after this all five veered off and left us. One of the other men took the wheel and we tried to follow the dolphins, but wherever we went they came up somewhere else.

"Simon was impressed, and remarked that never before had the *Tursiops* stayed with *Corofin* that long! I felt rather smug so I said in a joking voice (although I really did mean it), 'That's because I'm here.' Simon looked at me for a while and then said rather seriously, 'Yes, Val, I think you are probably right.'

"We carried on, and halfway to Tiri Tiri we met a group of *Delphinus*. This lot came close to us more readily so Simon stopped the boat and said he was going to get in the water with them after he'd taken some pictures. Out came the cameras again and Simon started making orca noises. As soon as he did this the dolphins moved off rapidly. To be with them we had to follow. This happened so often that I was convinced that although the *Tursiops* thought the orca noises were a big joke, the *Delphinus* didn't care for them at all.

"Eventually he stopped making the noise and as everyone was on the bow again, I started to go back along the boat to watch a small dolphin in the pressure wave at the side. I had just said, 'Look at the baby,' everyone looking back at me. At the same moment two dolphins leapt right out of the water, level with me and at about the same height. They were in a perfect Interlock symbol formation. Again everyone gasped and no one thought to click a shutter.

"Simon then leapt over the side, but no matter how he swam, or what he did, those dolphins wouldn't go near him, or let him near them. I am quite sure they knew it was he who made the orca noises and so avoided him."

Delphinus can be very shy, regardless.

"We all had a marvellous time. You well know how time flies by under those conditions. Too soon the day was gone and we had to continue on to Auckland, all of us badly sunburned because we forgot to use protection in the wonder and excitement of the encounters."

Footnote: In early December 1979 American filmmaker Dick Massey met five bottlenose dolphins between the Mokohinaus and the Poor Knights. He was amazed to find the dolphins came right up to him and he was able to film full-face close-ups of one individual with a distinct scar on its side, "shaped like a human foot." Comparison with photos proved this was Simo.

PART FIVE

Towards a Global Network

"Just as we are beginning to glimpse the incredible nature of whales we are on the verge of exterminating them. This is the irony of the whole situation. We have found a being for the first time in our history, with the potential to communicate with us, and we are killing them off before they have a chance to do so."

— Dr Paul Spong

11

Project expansion

OUR INTENSIVE correspondence with Val Walter took its place in the new phase of Project Interlock: having established a procedure for winning acceptance by wild dolphins, Jan and I wondered if it would work for others. From an oceanic viewpoint how would the cetaceans respond if more and more people met them on their terms, in a communicative and creative manner? Would there be any increase in the quality and frequency of human/dolphin encounters which would give some degree of objectivity to our markedly experiential study?

To our great good fortune the editor of *N.Z. Dive*, Rob Lahood, agreed to publish a regular "Interlock" newsletter in his magazine which is distributed free to all New Zealand skindivers. He also offered to place on his free mailing list, any people whose addresses we gave him. For no cost we had a superb feedback channel — a hotline to the New Zealand diving world.

This entailed a major extension of our experiment. We would publish our approach to dolphin gamesplay along with a standardised report form and then, in successive newsletters, present any feedback received. If successful, this in turn should stimulate an even greater responsiveness among divers towards dolphins and vice versa. Ultimately we hoped this could be extended on a global basis, helping to develop a new era in human/cetacean relations. As I write there is already evidence of this from our overseas contacts in Europe, the United States, Canada and Australia. This book may stimulate it even further — a global interlock network is what we dream of.

Our first newsletter, in April 1979, established the groundwork:

Dolphin games

"For two years now we have been using a thirty-six-foot 'Raka' catamaran for a series of experiments with wild dolphins, establishing friendly contact with groups of them and learning about their social behaviour at the same time as we show them ours.

"We are keen to explain our methods of approaching dolphins to other people who may be interested in playing with dolphins in similar ways. It would be an extension of our experiments if people approached dolphins in similar playful and creative ways in different parts of the world, and then pooled their experiences.

165

"The sailing catamaran is perfect for man/dolphin interactions. Our vessel is named 'Interlock' after the project. The term created by Dr John Lilly means 'interspecies communication'.

"We have fitted it with a double hammock in the bows which makes for easy access to and from the water, and facilitates contact with dolphins. We also have a twelve by eight foot diving platform which hinges down from the rear beam, necessary for scuba diving, film work etc, but not essential for dolphin games if you have the hammocks, or easy water access.

"Our craft has twin nine-inch speakers in each bow compartment which beam stereo sound out through the hull. It is difficult to say which ingredients in our set-up are essential, but we have had many successful, prolonged interlocks. Most people find that while dolphins bow ride, they leave if you get in with them. They may be frightened or holding out to establish equable human/dolphin rules."

We also included general observations based on our own experience. The newsletter explained:

"We feel it is vital that we avoid any tendency towards manipulating dolphins to our own ends. We must not harass them, encircle or in any way force our presence on them. Remember the Marine Mammals Protection Act. Even using a camera should be done with discretion — it forces you to behave in an active, manipulative way and can spoil the spontaneity of interlock. A receptive mood is best for all on board. It is better to leave cameras out of it for a while or they'll find you dullsville — it's hard to be playful and spontaneous with a headful of 'f' stops.

"When we sight dolphins now we just heave to or beat quietly about in their vicinity. From our forward beam hangs a bell which we ring about six times when they surface for air. This establishes our acoustic identity. If they are not too busy herding fish, they will leap out and head over to us. We play carefully chosen music through our bows, especially flute and wind instruments. This tunes us in to their presence.

"When they come on our bows we play a special 'message tape', which would take a lot of space to explain but only seconds to demonstrate. The tape is an analogue statement about the low frequency sound channels we and the great whales use and the high frequencies used by dolphins. Meanwhile we are on the bows and in the nets enjoying being with them.

"Mutual trust can be established as long as we place ourselves within access of the dolphins — so that each species is equally vulnerable to the other. It seems wrong to us to try to touch the dolphins — a sudden lunge may succeed but that is really rape and startles the creatures. The interlock approach is to hold out your hand — show them a human limb — its joints and expressiveness, demonstrating this unusual limb to a friendly alien. The dolphins may examine it, swimming on their sides, and eventually one may approach and nudge your hand.

"With powerboats, bow-riding is potentially very dangerous and a safety harness may be necessary. That's why we prefer sail and we know they're not attracted merely by engine noise.

"We find when we meet a group of dolphins there are usually certain individuals that are most attentive and keep returning again and again.

166

It is important to observe any with distinctive fin markings — you may then be able to recognise this group when you meet again and a body of shared experience will develop: friendship. A twenty millimetre and a telephoto lens with highspeed film are very good to record any distinctive fin markings. We have a cardboard dorsal fin as a template on the outline of which we record distinctive markings, with the date and location.

"Once mutual trust has been established you can slow the boat right down, while one diver at a time leaps in and engages their interest by dolphin-diving down. Meanwhile the boat circles back and stops. If you are all frolicsome enough the dolphins may stay — even teach you tricks.

"Don't be too disappointed if interlock is not successful. Dolphins may have a variety of reasons for not playing — an important fish-herding manoeuvre may be in progress — like cowboys on the big roundup. There is considerable evidence that dolphins may sense if there is somebody on board who does not want to be involved with them and would prefer to be fishing — or actually fears them. So if it doesn't happen — leave it for another day. In some cases the dolphins may return later in a playful mood — work over for the day.

"We feel it is essential to extend to dolphins the same courtesies and thoughtfulness as when visiting people in a strange village. Remember that man is inherently boring to these ocean nomads — many of the things we do are to heighten interest in us — the message tape, the rondels and the dolphin suit we wear may not be essential but our system appears to work.

"When you enter the water it is important to avoid swimming straight at them. Treat them like villagers on a strange island, or oceanic nomads who may have a low estimate of human intelligence but are curious to explore our behaviour and our capacity for joy, if we meet them in a humble and creative manner.

"With snorkelling gear start diving down, always doing the dolphin-swim or kick and stay below as much as possible. They start to mimic us, and seemingly lampoon our attempts to mimic them! This is the beginning of body language communication, just as between mother and child or people from alien cultures.

"So far the dolphins have responded in a variety of surprising ways, which suggest this line of research, if carried out more extensively, would produce some very interesting insights into the nature of their social patterns and the purpose of their large brains, quite beyond what can be learnt from individuals in captivity.

"On three occasions while wearing her dolphin suit, Jan has had individual dolphins bond with her, like friendly puppies not wanting to leave her side, seemingly indicating she should swim off with them. We have had *Delphinus* play with us for up to four hours twenty minutes and in each case it has been our side that had to break it off from sheer exhaustion.

"From these gamesplay sessions we are learning constantly and we keep modifying our approach flexibly in the light of new findings. We have learnt to identify individuals from the fin patterns and often know when we are meeting old friends."

167

INTERLOCK QUESTIONNAIRE

Sea & weather conditions:
Date & time of day:
Boat name:
Position:
How did boat/dolphins first approach?
How did dolphins behave *before* you got in?
Number of divers in water?
Number with scuba?
Person first in?
Dolphin species?
Approx. number of dolphins?
Any with peculiar markings?
Were there any young present?
How small?
Any surface or U/W shots showing recognizable fins?
What do you think held their interest so long?
How many cameras in water?
Owners' names and addresses:
Any unusual items of dolphin behaviour such as:
— tail first sinking?
— jaws opening and closing
— seaweed trailing from fins, jaws etc.
— bubbles gushing from blowhole.
— defaecating as a possible signal (ie close to a diver and right in his field of vision).
How did the divers behave such as:
— snorkelling down frequently?   — dolphin kick?
— swimming coordinately in pairs etc?   — fancy manoeuvres?
— forward rolls?
How close did they approach divers at any time?
How did interlock terminate: did the divers/dolphins withdraw first?
Duration of Interlock (approx):
Any special remarks:

This initial letter, with its questionnaire and report forms, really started the ball rolling. Our file is a rich treasury of dolphin/diver encounters — especially in the Poor Knights area, where it seems certain individuals belonging to a group of twenty to thirty *Tursiops* are specialising in close encounters with diving charter groups. For this reason we are very keen to obtain duplicates of any underwater pictures which show fin patterns clearly — we may be able to establish recognition patterns for a number of individuals, and trace their wanderings.

Our third newsletter carried an account of a Poor Knights interlock by Graeme Thomson of Wairoa. On 13 June 1978, Graeme was aboard *Lady Jess* near the Pinnacles when some two hundred *Tursiops* approached and several began bow riding. The vessel anchored and fifteen divers (only two without scuba, including Graeme) entered the water. Some divers began doing the dolphin-kick, snorkelling down frequently with fancy manoeuvres and forward rolls. Some of the dolphins remained with them for about forty minutes. There were young present, about six to eight in the group that stayed.

Graeme remarks: "The dolphin in my photo (one which Project Interlock had met frequently) was by far the most playful and seemed to be the instigator in evolving games we attempted to play. The others played and observed us, but he was the most interested. He would come

168

straight towards us at breakneck speed and stop instantaneously about two to three feet away, then spin round and round us two or three times before zooming in again. We saw the jaw open and closing gesture. If we did the dolphin-kick at least two or three dolphins, sometimes more, would swim parallel with us. We tried doing forward and backward rolls. My camera housing made this difficult.

"My buddy, Andy Smyth, managed some strange antics which attracted a fair bit of attention. Andy proved the sort of guy you want when playing with dolphins — seemed to know when to sit back and watch and when to play. Mothers were bringing their young in fairly close, four to five feet and the young were on the inside towards us, as if mum was saying to them 'Go on, have a good look. They're too clumsy to hurt you.' This sort of thing lasted around forty minutes until we were exhausted and had to retire to the boat.

"On board we could see they had broken up into separate groups — some with each pair of divers. People wearing scuba couldn't get anywhere near as close as we just on snorkel. The dolphins hung around for most of the day while we had two scuba dives, joining a number of divers while down on scuba.

"There was no real topside action (fancy leaps etc) other than coming up and checking on the boat when it was moving around picking up divers. Interesting to see the number of snapper* feeding below the dolphins."

Then in February 1979, Graeme and a diving group chartered a dive boat for several days along the coast between Tutukaka and Cape Brett. Graeme writes:

"On the shore side of Danger Rock in the entrance to Bland Bay we came across a school of dolphins — bottlenose — on two separate days. On 28 February, for one hour twenty minutes, we had a great time with them; barrel rolls and chasing each other. One of them, easily recognisable by the pieces missing in its tail fin, was a real sportsman. It would have races with you.

"I found that by descending to say ten or fifteen feet and remaining there until this particular animal drew level, then doing the dolphin-kick, it would race you until you ran out of air and then, just as you started to surface it would speed up and pass you, only to remain in the same area till you recovered for another race.

"The next day, 1 March, we saw them again in the same spot and had the pleasure of their company for one hour and ten minutes. It could have been longer but they being fitter than us, outlasted us easily. We performed basically the same manoeuvres and games as the day before and had lots of fun. The guys on the trip who had never been with dolphins before were really blowing their minds. I tried getting towed behind the boat (we had done this at Mahia previously when they weren't very interested in playing) and found it quite successful.

"I had 150 feet of rope out and was hanging onto a buoy at the end of it. It took a while but eventually they came and swam right next to me and together we performed barrel rolls at a slightly higher speed

*A common observation that matches Maori tradition. Dolphins don't eat snapper (too spiny), but the fish have been seen eating dolphin faeces.

than I could attain on my own. Up until this point they had been quite active on top of the water but the moment that I hopped in all topside activity ceased. I was told this by the guys in the boat. During this time they never got as close as before: about three to four feet was the limit.

"I eventually got tired and couldn't hack the pace, so I pulled myself back on the boat. About thirty seconds later a group of about eight dolphins charged the stern of the boat and at a distance of around five feet from where I was sitting four of the group leapt into the air in unison. I could have reached out and touched them. As they landed in the water right next to me all the boys on board clapped in response to the show. Then the dolphins went on and played among themselves performing leaps in the air. As many as three or four would be in the air at once. Twice they actually touched, glancing off each other."

Dave Munro's report

On 23 June 1979 at 1 pm, Dave Munro was aboard the diving charter boat *Lady Margaret* when she entered South Harbour at the Poor Knights Islands.

"We entered from the south and saw bottlenose dolphins lazily swimming and milling around near the eastern entrance to Blue Maomao Archway. As we crossed South Harbour two or three dolphins joined us, crossing and recrossing our bow. When we stopped, the dolphins moved away but returned in a tightly packed 'school' as soon as the divers entered the water."

"Five snorkellers leapt in to meet from twenty to thirty dolphins. Dave noticed one large dolphin with seaweed trailing around the dorsal and remarked that he had never seen dolphins defaecating so frequently, in what would be a gestural manner. The divers descended frequently, some doing the dolphin-kick, and for twenty minutes the dolphins played with them, coming almost within touching distance at times. On one occasion he saw bubbles gush from a dolphin's blowhole. The dolphins withdrew first."

Being interesting

By early 1980 I had begun to notice a pattern in these reports. Duration seemed to be the only objective way to evaluate such human/dolphin exchanges in the wild. Our dolphin games aboard R.V. *Interlock* were the most elaborate on our records and to date had produced the most complex and lengthy interlocks, lasting four hours twenty minutes with *Delphinus* and two and a half hours with *Tursiops* — in both cases being terminated from our end chiefly through exhaustion.

Human fear seemed to be another important factor in cases where dolphin approaches to people were brief. We suspect that it was this response to a supposed "shark attack", plus the diver's uncertainty about sharing the ocean with very large dolphins, that led to the typical hullo/goodbye meetings which, old hands will recall, were once the norm. To illustrate this, our fifth newsletter contrasted several lengthy and complex interlock reports, such as those already quoted, with a set in which fear seemed to have had an inhibiting role.

170

Fear responses

"On 17 November 1979, two boats were anchored about three quarters of a mile off Mahia Peninsula while divers decompressed from a deep dive; they were having lunch of hot crayfish and beer — the occasional water ski — the sea was perfectly flat! One of the divers on scuba, was playing around down below, in about twenty feet of water, feeding fish, and we were all watching him. We had seen the dolphin herd (*Delphinus*) quite a distance away but they were on the move so we didn't go over, when all of a sudden three or four broke off from the herd and shot directly towards this poor guy below. They covered the last 250 feet in a single breath at incredible speed; each one did a complete circle around him and then just as quickly took off back to the herd. While this happened there was this almighty cloud of bubbles, a Polaris powered diver, a scream that had something to do with copulation and our brave diver appeared." — Graeme Thomson, Wairoa.

"On 24 December 1979, in the late afternoon, a group of tourists got off a yacht anchored in our bay and came up to the station. One young man and his girlfriend were rather disturbed because they said they'd been 'attacked' by a group of big dolphins (*Tursiops*) as they approached our landing in their very small dinghy. I asked them what they meant by 'attacked' and they said the dolphins kept hitting the bottom of the dinghy and they were afraid of being overturned. This is a 'game' I've described to you before. Apparently there was a group of about twenty dolphins in the bay, but only five or six were playing this game. I went down to the landing but the dolphins had moved out to about Fish Rock and did not come back in." — Val Walter, Mokohinau.

Great Mercury

"My wife and I, along with a friend and his wife, have just returned from a sailing trip to Great Mercury Island. We called into Huruhi Harbour for the night. It was raining when we awoke on the morning of 28 December, so we decided to go diving for scallops.

"My friend, an experienced scuba diver, dived down in about twenty-five feet of water to check if there were any scallops on the bottom. He returned with a few, so I got a sack, put on my scuba gear, and joined him in the water. After checking the keel of our trailer yacht, we swam to the bottom and collected some scallops. We were having a general explore, when a large grey object swam past me. It was so close that I couldn't see exactly what it was. (I might add that this was only my third dive in the ocean, and that I am new at the sport.) I immediately thought it was a shark, and you can probably imagine my fright!

"It was not until they circled us that we realised that it was not one, but three bottlenose dolphins — two large and a baby. They circled us for a few minutes at a distance of about six feet. They seemed very inquisitive, their heads moving about, looking at us from every angle in a fashion similar to a seagull. We were a bit unsure of our feelings, having these creatures so near, but were reassured, remembering various articles on the dolphin family and their friendly natures. With one final look at us, they then swam away (the visibility was about fifteen feet).

171

I thought the best thing to do would be to go back to the boat, but after looking over to my friend, I saw that he had started to regather scallops, and I decided to do likewise. All of a sudden the dolphins reappeared. They circled us as before for a few seconds, being generally nosy, and then seemed to head seawards.

"We gathered up our scallops and headed back to the yacht about fifty feet away. When we surfaced we saw the women on board having a thoroughly entertaining time watching the dolphins from the safety of the boat. I heard them laughing. It was not until I was back on board that I learned that one of the dolphins had swum upside down between my friend's legs, brushing his chest as it passed by (a rare gesture). The women ribbed us for not playing with the dolphins who had shown that they wanted to play with us.

"Soon after, a large trimaran passed closeby, and the dolphins took off after it. They circled around it and to our amazement started a floor show by jumping vertically out of the water to a height of about ten feet. They made four jumps just like the ones that one would see at a Marineland show. The trimaran started circling to keep the dolphins jumping, but the dolphins circled a few more times and then headed out to sea.

"It was an enlightening experience to see these beautiful creatures — one that I thought you might be interested in sharing." — Mike Amphlett, Hamilton.

Delphinus interlocks

Initially most of our interlock reports involved bottlenose dolphins, *Tursiops truncatus*. Tony Ayling told us that, out of his fifteen dolphin encounters, "I've never been able to get in the water with *Delphinus*." The smaller species certainly seems much shyer, even though all our initial research efforts were concentrated on winning its confidence.

So we were thrilled when the first *Delphinus* report came to hand from Les Grey, down in Wellington. Les is a great dolphin enthusiast. Having been with us in the runabout on our first encounter back in 1975, and to sea with us several times on the catamaran, he is familiar with the playful manner of approach. In the newsletter I headed his report:

Lone diver interlock

"On 7 February 1979, I was driving around the coast when I noticed the familiar fins frolicking out in Owhiro Bay. I rushed home and grabbed my fins and mask and was back down at the beach as soon as possible — by this time the dolphins were a fair way out. I jet-finned my way out into the bay — sort of yelling through my snorkel at the same time. About three dolphins detached themselves from the herd to investigate this bearded apparition — and I duck-dived down to join them. I was so puffed from my hasty swim and so excited that I couldn't seem to hold my breath very long diving — (it also felt bloody cold on the skull under the surface). The dolphins didn't pay much attention to me when on the surface — but as soon as I dived down and dolphin-kicked they would 'buzz' me like jet planes in tight formation, racing up close and spiralling off out of formation to re-group.

"Of course, it was very inconvenient having to keep returning to the surface for air — feeling slow and clumsy.

"Some of them had quite noticeable scars and markings on them so that I was beginning to recognise various ones as they made repetitive runs — watching me intently with those wise eyes. It was very elating — as you both know — I guess I was in the water for about half an hour — before they lost interest in my limited performance and swam further out to sea. I returned ashore alone — grateful for the buzz of contact and really noticing the cold temperatures for the first time."

Then came a series of reports from snorkel divers meeting friendly *Delphinus* in the Cook Strait/Kapiti Island area. We were overjoyed to find they so closely matched our own experiences, hundreds of miles away. Alan Morrison and his girlfriend, Shirley Farthing, found the dolphins would stay around longer if they snorkelled down frequently. As with us, a small group would break off from the main dolphin body to zoom around the divers, disappearing into the gloom and returning from behind. (This rear approach is a recurrent feature in the fifty interlock reports now on our file.) Alan and Shirley soon learnt to recognise distinctly marked individuals that approached them repeatedly and recorded encounters lasting up to twenty-five minutes.

One day, in early January 1981, Alan and Shirley visited us at Ngunguru. Naturally we whisked them off to sea on the catamaran. The moment we cleared the harbour entrance, four dolphins approached our bows and performed a series of strange, slow motion leaps right under our noses. We all had a strong impression they had been awaiting us.

12

The film "Dolphin"

A human/dolphin celebration in the open sea

IN MAY 1979, we received word of an interlock experience that delighted us. Until then the reports on file were records of spontaneous encounters between divers and dolphins with little in the way of deliberate preparation for an interspecies exchange. They showed us that dolphins would respond to humans in the sea to a degree that depended on the mutual trust and interest manifested. They indicated a growth in such relationships in localities where interaction was frequent, such as the Poor Knights and Wellington areas.

But here was an account of an interlock which paralleled our own in many ways. Another species in another ocean; but the same playful approach, the deliberate use of music and body language to heighten interest, had led to an interlock as intensive and rich as any of our own, but all recorded on film.

Word of our research must have travelled farther than we thought, as the letter, dated 9 May 1979, came from San Francisco:

"I recently heard about your experience of swimming with wild dolphins and wanted to ask you about this. I am a filmmaker and have just completed a fifty-eight-minute film 'Dolphin', about our experiences swimming with, being with, and playing music underwater for a school of wild dolphins in the Bahamas. The film will be released in June in San Francisco and later in Los Angeles. Our intention in making the film is to raise human awareness about this magnificent creature and the benefits which could come to humanity through a relationship with another intelligence.

"Our film begins with basic background on the dolphin (evolution, history, brain size, intelligence, marine parks, tuna fishing, the Iki massacre in Japan) and quickly moves into our own research for dolphin contact in Hawaii, the Florida Keys and the Bahamas.

"My feeling is that we only scratched the surface. We feel that we were very fortunate in setting out to meet dolphins in the wild, that they were attracted to us and did play and swim with us and relate to us in their own environment providing us with absolutely magnificent film footage. Music was our primary means of reaching them although my sense is that our 'intention' — wanting so badly to join them — had much to do with our encounter: as if we were sending out 'psychic messages' as well. While the film does not get into this area directly, it is something I would like to explore, perhaps in another film.

174

"It's still too early for me to tell what I will do next as far as film-making goes, but my work with the dolphins has just begun. I would very much like to hear from you in as much detail as possible about your experience, sensations and reasons for swimming with the dolphins. What kind they were, the conditions, locations, and any other information you'd be willing to share. I heard about a girl south of you who is also experimenting with communication with dolphins. Any information you can give me about her and her work, or any other dolphin communication work taking place I would certainly appreciate. [He refers to Dusty Stewart.]

"I want you to know that my desire is to make a contribution through my filmmaking to human and dolphin relationships. . .to share the magnificence of the dolphin in a way that supports their life here. I've enclosed some information about myself, the 'Dolphin' film, and my other work, so that you can get a sense of me.

"Thank you for your cooperation. I look forward to hearing from you. Warm regards, Michael Wiese."

From this letter and enclosures a correspondence developed to the point where we desperately wanted to meet Michael Wiese and his co-worker, Morgan Smith, to see their film and share experiences — this was like one of those evolutionary convergences and the parallels could provide some invaluable pointers towards interlock procedure.

Then one day I had an inspiration: for many months we'd had two return air tickets to the United States. I'd won them with a science fiction piece about dolphins, published as an epilogue to my previous book *Islands of Survival*. We felt the tickets had to be used to further the dolphin study in some way and could see no purpose in visiting the United States at that stage in our work. That would come later. . .

Michael and Morgan accepted our offer and arrived in Ngunguru in early December 1979. My editor Neil Robinson and his wife, Flora picked them up at Auckland airport, gave them breakfast and brought them 140 miles to our door for lunch. We shared an intensive eight days together, viewed their film twice, showed them ours and took them to sea. In the course of all this I was able to put together the story of their Bahaman dolphin experience.

As Jan wrote in her journal, Michael and Morgan were some of the nicest people we had ever met — "very gentle and truly dolphin people, all the way from the other side of the world yet approaching dolphins in the wild in the same manner as we have been doing and achieving the same results."

We were very sorry they could not stay longer in New Zealand. On the mangrove-lined road to the airport Morgan asked us to stop the car. They had something they wanted to do in private. We were told to shut our eyes and both felt something being placed around our necks. We each had a tiny gold dolphin on a golden chain.

"Don't feel you have to keep them," said Morgan. "Give them away if you want, or throw them to a dolphin."

The seed for their "Dolphin" film was planted in 1967 when Michael Wiese was walking along a beach south of San Francisco and encountered a dolphin stranded in the shallows. He assisted it back into deep water and as it swam away he was overcome with the intense resolve to make a great film some day about dolphins in their natural habitat, as a plea for their protection. He was impressed with the sounds the dolphin made and the general presence of the creature. "I sensed something very special that was not going on with other animals. I'd swear it was trying to communicate with me."

Ten years later he met Hardy Jones who shared his determination and they raised a $200,000 budget to make a feature-length film. Buckminster Fuller narrates a segment of the film reviewing the history of dolphins over the past thirty million years and their amazing brain capacities. The film takes a look at their plight today, drowning in the giant nets of the American tuna fleet and being slaughtered en masse by Japanese on the island of Iki. It reviews the approaches being used to understand dolphins in captivity with a sequence showing dolphins being taught sign language at Flipper Sea School in the Florida Keys. And then they started to hunt around for stock footage of free-ranging dolphins.

"We very quickly found out that nobody had filmed humans and dolphins together in the wild." At that point their documentary became a quest.

On the Hawaiian island of Maui they met a whale-filming expert, Jim Hudnall, who agreed to help, but an attempt to film the Hawaiian "spinner" dolphins yielded little human/dolphin interaction. Next they tried Southern Florida, assuming it would be easier down there — but found they could not get near them. In Florida many bottlenose dolphins have been captured and tagged for research.

Around 17 June 1978, having been given a tip by the treasure-hunter, Bob Marx, they set sail on the seventy-foot schooner *William H. Aubury* for a remote location forty miles from Florida called the Lilly Bank. There they encountered a group of some fifty Atlantic spotted dolphins *Stenella plagiodon*. They played with them for three days for periods of forty-five minutes to three hours, each day ending when they were too tired to swim any longer.

At the outset the dolphins rode the bows of the schooner while eleven men and two women crowded around the bowsprit. Then Hardy Jones and cameraman Jack McKenney, clinging to the chainplates, dangled their bodies in the bow wave amidst the dolphins, establishing mutual trust.

Although the film shows a different sequence, it was a flute that initiated the interlock. When the boat anchored, two hydrophones were suspended beneath her keel over the shallow ocean floor. Through them Mary Earle played "Appalachian Spring" on the flute. To their delight the dolphins returned to the boat and members of the party began to enter the clear water.

One of the most successful at relating to the dolphins was Dr John Siebel, an experienced snorkel diver, who could hold his breath a long time. He imitated the motions of the dolphins and would often hum to them.

The interlock developed into an elaborate and graceful interspecies ballet when sound engineer Steve Gagne drifted down, cradling in his arms a pneumatic underwater piano. Using the exhaust of his scuba

Steve had devised a keyboard instrument which produces high-pitched crooning notes.

Morgan Smith was dolphin-kicking when a dolphin swam above her, gently touching her on the back. Humans and dolphins cavorted in perfect conditions: water that was extremely clear with more than 100 feet visibility, eighty-three degrees warm and only twenty to thirty feet deep — a featureless, white sand bottom. Only the two cameramen Jack McKenney and Jim Hudnall and Steve wore scuba but the dolphins showed no fear of them.

On the second day contact began at five in the afternoon. "Three of us were on the bow," Michael told me. "Beautiful weather and light. We said, 'It's so perfect — now if only we had dolphins!' Seconds later the ocean was filled with leaping dolphins, heading to our ship to ride the bow wave.

"When I was with the dolphins I felt as though I was communicating with them telepathically about the film. Certain dolphins seemed to pick me out of the bunch of humans and I felt that if we had been able to remain on location longer individual relationships might have developed.

"On the third and final day the dolphins were summoned by Steve's underwater piano. At first about six to eight dolphins came in, almost like a scouting party, and then others arrived. About twenty minutes later they left, apparently to feed. We could see birds feeding a mile or so away in the direction they headed. That evening the dolphins hung around the ship and watched us. They played games with one of our rowboats, twisting and pulling on the tow rope, tangling the boats up.

"The most powerful communication to us from the dolphins was this. We had spotted some very large and nasty-looking barracuda one day while swimming with the dolphins. They obviously knew of our fear because occasionally they would chase the barracuda away. The next day, in one of the motorboats towed behind the schooner, we found a very stiff, dried out and very dead three to four-foot barracuda with curved tooth marks in its back. The dolphins seemed to have tossed it up like a gift during the night as if saying, 'Hurumphff. . .barracuda — nothing to be afraid of — here!'"

Following the success of this filming expedition Hardy Jones had made three return trips before, in June 1980, after an eight-day search, his team re-established contact and filmed a sequel to "Dolphin".

In a brief note Hardy said, "We identified sixteen individual members of the pod. The dolphins began to mimic our musical output and would touch my flipper when I took it off. We are beginning to discern the social order/hierarchy of the pod."

13

Interlock accounts with surfers, swimmers and mariners

DURING 1979 understanding of the dolphin-games project extended through our television film, newsletters, articles in magazines and newspapers and our illustrated lecture tours for Conservation Week. Jan conquered her shyness to deliver a lecture in Christchurch and write for a woman's magazine. Only dolphins could have induced her, she said.

From the feedback it became apparent that interlock was not just going on between divers and dolphins: our files swelled with anecdotes from surfers, bathers, beach strollers, yachtsmen, fishermen and even one very surprised Whangarei city-dweller who met a dolphin in the Hatea River, many miles from the sea.

With surfers, as with divers, it seems fear is a hindrance to interlock — a certain uneasiness at the appearance of dolphins may inhibit playfulness. We even heard of teenagers fleeing from the surf when dolphins were sighted. With many people, we suspect it is just a lack of understanding of the potential for human/dolphin interaction that leads to a stand-off. After all, for twenty years of my diving life dolphins were of only marginal concern. We heard of Australian surfers sharing the waves with dolphins but taking little more interest in their presence than a passing seagull.

But in a world where dolphin consciousness is growing, stories are gradually coming in that indicate a potential for creative gamesplay and joyful communication between surfers and at least three species of dolphins.

In February 1979 Laurie Brett, a young Whangarei dentist, was enjoying a beach barbecue at Sandy Bay with a party of friends. On the coast directly opposite the Poor Knights Islands, Sandy Bay is one of the most popular surfing beaches in Northland.

It was around dusk, "one of those beautiful still summer evenings," Laurie wrote, "and a number of people were ambling on the beach enjoying it all when some noticed a small group of dolphins gambolling about 200 yards off the right-hand point of the beach. We were playing music on a tape-deck and we all felt that the dolphins were aware of us. I paddled out a little apprehensively, stuck my head under and tried to call them over — I had heard of the Maori word 'Tepuhi' and I was trying all sorts under water — squeaks and groans as well.

"Two large and quite scarred males (I take it) and a smaller female came very close over a period of about five minutes and the males did some amazing gymnastics — backward flips and high jumps etc. I could see the female was nursing a youngster about two feet long and this young one moved in perfect coordination and almost seemed glued to its mother's right flank. Finally, after about twenty minutes, one of the larger dolphins came underneath my board and lay motionless, in the long axis of my board, about three feet beneath it. It stayed thus for a period of about half a minute or so and I experienced a most wonderful feeling of peace, and belonging in the world (this feeling endures when I reflect on the incident). Shortly after that they disappeared. These were smaller animals, the female about five feet and the males (?) about six or seven feet. I have spoken with other surfers and just about all of them have had some sort of close contact with dolphins."

Later that same month, on 25 February, Laurie Beamish was surfing alone at Sandy Bay, watched from the shore by Malcolm Pullman who had a 650mm tele-lens camera. Malcolm saw fins appear around Laurie and watched the ensuing events, taking pictures where possible.

For forty-five minutes Laurie enjoyed surfing games with these bottlenose dolphins. They came very close to his board, so at first he was afraid of hitting them, but soon it was obvious there was no risk of this. The dolphins demonstrated a number of skilful manoeuvres. Laurie felt they were teaching him and accepted the lead they offered. Often four dolphins would ride a wave alongside him all the way to the beach.

For Laurie, out there alone with the dolphins, it was an intensely spiritual experience. He definitely believes that the length of the inter-lock was influenced by his being alone that day with no distractions. He spoke to the dolphins telling them how happy he was and how much love he felt for them. He lay on his board and put his head underwater calling to them. He practised speaking in tongues, which induces an altered state of consciousness.

Malcolm Pullman, who has lived at Sandy Bay for many years, remarked that such meetings between surfers and dolphins are most likely when the surf is small. He recalls seeing dolphins at play in four to five-foot waves, but they were alone.

That evening, Laurie Brett was surfing with three friends at Ocean Beach at around 6 pm. A small group of bottlenose dolphins appeared among them and made a number of surprising manoeuvres. Laurie describes a phalanx formation like an arrow: four, three, two, one, in which the dolphins appeared in the wall of a wave, before veering off and vanishing.

"They milled around in incredibly tight turns amongst us four and came easily close enough to touch, if you were fast enough. We weren't."

From the Wellington area Alan Morrison wrote:
"Before I took up diving I surfed for about seven years. I encoun-tered dolphins twice. One encounter I still remember vividly: a late

afternoon session on a really warm day about 1974. I was at Waitarere Beach, near Foxton, with two friends. We were sitting about fifty yards offshore just behind the break in the waves. Three dolphins, *Delphinus* I should imagine as they were not large, appeared from behind and startled us. It was quite sudden and my first reaction was fear. I recall them making some form of chattering noise. Then they raced off along the wall of an approaching wave before returning. They actually looked at us, almost upright and half out of the water. This was the first time I had ever seen wild dolphins.''

One of the rarest species in the world is Hector's dolphin *Cephalorhynchus hectori*. It is a small, dumpy, black and white creature, growing to about six feet in length. It has no beak and its flippers and dorsal fin are rounded, the trailing edge of the dorsal being convex rather than the usual concave. This configuration suits the dolphin to its usual habitat: it is an inshore species found in small groups seaward of river mouths mostly in the northern half of the South Island of New Zealand and occasionally further north and south.

We had a report, from Donna and Mike Baker, of a group playing around their boat off Akaroa in the usual friendly dolphin manner, but then we received a detailed account from Ian Surgerson of surfing with Hector's dolphins in Pegasus Bay, just north of Christchurch. As in many surfer/dolphin episodes he only saw them when there was a light surf. His first glimpse would be when they shot under his board while awaiting a wave. His usual initial reaction was ''Shark!'' but then the rounded dorsal fin would pop up beside him, with a puff from the blowhole and his heartbeat settled down. When the surfers tried to paddle after and touch them, the dolphins never panicked, but continued to circle just out of reach.

Ian described a meeting at Amberley Beach when there was a three-foot surf running. He took off on a wave and was riding out on the un-broken wall of it when he found a dolphin beside him. He kicked off the wave and watched to see what it would do. The dolphin stayed in the wave until about to dump in the shore break, leapt out of the back and repeated the experience. Once when Ian cut back he nearly collided with a dolphin but in a flash it turned, slipped out of the wave and reappeared seconds later right beside him.

We have a file of encounters between yachtsmen and fishermen which go beyond the bow-riding stage. Of these, perhaps Sam McHarg's* would be representative. Like him, most people who have unusual dolphin experiences invariably respond warmly to them at every meeting, whistling, approaching them on the bow and generally showing a high regard.

Sam writes:
''Is it possible that dolphins remember the underwater shape of boats? I used to own an old kauri twenty-two footer that has sailed the coasts for forty years. On two occasions I've let the yacht sail herself

*Earlier letter page 89.

180

while I stood on the bobstay and stroked dolphins. On the first occasion, only one was close enough, and then they moved off several feet out of reach. On the second occasion I stroked six or seven. Now why, when I was racing my boat several weeks later, in a fleet of twenty-five, should dolphins all head for my old tub and keep clear of the others?

"Several times when there have been a number of other boats about the dolphins have headed for us and not other boats! When they are about I always do my whistling, Tepuhi thing.

"On one occasion bottlenose dolphins followed me on the calm, early morning flood-tide from four miles south of Cape Brett to past Old Woman's Island in the shallow (three metres) water, right near the head of the Kerikeri Inlet. I was under motor all the way at about five knots. There were other yachts and launches coming and going in and out of the Kerikeri Inlet at the time, but the dolphins stayed with us. In the very shallow water they left us and appeared to head straight down the inlet for the open sea with no playing around.

"In November 1976, I was off Doves Bay in Kerikeri Inlet in a light southwest breeze and the boat was moving at about four knots. I owned a fast nineteen-foot GRP fibreglass Hunter sloop *Rata*. It had red topsides and was black under water. Her shape was *very* dolphin-like.

"We were overtaken by about ten to twelve bottlenose dolphins who had been playing in shallow water at Rangitore. The GRP hull enabled us to hear their conversations, and they were talking flat out. They circled *Rata* twice, one rubbing his fin alongside the hull. One came very close and slowed, so I leaned out and touched his dorsal fin. He moved out not too rapidly to about four metres off the port quarter, and slowed to the speed of *Rata* for about ten to fifteen seconds. He then joined the others as they moved on, and left us to move out past Cocked Hat Island and open water.

"Good luck with Project Interlock."

Cindy Slark and her brother Jon spent a night (15 January 1980) becalmed in their yacht *Manukarere* between Auckland and Great Barrier Island. For twelve hours a dolphin played around them in trails of phosphorescence: leaping, gliding back to the boat, swimming under and around, vanishing and returning. The two young people were deeply affected by its presence and played taped music out into the night. As soon as the wind arose, the dolphin left.

Cook Strait dolphin girl

One day a friend sent us a newsclipping from the Wellington *Evening Post*, dated 3 April 1978, showing a girl in mid-ocean surrounded by dolphin fins. It is an interesting comment on the low general level of dolphin knowledge that the newspaper had not stressed the uniqueness of the photo, even though such close encounters are rare.

I had a hunch there was more to this story and wrote to the girl, sixteen-year-old long distance swimmer, Meda McKenzie. Her name was already familiar to us for her exploits. Meda was the first person to thoroughly conquer the powerful currents of Cook Strait, by swimming the windy gap between the two main islands from both north and south.

She has swum the English Channel, the Bristol Channel and grimmest of all, the chill southern waters of Foveaux Strait.

Maori tradition surrounding the famous Cook Strait dolphin, Pelorus Jack (1888 — 1912) tells of Hinepoupou who was marooned on Kapiti Island and swam Cook Strait to her South Island home, aided by a dolphin she called to assist her.

Today the fishermen of Island Bay, Wellington, fondly call Meda their "dolphin girl". The newsphoto showed her swimming from Kapiti to the mainland. Her story could just as easily become a legend.

To us she wrote:

"I hope my answer to your letter is not too late. I have had a number of encounters with the dolphins and I feel a certain kinship with them as they always appear when I am in Cook Strait and I am quite sure that they come to protect me, especially when I am swimming in the dark as I can hear them calling long before they reach me. When a swim is abandoned they don't leave until just beforehand and each time, one dolphin has surfaced right beside me, flipped in front of me and back again as if to say, 'Don't go on.'

"Quite different from my successful swims when they have frolicked beside me and been very playful as if they knew the tides and weather were going to hold.

"On the Kapiti swim it was very rough and a strong rip was running about a mile off the island. A school of dolphins appeared and one mother and baby came up beside me; the adult or mother swam beside me but the baby swam in front and kept flipping over and coming up so that it brushed across my face almost as though trying to kiss me. It would then swim a few yards in front of me and sort of waggle its tail, then look back and I'm quite sure the look said, 'Come on, you can do it. Follow me.' They stayed till about 400 yards offshore. Then they circled me, joined the rest of the dolphins and swam off out to sea.

"I know when dolphins are playing and when they are serious. I guess you do too. With me, if there is danger ahead, they time my arm movements and when my hand goes into the water to start my pull through they flip it away so that I can't swim. If they are playing they then dive under me and come up when the next arm pull is ready. If they are serious they stay right beside me and make a funny noise, almost warning me that I can go no further."

On receiving this I sent Meda a list of questions on her dolphin encounters and from her replies, learnt as follows:

On her first Cook Strait swim, from the North Island to the South (3 February 1978), Meda met dolphins three miles out, after leaving Ohau Point at 10 am. Two miles off Perano Head, on the other side of Cook Strait, they left. She set foot on the South Island at 10 pm, after swimming 28.4km in twelve hours seven minutes.

Her second Cook Strait crossing, from south to north, took place two weeks later, 17 February 1978. Meda set out near Perano Head at two in the afternoon. Four miles out she met dolphins who stayed with her to within one and a half miles of her landing at Pipinui Point an hour before midnight.

That April, on an easier two and three-quarter hour training swim from Kapiti Island to Paraparaumu Beach, Meda met the dolphins a mile offshore and they escorted her to within a half-mile of the beach.

Next year Meda tried the Cook Strait crossing twice more to improve her times. Both these swims had to be abandoned because of weather conditions. On the first attempt (14 February 1979) dolphins arrived when she was three miles from Pipinui Point and stayed with her until she left the water after four hours' effort. On her second attempt a week later (20 February 1979) dolphins arrived when she was four miles out. At seven that evening deteriorating weather forced her out.

"While I was in the shower the pilot and my father said one dolphin kept skidding on its tail and calling. It came right up to the boat. Fifteen minutes after my leaving the water the fog cleared and the wind dropped. I could have kept going. . ."

Meda believes the dolphins to be both *Tursiops* and *Delphinus*. "The small ones come very close, swimming round, under and beside me. I'm sure they think I'm one of them."

I wondered whether the dolphins might simply be riding the bow of the boat, but Meda allayed this doubt:

"The distance between the boat and the dolphins varies from thirty feet to a quarter-mile, while with me they are from two feet to mere inches!"

Wearing goggles she was able to watch their antics but hadn't learnt to recognise individuals except that she had a hunch, "One at least has come to me more than once. I don't know why. I just sort of feel it."

On other long-distance swims elsewhere in New Zealand and Europe she had never encountered dolphins. While it seems incredible, the behaviour of the dolphins suggested to Meda they were aware of her capacity and what she was attempting to do. She definitely felt a great assistance in having them by her side.

Finally Meda wrote, "I am starting scuba lessons and hope to come north this summer. I would love to come out with you and Jan to see if my dolphins only look after me in Cook Strait or if dolphins in other places will come to me." Meda's wish was to come true. . .

Near dusk on 24 March 1980, eighteen-year-old Belinda Shields crawled ashore on hands and knees at Cape Terawhiti, the tip of the North Island, after swimming Cook Strait in eight hours thirty-two minutes. About one hour after leaving the South Island a group of sixty common dolphins had joined her.

"I heard them coming — strange underwater noises that got very loud. I realized they would probably be dolphins as I'd seen a school of them beside the launch the day before when we crossed to the South Island.

"They came very close and actually rubbed against me, underneath and alongside. It scared me a little as I had no previous experience of dolphins, but I knew as long as they were there I had no fear of sharks. It seemed they actually wanted me to play — very excited, jumping out of the water and chattering between themselves. It certainly broke the boredom for me.

"Prior to their arrival I was feeling a bit disillusioned with the cold water — between ten and thirteen degrees centigrade. It gave me a splitting headache. The sea was rough and the sky very dark. I was uncertain of making the swim, let alone breaking the record. When the dolphins came it took my mind off the cold and I was excited to have these beautiful creatures swim with me. I watched their behaviour and it pumped my spirits up. I'm not sure if there were any babies with them, but they came in many sizes, so perhaps there were. After about two hours they disappeared only to return half an hour later. Again I heard them coming — it was very loud underwater. They still seemed very excited and stayed with me until within three miles of the North Island.''

On this crossing Meda McKenzie was on board the launch and paced the swimmer towards the end.

On her honeymoon Meda and her husband, John Sweetman, came to Northland. At 8 am on 15 December 1979, Meda swam from the Tutukaka coast out to the Poor Knights Islands, a distance of twelve miles. Her main worry was that the warmth of the water might make her go to sleep. She reached the island near Rikoriko Cave at 4.27 pm.

Three miles from the mainland common dolphins had appeared. Following the swimmer with our catamaran, Jan and I were surprised. Almost every day for the week before the swim we had been to sea and sighted no dolphins in the area. For a week afterwards we were out frequently and still saw none. Yet there they were, after Meda had been swimming offshore for ninety minutes.

It was a weird day for a long-distance swim. A thirty-knot offshore breeze nearly put a stop to it, but Meda was determined to try. Her original intention was to swim from the islands to the shore but sea conditions ruled that out.

The moment we put the catamaran's noses out of Tutukaka Harbour we learnt there would be no need of sail or engine. With Interlock supporters Joyce and Graeme Adams to assist us, for once Jan and I broke our rule about not going to sea when winds greater than twenty knots were forecast. We found ourselves moving at nearly three knots with a bare pole and were obliged to tack to and fro to keep pace with Meda.

Just ahead of the swimmer two men, her father and coach, huddled in our inflatable giving her encouragement, and keeping her on course. The mother ship, a forty-foot motor vessel *Geisha*, hovered nearby.

This dolphin girl hardly used her legs, just hauling herself through the following seas with powerful armstrokes. Our hearts went out to her, so tiny and alone in all that wild ocean. With C.B. radio we were linked to another long-distance swimming event some 250 miles south, where eight people were racing from Whakatane out to Whale Island and back to shore, right through the area of Ramari ("Dusty") Stewart's Interlock II dolphin study. We wondered if those swimmers would encounter dolphins too.

It was 9.30 when we noticed dolphins about 200 yards away heading south toward the coast, as if going right past us. Jan called to them. She knew their presence would help Meda enormously if she were to keep going in such hectic conditions. To our delight the dolphins slowed and milled around before turning directly towards us, their fins slicing the waves. Jan and I were hugging each other with joy when they surfaced alongside Meda. There were six: four on one side and a pair just ahead.

Meda saw a baby dolphin flanked by its mother and an "auntie". The mother was closest to her. They then circled, playing around for several minutes before being lost to our view in the whitecaps. Twice more on her journey dolphins appeared around the swimmer briefly, as if checking her out. Meda was ploughing along strongly when only a mile from the steep cliffs, a fierce squall swept her away to the north. With utter tenacity she just kept on stroking. She seemed to claw her way to her goal.

On the long hard slog home we really learnt the wind's strength. With power and sail it took us six hours — not much less than Meda's 8 hr 27 min. Twice (at 5.10 and 6.27 pm) we were visited by the same small group of common dolphins. Their company made us feel a lot less lonely.

Following the progress of the Whakatane offshore race, we discovered no dolphins were sighted by the swimmers down there.

Footnote: When Dusty Stewart of Project Interlock Base II (see next chapter) left Whakatane River at seven that morning she met fifteen familiar-looking *Delphinus*, all with newborn babies, some only hours old, just off the entrance. For two and a half hours they accompanied her catamaran *Interlock II* cruising slowly along the coast. When the eight long-distance swimmers appeared Dusty left the dolphins and sailed out to Whale Island.

The following Sunday she met this same group of mothers and babies again. As soon as she changed from motor to sail the babies, brimming with vitality, all came between the hulls, with their mothers on either side of the vessel, while Dusty played the flute to them.

14

Interlock Base II

RAMARI STEWART, or "Dusty" as she is better known, is a highly trained, part-Maori nurse who became so fascinated with the possibilities of studying cetaceans in the wild she chose to devote herself to it fulltime.

After her "Follow Home Day" experience with us (page 146) and several other sea trips aboard R.V. *Interlock*, Dusty set about developing a second research base on Whale Island, three miles out from Whakatane in the Bay of Plenty. From the outset, dolphin enthusiast Des Crossland assisted her greatly. Aided by local fishermen they constructed comfortable living quarters on the island and completely refurbished a seventeen-foot sailing catamaran as a miniature replica of ours.

Just before sunrise one morning in August 1979, I participated in a moving little ceremony at the mouth of the Whakatane River where, knee deep in the chill water, a Maori priest performed the rites of a traditional canoe launching and the twin hulls of Dusty's *Interlock II* slid off the trailer into the dark sea.

From close liaison with fishermen and her previous year's observations Dusty was able to establish that a resident group of common dolphins, *Delphinus delphis* stays in the Whale Island area during the winter months in contrast with our own observations further north where these dolphins are more transient. Gradually, Dusty recorded recognition data from increasing numbers of individuals and we exchanged fin observation sheets regularly. (In her area, bottlenose dolphins are seldom seen.)

One day we discovered some of Dusty's dolphins in the Poor Knights area — evidence of coastal movement in summer and an exciting extension of the dolphin study.

Dusty's research took on a special urgency when she learnt of dolphin mortality in association with commercial fishing. Currently she is working with fishermen and local authorities to find a solution to this problem — one which is emerging in many parts of the world where commercial fishermen are competing with dolphins for diminishing stocks of seafood.

In many ways Dusty's observations of *Delphinus*, 250 miles from the initial study area, provide valuable parallels, helping us understand patterns of dolphins' response to people more clearly, discerning basic behaviour and local variations. While dolphins in both areas share certain patterns, the divergences make us cautious in generalising about behaviour from observations so limited in time and space. On the threshold of a new field of inquiry, we are more concerned to establish methods of gaining acceptance with wild dolphins than with making definitive statements about them which would rapidly require revision. Already there is too much of this in writings where behaviour of captive dolphins has been extrapolated to free-ranging social groups.

Besides, in meeting dolphins in their natural habitat, we must be equally concerned with patterns of human behaviour towards them. With such complex creatures observation cuts both ways. Using an approach pattern so similar to our own, Dusty's initiatives, and her acceptance by the dolphins, encourage us to feel interlock is an inter-species event repeatable wherever people are enthusiastic enough to persevere.

Snippets from Dusty's letters to us will give some idea of her work which will eventually warrant a book of its own.

Paleface day

27 September 1979: "This day we met the dolphins again for the first time since our return from seeing you at Tutukaka. Most notable of the many things they did, was a game initiated by one adult. . .Paleface. He enjoyed quite confidently racing up between the hulls — always stern to bow. The bow net is not yet installed.

"When we approached them, off the east end of the island, we were under power as there was no breeze. With the dolphins all around us we decided to put the sails up regardless. Out of gear, the motor was coughing and spluttering on the verge of stalling, and while we tackled the sails, it did stall! Just as we returned to the stern to steer, a dolphin started 'coughing' and came up right below the motor and blew enormous gushes of air bubbles beneath the surface.

"Between the bows, just forward of the centre deck, where the net should be, three dolphins were doing complex patterns. For example, one dolphin would appear close to the surface and then as if a bud were unfolding from below, there would be three petals. We were stationary, and so were the dolphins, except for these intricate movements. I exclaimed, 'How do they do it?' Slowly they performed the patterns, perfect and complex. During one sequence, I instantly recalled Dan Tana's drawing — is it possible for us to have a copy?

"We love the boat as we are so close to the water from all points. When I lay on the deck, my arm outstretched in the water, dolphins approached and audibly 'buzzed' my hand. The main group was spread out over an area of two to three miles. We maintained our position — almost stationary, for an hour, with a group of fifteen of them."

Mothers and babies day

7 October 1979: "The day before a storm, sea conditions were rough. Bruce McIntyre gave us a call on the C.B. from his vessel *Takapu*, to say that he could see activity one mile off the northwest point of the island. We were on our way out at the time, passing the Boulder Bank. We were joined by four mothers and their young. Each mother was accompanied by a baby, all the same size, a few months old. Immediately on arrival, they approached the stern. The mums and babies all cruised through between the hulls. We were under sail all the way. Since Paleface initiated this game, it has been repeated with each encounter. At no time did any of the babies leave its respective mother's side. If the mother was shooting the bows, or stationary on the surface between the bows, then her offspring would be right there with her.

"We could not locate the main group which we thought to be out further. One lone dolphin appeared at the stern and then raced off out to the north. Des, who was at the tiller, got a good look at this dolphin when it stuck his head out beside the boat — it was Paleface."

Rudder day

12 October 1979: "The dolphin patterns are now on the sails. At the northwest point of the island, about three miles out, we saw twelve adult dolphins. They were all recognisable with distinctive fins. All the dolphins immediately commenced shooting the bows. Des was at the tiller when two dolphins appeared, one positioned off each rudder. Whenever he turned the rudders they synchronized their movements. Later, one of this pair turned upside down at the surface and gazed up through the two hulls. I was on the port bow, forward of the deck, and peeped under at him. Des and I burst out laughing when this dolphin turned right side up and somehow sculled *backwards* for about twenty feet, curving right around until his tail was to our stern. The boat was into the wind and relatively stationary. We wondered if he was also looking at our new dolphin sail patterns."

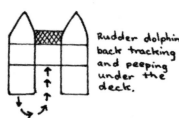

Rudder dolphin back tracking and peeping under the deck.

Teenage day

13 October 1979: "About one mile off the northwest point of the island we spotted them. The main group was hunting, spread over an area of one to two miles. There was a big group of teenagers who cavorted with us. They were visited by one or two adults who periodically joined in. One was Paleface.

"The wind was gusting, and we were expecting a big blow, so we were under power, but went out for the sake of keeping up the rendezvous. We set our course for the east end of the island, and the teenage group came home with us most of the way. Because we had our outboard going, they would sound at the stern to avoid it, and pop up under the deck. They kept racing out after the two adults, whenever they left the group, and then returned to continue the game. It was as if they were having a ball, but had to race off from time to time, to make sure it was all right.

"Each time most of the dolphins we encounter are on the seaward side. We have observed scout groups racing inside the island, but the main population has preferred to remain north.

"Each time, we circumnavigate the island clockwise. As we do not have a bell to say 'It's us,' I always use my whistle. If the dolphins are heading away when whistled, they always turn and come over. They have not as yet come to us when we have simply sighted them.''

Orca need better PR

"On Sunday, 11 November, a quarter-mile off the eastern end of Whale Island, we encountered three orca," wrote Dusty. "To our horror, one was ensnared in a gill net. It was being assisted by two others. We spent two hours trying to get close enough to free it. They came very close to the boat, but in each case one of the flankers got nervous, and kept nudging the ensnared one away to a safe distance.

"Des and I were both ready to leap in, clothes and all, but I reminded him that one of us had to keep an eye on the boat, which had all its sails up. We decided that I should go in and try to get the orca to accept me, and then he would come in and release the trapped one. I got close enough to touch it, although I didn't. The flanker kept between me and the captive. The one in the net was a young female about the same length as our boat (seventeen feet). One flanker was an adolescent, two to three feet shorter, and the other was a juvenile. The juvenile was the nervous one who, unfortunately, kept getting in the way. Somehow, the young adult had hit the net and spun, probably picking up the ground rope with all the lead weights, so the net was wrapped round twice and tightly bound. There was no way for the orca to free itself without assistance. I could tell the ropes were very tight by the compression of the skin. Also, number two was cut deep into the flesh. Number one was close to the blowhole. I could have grabbed the trailing net at one time, but I didn't when I had the chance, as I thought she was settling down and I would only frighten her.

"Eventually we gave up, as the orca decided to head out to sea. You can imagine how we felt. We headed in and talked to one boat after another. Hopefully, we thought, someone might be able to help us locate the main pod which could have calmed them, giving us another chance, but we failed. A large pod had been sighted the day before. Boats in the vicinity, that might have been able to help us, left quickly, afraid for their safety with 'killer whales' around! If only someone could help the orca, yet I don't blame them for not trusting us.''

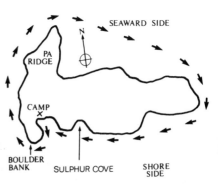

WHALE ISLAND

189

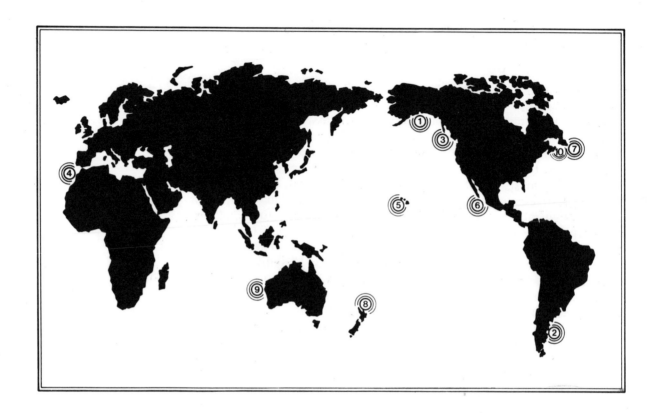

Cetacean Hotspots: World-wide. (This list is not exhaustive and can be expected to expand, especially when all whaling and dolphin killing ceases). (1) Alaska — humpback whales, grey whales. (2) Argentina, Valdez Peninsula — right whales, dolphins. (3) Canada, British Columbia — orca. (4) Gibraltar* — dolphins. (5) Hawaii* — humpback whales, dolphins. (6) Mexico*, Baha California — grey whales. (7) Newfoundland*, Trinity — humpback whales. (8) New Zealand coasts — dolphins, whales. (9) West Australia*, Monkey Mia — bottlenose dolphins. (10) Gulf of St Lawrence*, Mingan Islands — blue, humpback, fin and minke whales.

*tourist facilities, whale watching etc.

15

Playing with whales

IS INTERLOCK possible with other cetaceans besides dolphins? Can humans get close to whales? Will they respond to music, playfully mimic our body language or let us touch them? The visit to Ngunguru in December 1979 of Jim Nollman, director of Interspecies Communication Foundation, convinced us this has already begun.

First it must be appreciated that for whales there are several barriers to creative gamesplay with a species as small as man. Their vast size presents problems rather like elephant/mouse friendship. Human fear of close proximity to a creature many tons in weight is understandable, although it now appears whales are aware of this: several species have shown great care when close to swimmers.

Their ocean habitat makes them remote from the experience of most of humankind and near our populated areas it is usually too murky for visual contact. Thirdly, whales have been at much greater risk from human exploitation than most dolphin populations.

But today a change is under way. Never fast enough for cetacean lovers, each year significant progress is being made towards a global consensus that could eventually halt all exploitation and killing of cetaceans. We fervently hope this may not be too late for endangered species. Meanwhile, in a number of parts of the world, mutual trust is growing between humans and whales. Most popular for human/ cetacean rapport are areas where man has found ready access to cetaceans year after year and where hunting has ceased for some time: for the most part, breeding and inshore feeding grounds. In such situations an unusual degree of accommodation has been developing in the past few years. We have documentation on file which shows people scratching the heads of grey whales in Baha California; climbing around on receptive southern right whales in New Zealand and Patagonia; exchanging musical notes with orca in Canada; swimming with humpbacks at close range in Hawaii. We have accounts of friendly exchanges with pilot, sei, minke, *Pseudorca* and sperm whales. Very likely, by the time this is published, the list will have extended. When all whale murder ceases and trust expands, the process of interspecies exploration can be expected to accelerate.

March 1980, saw us glued to a television screen to watch Dr Simon Cotton's film of his meeting with orca off Great Mercury Island in January 1979. We'd waited for more than a year to view those historic moments in the relationship of man and cetacean. Now I find myself sifting through orca/human history, particularly as we have seen it emerge in New Zealand waters.

Significantly, it seems to parallel the material on Project Interlock files with regard to diver/dolphin encounters. In both cases there has been an intensive input from divers who deliberately set out to meet the cetaceans on their own terms. This is followed by a marked increase in reports from other divers of friendly meetings.

Until relatively recently very few divers, even the bravest, would have dreamed of staying in the water if "killer whales" were around. In most reports divers withdrew when orca appeared. In the sixties I recall a spearfisherman boasting he'd bounced a spear off one! (Around then another diver transfixed a dolphin with a spear from the bow of a boat. . .)

In 1964, an Auckland diver was so terrified when two orca swooped to and fro past the cave at Canoe Rock (Kawau Island) in which he was getting crays on scuba, that he withdrew into the grotto and skip-breathed until the coast was clear. "They may have only wished to be playful but who would be game to frolic with thirty-footers?" he asked incisively.

As knowledge of orca from overseas, especially Canada, filtered in, divers became a little more confident. Then came Simon Cotton's chance encounter in October 1977 while scuba diving on the *Wiltshire* wreck at Great Barrier Island, when he made several attempts to film a male and an albino.

By a stroke of luck the following month Dr Paul Spong of Greenpeace, Canada, visited Auckland and Simon saw his illustrated lecture on wild orca studies near Vancouver in British Columbia. Paul (originally a New Zealander) tells us in *Mind in the Waters* how he paddled his kayak out in the mist with orca on all sides and played his flute to them. As in his film of captive orca, "We Call them Killers", he had put himself entirely in their trust, at their "mercy" and the orca accepted him and guided him to shore. (This account is a "must" for those interested in orca.)

So Simon became determined to film the wild orca of New Zealand and set out on an elaborate expedition in October 1978. Film of wild orca is, or was then, as rare as hen's teeth. A group in British Columbia managed a small amount of footage, incorporated in Paul Spong's lecture, but conditions were murky. For some months Simon's intensive efforts were frustrated. Aboard *Corofin* he searched and searched, even with the aid of spotter planes, but no orca. December *Sea Spray* carried his advertisement: a $250 reward for information on location of orca pods. Soon after, in early January 1979, he got a radio report from the fishing vessel *Celtic* which led to success: three days of diver/orca encounters off Great Mercury Island.

Even as he leapt in with his camera Simon felt some misgivings: while he could not be sure of his safety, there were no justifiable grounds for fear other than the lack of knowledge of the behaviour towards man of non-captive orca and our own history of random brutality towards them.

192

His footage shows two females making repeated passes in front of the camera. A male approaches him head on, its fin passing right under his arm. Later the orca move into shallow water and in the film we see them balancing delicately on their heads among the kelp and rocks, two females and a young male. Simon says the pattern was repeated four times, sometimes with four orca and each time including a juvenile. The final frame of his film shows a diver and an orca at once. Since that time Project Interlock has received a series of reports that indicate a warming in orca/human relationships.

Over a mirror calm sea on 3 February 1979, a pod of orca glided towards the stern of the launch *Hirawanu*. With the Aldermen Islands in the background, Gary Dods started clicking off photos as they advanced along the wake. He and his father became increasingly amazed as the whales just kept on coming. For Gary's last shot a huge female raised her head and rested it on the stern platform of the launch.

Penny Whiting runs a sailing school in Auckland Harbour. On two days, 26 and 29 September 1979, her classes were interrupted while they accompanied a pod of orca that entered the harbour and advanced up the channel, to pass under the Auckland harbour bridge. With them, on each occasion, was a group of bottlenose dolphins and both species appeared to be playing together. The instant the tide began to fall they all turned and left. Startled Aucklanders watched the event on their television screens.*

Two days later the Antarctic whaling season opened; Russian factory ships killed 906 orca, a catch three times higher than ever recorded for this species. Normally they would have hunted sperm whales but the I.W.C. had banned factory ships from this. Virtually nothing is known about the biology or population dynamics of the orca.

In November 1979, Ramari Stewart of Interlock Base II made her attempt to release an orca enmeshed in a gill net off Whakatane. And so it goes.

We think it is likely people will now meet orca with less fear so that the pattern of exchange deepens in complexity. Such a prediction is based on similarity with the pattern of human/dolphin relationships. Since Project Interlock publicised dolphin game procedures there has been an upsurge in reports of friendly contacts. Now the same is happening with orca. Consistently they have demonstrated friendliness towards man. In response, people are beginning to show a readiness to trust orca on their own terms.

Jim Nollman — interspecies musician

On the motel wall, Jim Nollman projected pictures of his orca meetings while a tape recorder played an exchange of sounds between musician and sea beast. We watched and listened in amazement. In December 1979, Jim had come from Bolinas, California to Ngunguru to show us the equipment he uses and see how we operate aboard R.V. *Interlock*. He was on his way to Japan for the second time to try to prevent another dolphin massacre on the island of Iki.

*In that same month the following year, what seemed to be the same orca appeared in the same area on the 28th.

Jim admitted to being a little anxious that August 1977 day in Canada as the huge, sleek forms focused on him, floating out on the water off Dr Paul Spong's cetacean research base. A thirty-foot bull headed straight for the wetsuit-clad figure sitting in a weird drumraft, something like an old-style school desk. Jim had been tapping out a drum rhythm transmitted directly into the sea. He told us that subsequently he'd met a scientist studying the various sounds orca make. Jim played him a recording of their response to the water drum. In all his research the scientist had never heard that sound.

Two years later, in August 1979, Jim Nollman returned to the Hanson Island base in British Columbia, to spend three weeks with the orca. This time a Japanese television team accompanied him to document the interlock. With better equipment and recording gear Jim graduated from water drum to electric guitar. He set up his studio on a cliff above the sea. Each night at eleven he would begin to play. His guitar notes passed through modulators that enabled him to mimic orca sounds. From a twelve-volt car amplifier the signal went along 300 feet of cable to a hydrophone out in the bay. Each night the orca came to his notes and an exchange of call and response developed. Each night the orca stayed a little longer. By about the fourth night the orca arrived *before* he started playing.

The final session went on for two hours and during it Jim felt things progressed beyond the level of simple call and response. It seemed to the musician the orca were trying to show him a new sound pattern.

"I really felt they were teaching me a song." When Jim flunked the lesson they broke the sequence up into components for him to rehearse before attempting the original sound pattern again.

For several nights after Jim's departure the orca kept returning at around the same time. From the recordings and photos Jim showed us one thing is clear: in Canada a situation is developing in which orca exchange sound patterns with musicians. (Besides Paul Spong and Jim Nollman, jazzman Paul Winter and a moog synthesizer player have been involved there.)

During daylight hours Jim had first established a trust relationship with the orca in the water. In these daily sessions he cradled a waterphone in his arms: an acoustic instrument consisting of a metal hemisphere with a tube protruding from the north pole; from the equator, spiral brass rods of varying lengths. When a violin bow is drawn across the rods weird whale sounds are transmitted directly into the water. If the open tube is placed to the ear, underwater sound can readily be heard too.

Wearing a gaily coloured hat for recognition, his polar wetsuit inflated for buoyancy, Jim would enter the frigid water 300 yards in front of the orca formation and play his instrument. As they came nearer and nearer, Jim began to feel they were testing him. Once they regarded him from below. Another time two juveniles rushed at him over the surface, diving at the last second to emerge on the other side, turn and repeat the performance. Jim wasn't ready for that. His heart pounding he had to get out. The leading male with its six-foot dorsal fin came up to the boat and five feet away rolled over revealing its white belly. To Jim it seemed to say, "Come on back in. Let's play some more." So he got in again and this time the dramatic sequence of photos we saw, was taken.

For Jan and me the climax of Jim Nollman's visit to New Zealand was the December day we ended up at sea with Meda the dolphin girl, filmmakers Michael Wiese and Morgan Smith, and Jim on board: four people with interlock experiences from different parts of the world sharing our catamaran with us. A nice stroke of coincidence which restored confidence in our sanity as we exchanged interlock experiences with our visitors.

In September 1980, Jim Nollman returned to Hanson Island for a third recording session with the orca.

"It was my strongest orca experience yet," he wrote. "They were vocalising so loudly and so close to me — at one point there were twelve or so directly under my feet — that I felt the sound was actually a form of massage — massage that I could feel all over my body. A very strange experience. I have never *felt* sound before. This may be one of the major ways they communicate. There is no such thing as a 'blind' orca. The communication between us was of the highest quality — at one moment we shifted keys simultaneously, as if we all knew in advance the piece of music we were performing. Both myself and the men recording sound for me, agreed later that this one afternoon was as close to a 'satori' experience as either of us has ever experienced. I cannot say enough to give you an idea of the kind of event that transpired that afternoon; but I have never felt that kind of closeness and 'suchness' ever before. The orca are my teacher."

The great whales

It is not surprising that orca have been next to the dolphins in relating to man. For reasons of size, habitat and relative freedom from exploitation they are much closer to us than the great whales.

But from 1978 onwards we began to notice a growth in the friendliness of sei and minke whales in our study area. As our research extended overseas we found this process became significant, during the mid-seventies, in several parts of the world.

For us it started with a letter from Dr Tony Ayling at Leigh Marine Laboratory, fifty miles north of Auckland.
"Dear Wade,

"Yesterday we experienced the ultimate interlock (or rather INTERLOCK). A student assistant and I had just come up from a dive on the outside of Goat Island and were sitting in the boat putting our gear away when something larger than a dolphin surfaced about fifty yards away. I couldn't tell what it was but thought it was either a female orca or a pilot whale. We headed in the direction it had been going with some vague idea of being able to get close. We saw it surface several times. The distance between us decreased rapidly. Just when we thought it had sounded, it surfaced about twenty feet from the boat!

"We were joined by two scientists in another boat who had been diving nearby. This time we got a clear view and I think it was a sei whale about thirty-five feet long. Still it didn't sound even with two boats following. Several times we got close enough to see it just beneath the surface. By putting my head over with mask on I could watch the huge tail flukes. Again it didn't appear for some time and we slowed down. Then it surfaced just *behind* the boats!

"We leapt in just with masks and snorkels and with forty-five feet visibility this huge and beautiful animal passed, oh so slowly, under us, turning on its side about twelve feet beneath us and looking up! What a mind-blowing experience! We leapt back in the boats after it had passed, followed it up and repeated the same scene four more times.

"On one pass the whale stopped underneath two of us, about five feet below, a huge expanse of sleek and beautiful beast. At no stage did he appear worried and certainly none of us felt anything except tremendous excitement.

"Finally we had to leave the whale — it didn't leave us. By this time we were over two miles down the coast and a mile off Cape Rodney. As we were leaving the whale broached three times in a row, rearing half its body out of the water and crashing back. I think we all felt it was the most astounding experience we've had. Certainly it's the sort of thing you never dream could happen. I thought you'd like to hear about it."

Following this, we experienced several close encounters with these smaller whales in our catamaran and on two occasions accompanied them under sail for lengthy periods. Over twelve consecutive dives we studied a whale's breathing cycle and found each dive lasted around eight minutes, preceded by three (occasionally four) shallow work-up dives of around thirty seconds. We soon learnt to foretell when a whale was sounding by the distinctive heaving motion and knew when to expect its reappearance.

During the spring of 1979, we heard of several other boats in the area having close visits from whales. One stayed within twenty feet of *Marco Polo* for an hour, Ross Cotterill told us. Some scientists suggest this "friendliness" may be related to the habit of small fish seeking refuge near boat hulls.

Meanwhile material was coming to us from overseas that broadens our view of the emergence of whale/human interlock.

In South America, off the Valdes Peninsula, Patagonia, there is a nursery of southern right whales. Each year these cetaceans migrate from their Antarctic feeding range to two large, calm bays. There, in fairly shallow water, for three or four months they breed, give birth and nurse their young.

Swimming along at fifty feet on scuba Dr Lyall Watson came upon a mother and her calf alone. The mother was lying on her back, scratching herself against the sea bottom. He could see the pleats on her belly. The calf was perturbed at Lyall's approach and left quickly. The mother, obviously aware of his presence, just lay there and kept on scratching.

"As I got closer," he said, "I knew she could see me. She raised her head and looked at me. I swam over and she raised her flipper, hooking me down — a frightening thing at first. But I quickly realized she was being very gentle with me, obviously aware of my position and size and how much force was needed to push me gently. She pulled me down onto her belly and I slid down the pleats and grooves of her throat. I swam up and she pushed me down again. We played this game for an hour, just the two of us, the calf hovering anxiously around, wondering what I was doing with his mum.''

Ethologist and author of many popular books, Dr Lyall Watson has travelled around the world for ten years on the expedition ship *Explorer* and seen in the wild eighty-two of the world's ninety-two species of cetacean. He is now actively engaged in setting up a cetacean research centre in the Seychelles, to investigate pathways to communicate with cetaceans as intelligent beings.

An underwater photographer, Armando Jenik, sighted a baby right whale close to the shore, while diving in Patagonia. He grabbed his camera and rushed into the water. Watched by its forty-foot parents the baby whale responded to the diver by offering her tail repeatedly for rides, both above and below the surface — *Skindiver* magazine, January 1979.

I must admit that I found these accounts of physical contact with whales much easier to accept when I received a magazine with photos and article by Robert Merlo showing Italian divers doing similar things with right whales in the same area. (*Mondo Sommerso*, September 1979.)

Near the Florida coast is a small group of islands called the Dry Tortugas. On 25 July 1976, oceanographer Dr James W. Porter came upon a pod of thirty *Pseudorca* resting on the lee shore of one of the sand cays, facing towards the shore. The whales' backs were awash in the clear shallows: seventeen females and thirteen males. At the centre the largest, an eighteen-foot male, was sick. Blood seeped from his right ear. The other whales were not stranded and periodically would shift towards the middle of the wedge-shaped formation.

Nearby Dr Porter entered the water, intending to snorkel amongst them. The outermost whale headed over, lowered its head and slid beneath him. Slowly its body rose, lifting him almost clear of the water and bearing him towards the beach where it slowly submerged. The whale circled him and approached again. James Porter dropped his snorkel on the verge of calling for help, but at the release of his snorkel the whale seemed to lose interest, veering off to rejoin the group. The pattern was repeated three more times.

At that, the scientist walked along the beach to re-enter the water on the other side of the group. The flanking female responded in the same way an equal number of times.

The *Pseudorca* accepted his presence to take intimate underwater photos of them when not using the snorkel. James Porter wondered whether it sounded like a clogged blowhole. He recalled tales of drowning people being pushed ashore by dolphins and small whales. After three days the large male died and the rest of the group returned to sea. (*Oceans* magazine, July 1977.)

Fortune smiled for me in May 1980, and I was able to travel, with all expenses paid, to the United States: Los Angeles, Washington D.C., San Francisco and several islands of Hawaii. In the course of these travels, discussed in the next chapter, I met a number of people with experiences of cetaceans in the wild. My investigation into the potential of human/whale interlock took such a leap forward that this theme alone could easily fill another book. At this stage I would just like to present sufficient to complement our studies with dolphins and indicate the enormous potential of such exploration for the future.

Each winter humpback whales of the north Pacific migrate from cold Bering Sea and Alaskan feeding grounds to the warm waters of Hawaii and other tropical islands where they mate, calve and rear their young. This population of humpbacks is only a remnant of a tribe which in 1905 numbered about 15,000. Now only about 800 creatures survive and of these about sixty percent visit the Hawaiian nursery.

In early November, whales begin entering the sheltered Four Island area adjacent to the island of Maui and by mid-January significant numbers are present. The population peaks in mid-February and remains relatively high until mid-March. By the end of June they have virtually all withdrawn. This humpback nursery is close to high density human population centres and intensive tourism.

Snorkelling very quietly, Jim Hudnall could hear a humpback singing somewhere below him in the blue depths off the west coast of Maui. A few minutes earlier the researcher had seen the whale raise its flukes and vanish. He knew humpback songsters spend from eighteen to twenty-two minutes below but no human had ever seen one performing. Peering to and fro, he hunted for a glimpse of the whale as the sounds grew louder. Then a trace of something white appeared in the blue abyss. Jim switched from snorkel to the tiny scuba tank he uses for whale study.

"As I descend I can clearly see the outstretched flippers of a motionless humpback. I pause a few feet above its huge flukes. The whale sings a note that is shorter than usual, then turns to look at me. The song ceases and the whale approaches until we are eye to eye. A slow roll and its genital slit faces me. Are we to 'rub bellies' as dolphins do? No longer do I wonder what sex this humpback is. Very definitely a male. Finding me unresponsive to his first advance he glides off, turns around and repeats the performance. Ignored again, he slips away into the near distance and resumes his song."

When Jim Hudnall first came to Maui in 1974, not much was known about the humpback nursery, the singing whales and their living patterns. Jim returned in 1975 and commenced his study using the simplest of equipment, a small inflatable boat, snorkel and his lightweight mini-scuba rig. Jim often operates alone leaving his boat drifting on a sea anchor while he observes and films the whales.

In 1975, he began recording their songs with a hydrophone. This began when he found himself within audible range of a singer. He and his companion, Jim Darling, made snorkel sounds in reply and suspect that the whale may have mimicked them. So Hudnall obtained recording gear to document the songs. From that time he never again ventured a communicative approach, believing it was more important to document the unmodified songs initially.

When I visited Jim in June 1980, the whales had migrated. We discussed our communication model for approaching cetaceans. He was very enthusiastic and felt the time ripe for such an initiative. These days, he said, there are four or five hydrophones in the water off Maui every day during the breeding season. The historical period is over and it is time for an innovative approach.

In his first year of study Jim identified individual whales from the pattern on the underside of the tail flukes. In 1977 he and Jody Solow first met the whale they call Notchy, from a deep notch on its left pectoral, on its dorsal and its tail flukes.

By 1976, he had realized that this technique was ineffective for identifying females with young. Nursing mothers don't dive deeply showing their tail flukes, as their young are incapable of such dives and would be left behind. Jim then discovered the upper surface of the pectoral fin was a distinctive and comparatively easy feature to photograph. With assistants he began a programme of clifftop observation and was able to identify increasing numbers of whales, observe births and maintain a continuous watch on cow/calf activity.

By 1977, whale-watching was in full swing with many observers working in the field and whale tourism was flourishing. In 1979, Jim established the Maui Whale Research Institute which has a photographic catalogue of individual whales, available to researchers.

While with Jim on Maui, I was able to see his films, hear his tapes of whale song and compare notes with him on interlock. In approaching whales Jim shuns the earlier techniques of leaping in front of them from fast boats for a fleeting glimpse, or confusing them by racing around in tight circles. As long as he moves gently towards them over the surface the whales show no fear and approach him curiously. His longest encounters have been with humpback cows and their calves. Baby whales are playful and curious to explore their environment. Often a calf would lead its mother to investigate Jim, coming so close at times he expected to be touched — but at the last moment contact was avoided. Even young calves had this precise body control.

Jim remarked on the special friendship that had developed with Notchy since their first meeting. For three consecutive years he had met this same whale. Gradually it stayed around him longer and longer. He thought it was sick when it came so close he was able to touch it, but days later he saw Notchy with another whale, leaping and racing about in perfect health.

"Do you agree that it is necessary to behave interestingly if you want to extend your time with whales or dolphins in the wild?"

"Absolutely — the whales seem to be very quick to lose interest in people who are not doing anything in the water. But with Notchy it is always we who break contact."

As with our dolphin observations there seems to be some link between the distinctively marked individual that draws our attention and the extra responsiveness of this particular cetacean towards humans.

Besides his work with humpbacks, Jim Hudnall has had considerable experience with grey whales on the west coast of North America from Vancouver Island to Mexico. From him I learnt of another whale nursery — the grey whales of San Ignacio lagoon.

Each northern winter the Californian grey whales migrate south along the North American coastline to warm-water breeding areas in the Baha lagoons of Mexico. By January, the thirty-five-ton cetaceans are beginning to enter San Ignacio and Scammons lagoons and Magdalena Bay where they will court and calve and nurse their young until their departure for the north in May.

In their twelve-foot inflatable, marine ecologists Steve Swartz and Mike Bursk were motoring across the morning calm of San Ignacio lagoon. Sighting three whales leaping acrobatically, they went over to investigate. At close range they observed a courting ritual, the whales seemingly oblivious to their presence. Suddenly the whales vanished — but not for long. The female surfaced ten metres from their boat, circled it slowly and disappeared.

"Moments later," wrote Steve, "she is directly beneath us. Imagine our excitement, watching a huge form rise through the murky water and gently nudge our boat. The two males return and seem eager to participate. They too shove the boat, ever so gently. A whale surfaces vertically and, with a graceful motion, rests its head on a pontoon. Mike touches the rostrum and the whale abruptly backs away. But after the initial contact the whales grow bolder. They continually keep their upper and lower jaws accessible for scratching and massaging and we are willing to accommodate. We completely surrender to this astonishing phenomenon." (*Whalewatcher, Vol. 13 No. 1, 1979.*)

This episode took place during the 1977 breeding season. The whales were not always like this. When Jim Hudnall visited the area in 1974 on a whale observation trip, he saw nothing in the nature of the friendly whale behaviour so common there now. As far back as the early sixties there were stories of grey whales lingering around skiffs and tour boats, but in those days the whales were not trusted near boats and most fishermen avoided them. Commercial whaling of greys had ceased in 1947 but they were still notorious for "violent attacks" on whaling vessels.

With the growth of whale tourism in 1975, reports came in of individual whales following tour boats for periods of up to three hours, circling and rubbing themselves on the hull. Dr Raymond Gilmore tells of a female presenting herself alongside whale-watching skiffs and allowing passengers to pat her head. In 1976, Dr Bruce Cauble had three females with a calf accompany his drifting skiff for an hour with all four repeatedly surfacing to be touched.

Each year the interactions have increased in frequency and quality. During the 1977 season, Steve Swartz found there was a change in the whales' attitude to the presence of observers. Initially the whales showed little attention to scientists watching their daily rituals, but soon individual whales would remain with them for an hour or more. By then up to 1000 people were visiting the lagoon each season. Tour operators can now guarantee every one of their thirty passengers will be able to touch a whale.

One particular female named Amazing Grace has delighted whale-watchers for three consecutive years, with playful innovative behaviour, such as submerging her blowhole to spray people, spy hopping beside the boat to look at occupants, accurately wetting them with side sweeps of her tail and imitating the gurgling sounds of an idling motor with her blowhole just below the surface.

Jim Hudnall showed me raw footage of a film he shot in San Ignacio lagoon in 1980 when, for two hours, eight grey whales circled the tourist skiff, mothers with young playfully interacting with the people. When the time came for the skiff to return to the mother-ship for more tourists the whales seemed to block its path repeatedly. Each time the engine was put in gear a whale would surface at the bow. Eventually the skipper managed to slip through a gap but Jim would have liked to see how the game would have progressed.

The waters of the lagoon are murky and make underwater observation difficult. On two occasions swimmers who approached whales silently, startled them and received a tail slash which, in one case, broke three ribs. Jim Hudnall urges that divers should not enter their private space in this manner. When whales are aware of a human presence their gentleness and the fluid coordination of their movements leave no cause for any fear.

Scientists and lay people are puzzled at the friendly whale behaviour in San Ignacio lagoon. Some say the whales are just curious. Others see it as interspecies communication. Some scientists have used the opportunity to take samples of expired air from blowholes, sample skin parasites or measure heat flow through the skin. Others, less benign, have attached radio transmitter tags. There are indications that this may affect the tagged whale's relationship with its group and others of our species.

A surprising aspect of the "friendly grey whale" phenomenon is its limitation to this one lagoon, but there are indications it is extending — as people along the west coast of North America become ready for it.

For three consecutive years Jim Nollman has played music to migrant grey whales passing his home at Bolinas, near San Francisco. In March one year he was asked to accompany an ocean burial near the Farallon Islands, twenty miles off shore. A small boy's last wish was to be buried with the whales. To Jim's surprise two whales were present, and stayed around the boat for four hours.

"When I got in the water with them they let me come right up to them and, as with the orca, I got scared. I was right next to them — so big and writhing around, you can't tell where one begins and the other ends — just these huge shapes and once in a while I'd see an eye. I said to myself, 'What am I doing here — this is ridiculous!' At that split second they left. I was startled. It was as if I'd slapped their faces. After four hours with them they just dove straight down and I never saw them again. They were reading me. I don't doubt it. It was too sudden. For us to have met whales that day and kept them from their migration for four hours — we felt we'd been honoured."

Dr Peter Beamish is a Canadian bioacoustics specialist who has established his own cetacean research base in Trinity, Newfoundland. Ceta Research Inc. is engaged in studies of humpback, fin and minke whales which are readily accessible in that summer feeding area.

Besides this he set up at Trinity a company, Ocean Contact Ltd which, from June to September each year, provides opportunities for human/cetacean contact. Twelve-member expeditions join Peter on charter yachts and assist his research.

Very soon Peter Beamish found he had a political problem: whales were doing two million dollars' damage a year to fishing nets. Twelve humpbacks had drowned after tangling in the leader section of trap nets. Peter set up a whale rescue service, and his teams have made twenty rescues.

While in Washington D.C., I met Peter and saw the film he has made of this work and was profoundly moved. Risking their own entanglement two scuba divers struggle to cut clear a web of heavy ropes enmeshing a humpback. Eventually they cut the last strand and the whale is free. The final frame, in Peter's film, freezes in a unique human/whale gesture: the whale gently touches the hands of the two divers with its huge rostrum. I was reminded of the traditional Maori greeting or "mihimihi", when foreheads are pressed together for a flow of understanding. (Europeans misconstrue this as "rubbing noses".)

David and Gundi Day were near Cowley Islet in the Galapagos Islands on 11 January 1978. Their fifty-seven-foot schooner was chugging along at six knots in light, sunny conditions when a broad, dark-grey back surfaced and blew, almost touching their port side. David instantly slowed to three knots fearing a collision, but soon realized there was no such danger — the whale began to frolic from side to side on their bow performing more than a dozen barrel rolls and revealing its light belly. A Bryde's whale, it began ducking under the hull and taking an interest in the dinghy trailing astern. It surfaced with its head side on to look at them.

David said to his wife, "Gundi, why don't you get into the dinghy. You can probably touch him. It seems he wants to make contact."

Several times the whale blew alongside and behind the dinghy and Gundi was able to touch it twice. She rubbed its lips and dark pieces of skin stuck to her hand. Before this it had not once touched the dinghy, so when it came up from behind and lifted the stern of the dinghy gently up and down with its nose, it seemed to them the whale was returning the touch. Holding its head high out of the water it nodded as if in response. It rose even higher in an attempt to look over the stern of the schooner. After nearly two hours the whale appeared to tire and the Days decided to increase speed, leaving it behind. (*Marine Mammals News*.)

202

Eric Morris was cruising between two atolls in the Tuamotu Archipelago. The wind was so light his thirty-seven-foot Searunner trimaran was ghosting along at less than one knot. He sighted the white plumes of whales a mile to leeward. Half an hour later he saw them alter course. Moving lazily over the surface two large bulls led their pod curving towards him. From the bulbous heads and distinctive spouts he knew these were sperm whales. One of the bulls did a deep dive towards him while a group of cows and calves began to frolic just ahead. Eric lowered his sails and to his own amazement found himself preparing to snorkel with the whales. On entering he found a huge tail hovering directly beneath him. It was the bull that had disappeared in a deep dive minutes before. It was floating motionless, head down, body vertical. When it moved its tail and swung its head towards Eric, he leapt aboard his ship in fear. As the rest of the whales slowly approached, his qualms reduced and he got back in. One of the cows swam very close. Eric again sought refuge on his boat. The whale then stood vertically in the water lifting her head clear to look at him, revealing her long, thin lower jaw.

When the whales left, Eric motored after them, keen for more contact. This time he snorkelled to within fifty feet of a female with three calves around her. They appeared to bolt in fear. A bull advanced. From his boat Eric watched it gnash its jaws and thrash its tail with loud cracks. It seemed clear he had gone too far in pressing his company on them and he left. (*Multihulls* magazine, November 1979.)

In May 1973, as the nuclear protest ship *Fri* entered the test zone near Tahiti, six crew swam with a whale. Approached for close scrutiny, Peter Yates felt a rush of fear. That instant, the whale sounded and then rose high out of the water.

In November 1980, the crew of the twenty-five-metre purse-seiner *Pirimai* were alarmed when a fifteen-metre southern right whale approached their vessel but when it returned two weeks later, they decided to accept its friendly advances. It was a glassy calm day off the Kaikoura coast of New Zealand. Within metres of the ship the whale poked its head out of the water, examined the old wooden fishing-boat, almost within touching distance.

The skipper Chris Sharp donned basic diving gear and joined it in the water. Several metres down, a huge eye scrutinized him only centimetres away. The human and the whale stared at each other and then both surfaced to breathe. The crew watched in amazement as the massive form swam slowly past their skipper, carefully twisting its tail to avoid contact. Two more of the crew decided to join him. Deckhand Simon Reid was lifted half out of the water on the huge tail. Peter Kelliher jumped in and swam over.

"The whale was arching through the water and lifted me up clear of the sea before gliding on out from under me."

Almost every newspaper in New Zealand carried their picture on its front page, Peter astride the cetacean's back, right alongside the fishing vessel. ("Pirimai" means in Maori, "Keep close to me.")

To the press Chris Sharp remarked, "How anyone could kill an animal as unique and intelligent as this is impossible to comprehend. There is no doubt it was communicating. It showed absolutely no aggression and made no sudden movements — even when we jumped from the deck into the water right next to it or climbed on its back."

Clearly there has been a major advance in friendly encounters between whales and humans in recent years, and it is hoped the process will have advanced even while this book is at press. To some extent it is related to the growing confidence people show towards whales, now that we are behaving more benignly towards them.

But already I forsee a new problem arising for the whales — a lack of human perspective in our anthropocentric approaches to them. As the grey whales of San Ignacio lagoon have indicated with their tail slashes, tourists, photographers and scientists must observe an interspecies ethic when we enter the whale's personal space. From Patagonia I have just received accounts of several incidents where divers have been injured when sneaking up silently on unsuspecting right whales to snatch photos of them. These whales have not deliberately injured anybody but make it abundantly clear when they feel harassed, charging boats at full speed and then making gentle contacts, splashing with their wide, flat pectoral fins while circling or filling their blowholes with water to expel it at occupants. Underwater they may swing their heads violently to indicate annoyance.

According to my informant, Dr Ricardo Mandojana, such incidents are provoked when a couple are mating and people get too close or, with a swimmer approaching from behind, a sudden hand or swim fin entering the animal's visual field may cause an alarm reaction — and broken ribs.

For the future of human/whale relationships we must remember: when we enter the sea in their vicinity, we may be intruding in their bedroom, or their nursery. After centuries of killing them, we must now extend to the whales the common courtesies we know are essential with our own species. Manifesting our own intelligence towards whales, who knows what rich relationships we may enjoy?

204

16

Cetacean intelligence and the ethics of killing them

OPENING THE MAIL on 18 March 1980 I found the offer of an expense-free journey to Washington D.C. A letter from Dr Ray Gambell, secretary of the International Whaling Commission, invited me to attend their special meeting at the Smithsonian Institution on the intelligence of cetaceans and the ethics of killing them. Just before walking down our long driveway to collect the mail I'd been drafting a "sorry but" letter to Dr Lyall Watson who had sent me the original invitation. A letter I'd begun some days before but hadn't felt like completing. . .

I immediately set to work preparing a paper for the conference titled "Towards a Communications Model in Approaching Cetaceans" in which I reviewed some of the things Project Interlock has learnt. Even as I wrote I had a sinking feeling that much of our knowledge was insufficiently based on scientific research for such an august body.

Then came a telegram from Maryland asking me to bring our film for screening and Dr Simon Cotton's wild orca footage.

With an hour's stopover in Tahiti, just long enough to take in a pastel sunrise, and a two-day break in Los Angeles, I arrived in Washington fresh from our forest world, like a dolphin in a new tank. In retrospect, Los Angeles is an excellent entry point to the United States. Culture shock can never be much worse than that, and in comparison springtime Washington with its old-world buildings, open spaces and deciduous trees was reassuring of some stability and order in a world gone mad.

As I entered into four days of conference on a subject so very dear to me, with people who largely shared my enthusiasm, it was hard to believe I was in that fabled capital — supreme target in the nuclear standoff — until one lunch hour I discovered the building I was passing was the White House.

Others must have shared my feelings, attending a conference on a subject that interests them passionately and meeting in the flesh a whole range of people already long familiar through reading and correspondence. For me it was sheer ecstasy, with so much to learn from the very frontiers of cetacean research — like being in the debriefing room after a journey to the stars.

At the thirtieth annual meeting of the International Whaling Commission in London, in 1979, it had been agreed to convene a special meeting to consider first, cetacean behaviour and intelligence as relevant to population assessment and management and secondly, the ethics of killing cetaceans. Financial support was provided by the I.W.C., the Delphinid Research Institute, Animal Welfare Institute and the governments of Australia and the United States.

With over 100 participants the conference included scientists, representatives of both whaling and fishing industries, conservationists, philosophers and bureaucrats. Some fifty papers were tabled and most of the authors were given the opportunity to speak to them before general discussion. The proceedings were taped and filmed. Several relevant documentaries were screened at various times.

Among the conclusions of the meeting it was largely agreed that no species of whale should be made extinct, nor any individual populations endangered; that cetaceans are a matter for international concern; that the infliction on them of unnecessary suffering and pain was unjustifiable and that there exist unique opportunities to investigate communication among cetaceans and between cetaceans and humans, and every care must be taken to ensure this is not jeopardised.

A strong plea was made for much more research on living cetaceans under natural conditions, especially underwater observations, as such techniques have so far yielded valuable biological information about a few protected species. Studies in which individual cetaceans are recognised and their lives followed over the years have yielded information on population structure unavailable from traditional means. The extent to which such benign research methods are compatible with conventional methods, or with continued whaling, is a question that was left open.

It would be beyond the scope of my book to do justice to the huge volume of material tabled at the conference. I was particularly interested in the scientific assessments of the cetacean brain, the reports of field research into cetacean behaviour and the ethical debate on whether whaling should be condoned. Five scientists presented papers which made the highest claims for the cetacean brain, each from a different angle.

Professor Harry Jerison, a neurobiologist at U.C.L.A., is a specialist in brain evolution and intelligence. Since I'd already studied his submission to the Australian Inquiry into Whales and Whaling (1978), I listened with deep respect to this scientist and spoke to him afterwards with equally deep admiration. For he and his colleagues, all leaders in their fields, have not been afraid to assert themselves boldly in the world forum concerning cetacean intelligence. The evidence of these brain scientists had a major influence on Australia's shift from being a whaling nation, to a leader in the battle to save the whales.

Jerison approaches the cetacean brain from the viewpoint of its gross anatomy. Comparing vertebrate species he noticed a trend toward the evolution of relatively larger brains that led him to a new definition of biological intelligence. He saw brain enlargement as an adaptation that enables the mammalian brain "to construct a real world as a possible world in which the events of a lifetime can take place." From an overwhelming load of neural information our brains consistently construct the real world of our experience.

Animals with bigger bodies could be expected to have larger brains to control them but Jerison established that there was a residual factor in brain size related to information processing *beyond* that required to control the body. This factor provides an estimate of an animal's biological intelligence which he calls "encephalisation" based on the ratio of brain volume to body area. Brain volume determines the number of brain cells and their interconnections: the brain's information-handling capacity. The body surface of an animal relates to the capacity for information processing that could be expected. The ratio of the two gives an estimate of the total processing capacity in relation to the amount of brain required to handle ordinary body functions.

Of the 40,000 known species of vertebrates about two-thirds operate with a minimal amount of brain. Encephalised species range through the sharks and birds to the mammals. The whales were highly encephalised at least twenty million years ago.

The biological intelligence of a creature should reflect the richness of the real world which its brain creates. Different brains construct different realities. Higher grades of biological intelligence would represent more complex realities — more elements integrated into a real world, a longer past, more alternative, possible futures and a more comprehensive present.

Jerison believes the most important thing may be that in this order of mammals there are species such as dolphins, orca and the sperm whale that have brains in the human range of encephalisation, the functions of which remain unknown at this time. There are no other animals in a comparable position. The enlarged brain alone is sufficient evidence that unusual information processing goes on in cetaceans, especially in highly encephalised species like the bottlenose dolphin.

It has been suggested that echolocation could account for the volume of the whale's brain, but Jerison discounts this explanation as insufficient for such a degree of encephalisation. As an organ the brain is too demanding for us to assume such expansion would occur without special needs. While both bats and whales have unusual auditory and vocal adaptations it is not so much the analysis of the signal as the final synthesis that would reflect the richness of reality generated by a highly encephalised brain. We could compare the eye of a frog with a human eye.

Professor Jerison believes we should assume that unusual mental processes occur in whales which will be quite different from those we know ourselves.

"A major challenge for the future is to discover this alien intelligence as it were, right here on earth."

Russian scientist A.V. Yablokov was unable to fly to Washington but sent along some penetrating comments on the agenda. In problem-solving experiments Soviet researchers have found the intelligence of bottlenose dolphins to be on a development level equivalent to four to seven-year-old infants. Yablokov said that the accurate assessment of cetacean populations by standard methods is made difficult by the possible presence of an efficient system of natural population control dependant not just on population level and food supplies, as with most animals, "but also on social-intellectual factors."

Stressing the need for new, more adequate methods of cetacean study, Yablokov claims that existing methods for investigating higher forms of intelligence are not sufficiently objective. The Russian scientist feels that it may prove altogether impossible for us to ever understand an alien, non-human system of thinking from the current anthropocentric viewpoint. Since some cetaceans have the most advanced brain associative regions of all animals, highly complex social structures and behaviours, "this all makes us believe that cetacean intelligence is a phenomenon with no analogies in the animal world."

The remarks of Jean-Paul Fortum-Gouin provide an apt conclusion to this section of the conference. The prominent anti-whaling activist said there are only two dozen men in the world working in the field of neuro-anatomy and they are all basically agreed in respect of the cetacean brain. He quoted Russian professor Alfred Berzin of the Cetacean Research Laboratory at Tinro: "The sperm whale brain must possess an extreme functional plasticity and practically inexhaustible possibilities for establishing links between stimuli and the form of reactions. Its structure is such that this can be said to be a thinking animal capable of displaying high intellectual abilities."

During the conference I learnt of three American research programmes in progress, each working toward teaching captive bottlenose dolphins a human language.

This research has been spurred on by the reported successes with chimpanzees and a gorilla. So far the ape level of naming and syntax, using a gestural language, is comparable to a two and a half-year-old human. Koko the gorilla, by February 1980, had a vocabulary of 756 signs.

Dr Louis Herman showed us a film of his research work in Hawaii where a pair of dolphins are being taught separate artificial languages, one auditory with computer-generated whistles and pulses and the other visual, using arm and hand gestures. Both dolphins have achieved the same learning speed and there has been a transfer between them from one mode and the other. They are both handling three-word sentences and have surpassed chimpanzees in syntax.

Watching the film I noticed that the dolphin responded to the gestures of the blindfolded researcher *before* they had been completed . . . Dr Herman explained to me later that the dolphin has 120- degree vision and so could move off to perform the signalled instructions before they were completed. I wish there could be a control against the possibility of ESP. . .

In California Dr John Lilly is well advanced with Project Janus, programming a computer language to interface with dolphins using high-frequency sounds in their normal frequency range. So far he is encouraged by an exchange in which captive dolphins matched high-frequency bursts with the machine.

Jean-Paul Fortum-Gouin, who owns the Delphinid Research Institute in the Florida Keys, told me he is confident that dolphins are so smart they can learn to respond to an oral human language. People in the Canary Islands communicate with complex whistle patterns. In their first year his researchers developed a fifty-word vocabulary with four dolphins based on whistle pitch and duration.

Somehow I suspect all three avenues of research may prove successful. Already the dolphins are showing significant progress which suggests they can meet us whatever bridge we construct. Progress may take unexpected directions when we allow them the initiative, by working with free-ranging dolphins, but as yet our oceanic limitations have made the pool approach more attractive to researchers.

Back in 1974, eminent ethologist W.H. Thorpe said that chimpanzee sign language studies make the distinction between man and animal on linguistic grounds far less defensible. Subsequent dolphin studies strongly reinforce this view.

Well known for his research into ape language capacities, Eugene Linden, author of *Apes, Men and Language*, presented to the meeting a summary of fourteen years of work in this field which he claims is redefining man's place in nature, but not without considerable controversy. Much of the argument has arisen from double blind experiments in which researchers have set themselves apart from the animals to dumbly record their responses. Such an experimental design breaks down because rigid controls interfere with the apes' interest in using the language we teach them to communicate with us. The more successful experimenters have developed a close rapport with their subjects but this is criticised by others as unscientific. The scientific world will have to adjust to a revolution in its view of reality, if we are to come to terms with evidence of intelligence and language in both apes and dolphins.

The biggest question remains: how do cetaceans communicate with each other? Dr Saayman of South Africa expressed surprise that so many researchers approach the problem with research strategies more suited to the study of human speech, or sound generation in terrestrial mammals. He said the hypothesis that dolphins may communicate complex information through summarised acoustic images or analogues has not yet been proven or disproven, but they have the capacity for it.

"Researchers Tietz and Taylor suggest that amplitude modulation of a single-frequency sweep within two khz to fourteen khz is the means of acoustic communication in bottlenose dolphins. Dolphin whistle modulations can be correlated with sonar echoes associated with specific objects but in 'summary' form."

The meeting reached a high point of excitement when several researchers presented evidence of cetacean intelligence based on field studies of free-ranging creatures. Because of inherent difficulties such work is all too rare and the audience registered a thirst for more.

With superb film footage Jim Hudnall told of his direct observations of humpback whales in Hawaiian waters, describing a solitary male hovering neutrally buoyant in the water column moving his pectorals slowly back and forth as they droop from his body while he sings. Stressing the need for much more underwater research into the realm of consciousness of the humpback whale and their capacities for communication, Hudnall described the way absolutely silent cows with calves appear to communicate without touching each other. He outlined a wide range of underwater humpback behaviours which emphasized the need for further observation in the ocean.

Dr Steven Swartz of San Diego University told of the way grey whales in San Ignacio lagoon have modified their behaviour towards tourists over the past five years and now solicit physical contact.

Dr Peter Beamish, a bioacoustician from Newfoundland, told of his research into the acoustics and behaviour of baleen whales. He has discovered they use sonar for navigation but not to locate food, and suggested that for these whales sound/touch may be one sense: a low frequency sound pulse could be felt by the bristle on their heads. He described social cooperation in feeding wherein one whale may assist those behind it, with no immediate advantage to itself.

Dr Roger Payne reviewed the global research into the songs of humpback whales over the past twenty years. Whales 3000 miles apart sing the same song but each breeding season it changes from an elaboration of the final phrases of the previous year's song. Atlantic songs differ from the Pacific but follow the same laws of composition. No other animal changes its song over a whole population like this. As ethologist W.H. Thorpe has remarked: "Surely one of the most remarkable discoveries concerning animal communication in recent times."

With contagious enthusiasm Roger Payne then described in detail the elaborate way humpback whales create spiral bubble nets to enmesh fish prey, varying the size of the bubble along a helical path so they reach the surface uniformly spaced. Such manipulations would have to be calculated precisely. He told us that in high winds Patagonian right whales have been observed using their tails as sails, gliding along for up to twenty-two minutes on a broad reach.

Roger Payne stressed that we are on the verge of discovering another culture in the ocean, in the light of which a new international ethic like the Nuremburg code must be established with the utmost urgency.

I envisaged the people speaking to us from the rostrum as archaeologists reporting discoveries of an ancient civilisation to a wondering world — not a story based on potsherds and ruins but the living remnants of oceanic tribes we are still engaged in slaughtering.

On my third evening in Washington I walked into a superb little theatre, fresh from an excellent buffet dinner — when the screen hit my eyes: a sandy cove piled with dolphin bodies at the edge of a crimson sea. Japanese men in wetsuits were hauling living dolphins out by the tails and stabbing them with lances in a picnic atmosphere. Helpless in repressed agony, a hundred viewers half a world away watched film-maker Hardy Jones' silent footage from the second Iki Island dolphin massacre. Bottlenose dolphins flapping like so many tuna acting out their torment for the cameras, their grinning faces expressing nothing of their suffering. A silent window into a hideous reality — the theatrette wet-eyed in pain. Just along from me sat eight Japanese delegates sharing the space while this sacred cow of western culture was fully revealed to them.

Fortunately for human relations Jim Nollman of Interspecies Communication Inc. had already spoken to the conference about Iki, whence he had flown direct to Washington; his companion Dexter Cate still in a Japanese jail for cutting the fishermen's nets to release the dolphins. Nollman's words helped build an important atmosphere. At the previous I.W.C. meeting in London, blood had been thrown at the Japanese delegates. Jim described the Iki slaughter in all its horror but stressed the point that these were just ordinary, decent human beings puzzled at the world's attitude.

"It's not us and them in this matter," he reminded the conference. "It's us and us." That hit home because virtually every nation there was a whaling nation in the recent past. A climate of cetacean tolerance and mutual respect prevailed and the keen arguments remained on an academic level. The Japanese listened to all that was said and their viewpoint was received with equal consideration. They attended all the social gatherings and communication with them was warm and sensitive.

The ethics of killing

When the conference shifted its attention to the second half of its agenda, the ethics of killing cetaceans, the Japanese scored some telling points as they questioned western attitudes to factory-raised domestic animals and explained why, to them, the fox is sacred to the harvest and foxhunting an equal affront in their eye.

That the ethics of man's exploitation of the cetacea could ever be discussed under the auspices of the International Whaling Commission is evidence of the major shift occurring in the locus of human thought, partly as a result of advances in our science. Modern research cannot decide our ethical codes, which are the decisions of collective humanity, but science does give us new evidence on which to base such decisions.

In recent times the old man/beast dichotomy on which western civilisation is based, has been chopped from under us. From Aristotle's "Great Chain of Being" to Darwin's misunderstood evolutionary theory, western society derives its ethics from the assumption that man is unique among animals, more evolved than the cetaceans, the only creature aware of its own existence.

Appropriate research was cited at the conference which refutes these traditional attitudes, showing that humans are not unique in terms of tool use, cultural transmission of technological skills, language or self-consciousness.

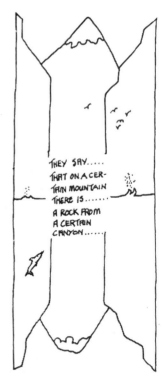

As Dr Teizo Ogawa
of Tokyo University
puts it:
The whale is
one of two
mountain peaks
of evolution
on planet earth:
on land,
human beings,
and in the sea,
cetacea.
Drawing by Hal Chapman

211

As a basis for ethics, man can no longer ignore that a continuum exists between humans and other species and an appropriate new system of ethics has to be developed.

Some would rest it on ecological imperatives, which urge that man should assume a role of ecologically sound stewardship in a new age of Earth-minding. During an exceptionally destructive period, western culture has achieved such power over nature that it is viewed as a resource, and its component plants and animals and delicate ecosystems, objects for human exploitation.

Dr Michael Fox complained that the ecosphere has been regarded as a self-serving "egosphere" and urged that human survival and evolution depend on the liberation of the human mind from such egocentricity: "We are on the threshold of such a transformation now."

Other arguments were voiced that rest on psychological grounds. It was suggested that in the new continuum we should extend human rights to other creatures following the same rules used in allocating rights to ourselves: granting to babies, children and mental retardates human rights according to their levels of consciousness but guaranteeing all of them, as self-conscious beings, the right to be free from the gratuitous infliction of physical or psychological suffering.

Since the cetaceans are now seen to be at least the equal of non-human primates many scientists regard their unnecessary and cruel slaughter as no longer ethically defensible. Cetaceans are the *only creatures* hypothesized to have a high degree of consciousness, which are commercially harvested even though there exist alternative sources of all the products derived. There can be no doubt that whales are caused significant pain by present-day whaling techniques. It takes between two and five minutes for a whale to die and in some cases up to twenty-five minutes. The killing of intelligent, social animals causes feelings akin to grief in mothers deprived of their young or members of a group deprived of one of their number. Philosopher Tom Regan asserted that the pain whales are made to endure is unnecessary, gratuitous, and stands morally condemned.

And so the question of cetacean rights is gaining momentum in a world which only decades earlier would have been puzzled at international concern over the morality of killing cetaceans. During the seventies scientists made many discoveries regarding the intelligence, playfulness and grace of cetaceans which were widely and rapidly publicised by popular books and articles. This same period saw the creation of many oceanaria where the public watched dolphins and other small cetaceans as trained performers. Television shows and films presented them in acting roles. Increased public exposure to cetaceans combined with the new appreciation of their intelligence and other "human" characteristics has caused a dramatic increase in public concern about the morality of killing cetaceans.

Dr John Lilly has been a proponent of the legal rights of cetaceans for several years now. To the conference, he pointed out evidence of ethical codes among cetaceans themselves and urged that they should no longer be considered as property, industrial resources or stocks but should have the freedom of the oceans with the legal rights of humans. He stressed the need for research into communication with cetaceans.

"We must learn their needs, their ethics, their philosophy, to find out who we are on this planet, in this galaxy. The extraterrestrials are here, in the sea. We can, with dedicated efforts, communicate with them. If and when we break the communication barrier, then we and the cetaceans can work out our differences and our correspondences."

Jean-Paul Fortum-Gouin spoke eloquently on behalf of the cachalot, or sperm whale, which is his totem animal:

"If whales are the common heritage of mankind, then one five billionth of each whale is my share. Why should a small, destructive industry profit from these gentle, friendly giants at the expense of the future?"

Therein, I thought, lies the fallacy which the whaling nations propound in making analogies with the consumption of domestic animals: the whales are inhabitants of the world's ocean, not a Japanese pond. Equally fallacious is the argument that whalemeat provides essential nutrition for mankind in a starving, over-populated world. The oil consumed by the whaling industry could more usefully be converted directly into stock feed. Whale flesh is an increasingly expensive delicacy.

For psychologist Graeme Saayman from Capetown, the pivotal question is whether cetaceans are self-aware. According to the ethics of psychology human subjects have the right to consent to experimental situations and may elect to withdraw:

"Accumulating evidence from recent field studies suggest that mammals other than man and including at least some of the cetacea, have the conceptual abilities to form abstractions of a kind which clearly imply the emergence of a degree of self-consciousness."

Saayman contends that no amount of scientific evidence can decide an ethical question of this nature. If man is an ethical creature he has to evaluate the outcome of his actions by the equally important feeling functions of his mind.

"He is answerable to that greater human collective from which, in the end, he requires his ultimate mandate. For what is ethical is what is prescribed by collective humanity and NOT by a limited number of individuals, whatever the investment they may have made in academic degrees and intellectual pursuits."

Saayman concluded by quoting Rudyard Kipling, in the words of Akela, pack leader, seated on the Council Rock: "Ye know the law — ye know the law. Look well, O Wolves."

17

Dolphin journey

WHEN THE CETACEAN Intelligence meeting had concluded, on 2 May I set out on the strangest journey in my life. In a receptive state I took a back seat and just let things happen. I had invitations from people at the conference whose work I was keen to explore further on their home ground: Toni and John Lilly in Los Angeles, Jim Nollman in Bolinas, Jim Hudnall and Dr Bernd Wursig in Hawaii, were on the top of my travelling list but I was not to know I was in line to meet so many others — to be passed along a warm chain of human contacts.

At Dulles airport Jim Nollman and I met up with the Japanese delegates and had an amiable breakfast together. With twinkling eyes the head of the Japan Whaling Association took Jim's dolphin lapel pin and put it in his own jacket. As we flew over to San Francisco Jim and I felt jubilant that humanity had been preserved in an arena wherein bitter conflict could so easily have prevailed. It seemed unbelievable that both factions were leaving the conference with a view of each other as normal human beings. Even though differing views on cetaceans could have led to anger and possibly violence, something in our common concern for them forged a bond both parties seemed to value. It was as if the refusal of cetaceans to retaliate violently towards their human persecutors had created a spirit that pervaded the whole conference. Never before have I been party to a dispute in which opponents avoided seeing each other as objects of hatred and loathing. It has been said that the Smithsonian meeting was a turning point for human/cetacean relationships.

As my dolphin journey unfolded I began to keep a journal and prefer to use this mode to convey the immediacy of it all, while at the same time conscious of the need for compression if this book is not to become unwieldy or steal too much from events that I suspect may lead to its sequel.

Journal, 2 May 1980: "This is the first peaceful moment since I left our forest home eight days ago. This morning I am stretched out on the sofa in Michael and Morgan Wiese's lounge here at Sausalito, San Francisco. I arrived at mid-day yesterday after flying in from Washington with Jim Nollman. Above me on the wall is a huge blow-up from their film 'Dolphin'.

"The four-day cetacean meeting is now a gross weight of paper in my suitcase and a kaleidoscope of memories so rich, it would take another book to recount them all. It was a tremendous success. I have made many exciting contacts and our film was surprisingly well received. Apart from that and tabling a paper, I didn't contribute much to the conference itself; as yet our research is beyond the point of academic acceptance, but on a personal level many people responded to it with enthusiasm. I have a clear insight into where things are at, what is going on in other parts of the world, and how things are likely to develop.

"Whaling is in retreat — the key issues are clearly defined and the pressure is going to become enormous to halt it — before it is too late for the whales.

"At this stage my view is that we should cease killing cetaceans not simply because of what we now know of their intelligence and behaviour but because we can never expect to discover the extent to which communication might develop while we continue to destroy them. Consistency demands we should first demonstrate some degree of ecological intelligence ourselves. What purpose could there ever be in voyaging to the stars if we fail to take the first step and bridge our loneliness on Earth?

"I've now flown right across the U.S. twice in window seats on clear days and glimpsed three huge cities at ground level. We New Zealanders are billionaires and they are paupers living on the brink of chaos — but they are used to it. People are extremely kind but Michael Wiese says I am meeting a special set. Maybe so, but generally as I move around I feel at ease with casual contacts and have not met with any unpleasantry as yet, which is incredible when you consider the pressures people are under. The sanity of car drivers in L.A. is food for thought. Best driving I've ever seen — a matter of survival as the road energy is colossal.

"L.A. is built in a desert area by a putrid ocean and has no food production in its environs. Supermarkets hold a four-day stock. Water and electricity comes from 700 miles away. A few small oil well pumps bow and scrape in the midst of all the swank seaside apartments. The beaches are the ugliest coastal scenery I have *ever* seen, yet competition to live in this zone is unbelievable.

"Today Michael has arranged for me to meet Dr Jeffrey Mishlove, author of *The Roots of Consciousness* and the first person to gain a doctorate in parapsychology. He has his own research laboratory and is keen to discuss aspects of our dolphin research.

Bolinas

6 May: "I am in a safe haven here at Bolinas with Jim Nollman. Tomorrow I am to give a talk and film to a graduate group at the parapsychology department of John F. Kennedy University, Orinda, and then fly to L.A. Ray Kleiman will meet me at the airport — a relief because it is absolute pandemonium at that hour on a Friday — taxis are impossible. I'd hate to be a tourist in this country!

"These few days of tranquility at Bolinas have saved me. I was at the point where I felt like bolting — just cutting loose, grabbing the first plane home and to hell with all these cities. I've had a royal time and people are so very good to me but ugh — the environment!

"I've spent two days out at Antioch with the New Frontiers Institute people, Richard and Cherie Gierek, who have been exploring the possibilities of ESP communication with dolphins through group hypnosis.

"On my last night in San Francisco, Dr Jeffrey Mishlove arranged a second showing of our film, this time to a group of his friends, all people interested in parapsychology and curious to know what has been going on in this field between humans and dolphins, through dreams, visualizations and physical transactions. (While I have hesitated to present much of this paranormal material in this book, I had with me a file of such reports, a fast expanding aspect of our project and something we were quite unprepared for when we set out to observe dolphins in the wild.)

"Among Jeff's guests were an architect involved with N.A.S.A., a top particle physicist, two authors of books on dreams, a Jungian scholar and several advanced students and lecturers in parapsychology. I was amazed at the interest our film aroused in these people and the acceptance this subject has gained in the U.S.

"Jeffrey Mishlove got on the phone and arranged for me to meet the Mobius Group, a parapsychic research team based in L.A., who have been using distant perception or ESP to locate undersea ruins in Alexandria, Egypt and Mayan relics in Cozumel, and wish to become involved with dolphins. The group seeks practical applications for what is now a proven human faculty since the publication of the research of Puthoff and Targ at Stanford University*.

"The following day Jim Nollman brought me out here: Bolinas would be the most interesting town I've so far seen. The name is Spanish for whale. A peninsula on which handbuilt houses are scattered in scrub and tree. Yesterday we had a day in the sun on a houseboat, transcribing tapes and recording an interview for my book. I saw my first hummingbird — like a large whizzing, highspeed bumblebee, or tiny meteorite.

"I've now met four authors of books all working in parapsychic areas relevant to this aspect of the dolphin study and have copies of their works. Dr Michael Samuels of Bolinas is a case in point. A qualified M.D., he tossed in his conventional medical practice and now teaches people to care for themselves using visualization techniques — very relevant to the dolphin communication hypothesis. His exquisite book *Seeing with the Mind's Eye* is really a do-it-to-yourself manual and uses art history and photography to instruct.

"As New Zealanders we are so very lucky to be where we are! This world is on the brink of collapse and few seem to realize it. But once it was very beautiful. Twenty miles from where I sit at Bolinas atomic wastes lie on the sea floor at the Farallon Is. Dumped long ago, before the rules were made, they have imploded. Huge, mutant sponges grow on them. The lagoon here is very shallow — it was once a navigable port

*"A Perceptual Channel for Information Transfer over Kilometre Distances." Proceedings of the IEEE. March 1976.

216

for the export of logs. Redwoods. Like our kauris the giant redwoods have gone — just patches of tertiary growth on the hills that rise to 3000 feet between here and San Francisco. The harbour silted up. The seaward cliffs of the Bolinas 'Mesa' are collapsing — soft, porridgy rock with patches of white encrustation on the lower third. The houses above are threatened by landslides. I found that the white patches are septic tank exudations. My nose told me that. It doesn't help the stability of the cliff and spoils the sea coast. A dead elephant seal, a dead skate, a cabezon, a bird — a litter line of dead sealife.

"Ten years ago Bolinas made a bid to save itself. An oil slick threatened to destroy the lagoon. People rallied round and managed to keep it at bay. The community awareness that resulted led to two major decisions: the Bolinas people bought up the remaining real estate and built a sewage farm on it. They established a complete moratorium on new buildings. Jim and I had our evening meal on a hill crest in the middle of the sewage farm. The birds, trees and grasses didn't seem to know it was there. Nor would I, if Jim hadn't explained it to me. But now, I am told, the energy and creativity that saved Bolinas has wound down. Those people are tired and have withdrawn to their homes. A town of welfare mothers, craftsmen and the very rich."

Los Angeles again

10 May: "I feel a lot nearer to New Zealand now — the Pacific is lapping the steps outside Ray and Miki's Malibu Colony home where I arrived last night after giving the lecture at Orinda and flying to L.A. Phew! This is the most strenuous endurance test I've ever taken. I keep getting the urge to 'scram' across the ocean on the next plane. But people are so very kind to me everywhere. This afternoon Miki will drive me out to Dekker Canyon to see Toni and John Lilly.

"This Malibu Colony must be one of the strangest villages on Earth — or its most expensive concentration camp. The natives act in films and collect Rolls-Royce cars — a neighbour has four. A seaside settlement, the colony has high wire fences on three sides, its entrance protected by a guardhouse and guns. If this is what great wealth provides Angelinos, I have no envy.

"I've explored the tidal lagoon that runs out of Malibu canyon and could not find a single living organism in it — apparently kids play in it on hot days and no doubt it abounds with viruses and bacteria but I saw no crabs, worms, molluscs, shrimps or sprats — just a telltale confetti of sewage particles. I would not have believed this could happen to a tidal estuary. In front of this house starlets and beach boys dabble in impoverished tidepools. Nearby, on the famous Malibu break, surfers are riding waves so contaminated by sewage they have to get injections. On smoggy days the surfers and tennis players of the colony must go indoors after half an hour's activity because their lungs hurt too much. Those Angelinos who can afford imported supplies never drink their tap water. "How long," my host Ray Kleiman asked, "will it be before we have to import our air?" And he was *not* joking.

"I am wondering whether a global conference on human intelligence is not long overdue. How can it possibly be that a people who have voyaged to the moon can allow themselves to poison in their own wastes? It is all so much worse than I had suspected: the water, the air, the sea, the earth are all in visible stages of destruction in Los Angeles. Its inhabitants frighten me the way they've become habituated to this degradation, resigned to it, evading its harsh realities. They call their dingy car-gas soup a 'fog' and enthuse at the brilliant sunset colours — to me like the rainbow rings of oil on water. Even an H-bomb blast has a certain deadly beauty.

"It seems that man is incapable of arresting this process — too inflexible in living patterns to heed such bold warnings and alter course. I would have thought the technosociety capable of overcoming these problems, once they reached such drastic proportions. But now I see the world's technological nerve centre is not coping. We have an enormous amount to learn from the whales, with their thirty million years of survival, without their ever speaking a word. . ."

The Lillys

12 May: "Arriving at the Lillys' at 1.30 yesterday I met two men polishing the floor tiles of an elaborate home. I found John, his teenage daughter and her boyfriend, in a room full of electronic gadgetry setting up computer hardware for the Project Janus experiment in communication with dolphins.

"After a lunch of chicken and white wine we had a pleasant rap in the lounge: they liked Jim Nollman's interspecies music tape and made two copies of it. John rang Burgess Meredith and arranged a videocassette copy of our film. He likes the idea of the dolphin suit but wonders whether our long arms might suit us to a humpback configuration. I shared with the Lillys much of the key material in this book, in the hope that when they are ready to field-test their computer array, they may know where to find receptive dolphins — like the remote Monkey Mians. One problem, I learnt, was that John is in great need of funds to get him through the next phases of his research. Project Janus is an expensive affair and desperately needs a benevolent sponsor.

"John gave me three of his books that I'd not read. One of them, *The Deep Self* is on the subject of isolation tanks. Flicking through its pages I asked if the isolation tank was still going.

"'Yes, want to try it?' asked Toni.

"I showered, donned a bathrobe and just on sundown picked my way up the hill to a nondescript shed. A hothouse warmth flowed over me as I entered a gently lit space, full of gadgetry and dominated by a large fibreglass tank with a curving, counter-weighted entry hatch. Boarding the innerspace ship nude I found ten inches of lukewarm epsom salts and stretched out. Just as in the Dead Sea the saline water supported my body perfectly and I relaxed into a nice drift of thought. My journey and all those I'd met sifted slowly through my mind.

"At times I rested my hands on my head or abdomen rather than let them float extended. This relieved a discomfort that developed in my armjoints, distracting the mind. The sound of a jet plane, the plop of condensing water or a sudden sting of cool, were major events. In the

218

steamy warmth there was no awareness of any odour or light, while touch and sound were almost absent.

"There was no question of sleep but my consciousness must have undergone quite a change when an emerald lake appeared on my mind screen with, at its centre, a dense black void. And then I caught a glimpse of the stars as through a steamy window. This gave me such a shock I jerked out of it, back to the blackness of the tank.

"I enjoyed eidetic displays of people's faces, undistorted and not emotionally charged. Lying in the isolation tank was a pleasant, low-key relaxation, a space I would like to explore further while listening to cetacean recordings. After what seemed like an hour I decided I should make a move. Reaching the house I was staggered to find more than three hours had elapsed. What I thought was a low-key experience had drastically altered my sense of time.

"When I got back to Malibu I read *The Deep Self* and found it contains the experiences of about eighty people who have tried the inner-space voyage. Most interesting was that of a Mexican shaman who said it provided the sort of out-of-body experience to which he was accustomed within his own culture. He then gives details of how he would communicate with dolphins while in such a state."

Post-Mobius meeting

13 May: "In the jacuzzi pool this morning I am mulling over the meeting with the Mobius group. I'd been told California was a mixture of the best and the worst on Earth. Now I've seen folk functioning and relating with a model that goes beyond egocentricity: a reintegration of humanity with the whole, the Gaia concept of a living Earth in a holistic universe embracing ecology, interconnectedness, multiple realities, space, time and beyond.

"The folk I met in Maryland; Jeffrey Mishlove and his friends in San Francisco; Mike and Nancy Samuels at Bolinas, the New Frontiers people at Antioch; and now L.A., for all its environmental horrors.

"Last night with ten of the Mobius group, five women and five men, I explained Project Interlock before screening 'The First Move'. This developed into an exchange concerning interspecies communication. I gave them a copy of Jim Nollman's interspecies music tape and a collection of reports from our files involving ESP phenomena.

"I was thrilled to receive from them a number of valuable cetacean anecdotes. David Keith, a former orca trainer, told me of ESP experiences with them. Brando Crespi told me of a boy travelling on a surfboard off Virginia, whom dolphins protected from sharks day after day; Lona Peoples told me of being on a yacht and afraid to tend the foresail because of sharks. At that moment five dolphins appeared and stayed with the yacht.

"Brando told me another complex story from the Amazon and Kathy Peoples described a recurrent dream in a huge sea cave, meeting beings that are half dolphin, half human.

"President of Mobius, Stephan Schwartz summarised it all neatly in his comment that it was inevitable people working along paths of psychic and cetacean research would converge, as during my visit to the United States. From an input by David the possibility emerged that through parapsychic channels we might ask the dolphins what they wish us to do along the cultural interface. This would lead to a new development of Project Interlock in collusion with Mobius.

"They screened for me the Mobius documentary 'Deep Quest', in which psychics plot the site of an unknown wreck in deep water off Catalina Island from places in the east, just using maps. Then Mobius set out with a special exploratory submarine and actually locate the wreck in 370-foot depth, including a predicted rectangular box lying in the mud. The aim of the film was to demonstrate the potential use of psychic faculties.

"They then showed me rushes of their latest film from Egypt wherein psychics plot the location of underwater ruins in Alexandria Harbour enabling divers to locate them in one day; then, in the desert, psychics establish the layout of an ancient house before it is excavated. Stephan gave me a copy of his book *The Secret Vaults of Time* on parapsychic archaeology and we rapped in the hot tub till 3 am.

"At daybreak we chatted with Dr Ron Nolan, a scientist in Hawaii, on a three-way phone link and the way opened up for the next stage of my journey. Mobius have decided to launch themselves into a full-scale interspecies exploration they are terming 'The Bluewater Embassy'. It may be that an initial field experience can be arranged with cetaceans in Hawaii in 1981. My trip will explore this possibility. Could this be the next move?

"Up till now Project Interlock has been a low-key network of people interested in free-ranging whales and dolphins. On this journey, one member has been able to meet an international field of people engaged in top levels of cetacean study, philosophy, ethics and conservation. Since the Smithsonian meeting multiple paths have opened out leading to meetings with parapsychic researchers. It seems cetacean interests may converge with these minds. One thing is clear: the need for a global sharing of advances along the interspecies interface. To this end the Mobius Group and Project Interlock have agreed to join forces.

"After an intensive two-day exchange with the Mobius Group I am finding this polluted seaside enclave, for all its glaring problems, a refuge from supercity: the wave sounds and family warmth bring me together again."

Oahu, Hawaii

20 May: "The psychic scientist, Dr Ron S. Nolan, picked me up at Honolulu airport in his convertible, handed me an iced beer and whirled me across Oahu to the weather coast. This island is one continuous suburb. Last night over a seafood dinner Ron told me how the psychic change came into his life. Now aged thirty-three, Ron heads the highly successful environmental and fisheries consulting firm, Orca Ltd., has a doctorate in marine biology and is a long-experienced diver and underwater photographer.

"While working for three years alone on the west coast of the island of Hawaii, the big isle (near a Polynesian temple), he had become aware of the spirituality of the place. Then he met Adele Tinning, a psychic in San Diego, and began to develop this faculty.

"He told me of his primal cetacean experiences: seeing a mother humpback teaching her calf to leap, and then the day he had a feeling of precognition that he was going to communicate with a whale. With scuba he was swimming along the foot of a typical Hawaiian lava-flow cliff. He began to feel as if something was inside him, scrutinising him. Expectations grew but nothing came. Ron swam up to the boat and climbed in, expressing his disappointment to a puzzled companion.

"Just then the water beside their Boston Whaler heaved in a glassy mound. Out of the centre a huge form thrust some twenty-five feet into the air and flopped over on its side in a crash.

"He told me of a mission to get photos of a captive *Pseudorca* at Sea Life Park. Inadvertently Ron fired his strobe very close to the creature. The cetacean seized his camera gently by the strobe unit and placed it in the centre of the pool. That was it — no more photos.

"Ron told me of a problem that exists around the big island of Hawaii: some game fishermen are killing dolphins. The men impale live bait on their marlin hooks and troll deep down. Dolphins remove the baitfish. Some fishermen try to wound a dolphin with a bullet so it will take the pod away. For all this, Ron says these dolphins remain friendly and can tell your intentions towards them.

"Ron is very keen to assist Mobius towards establishing a Bluewater Embassy interface in Hawaii and would provide logistical and personal support."

With Jim Hudnall

22 May, Kihei, Maui Island: "So this calm Maalaea bay with its nearby islands, Lanai to the right, Kahoolawe to the left, and just the western tip of Molokai visible beyond Papawai Point, is the world's hottest spot for human/humpback relationships. It was out here that the finest footage of humpback mothers and their calves was shot by whale researcher Jim Hudnall, and here the problem of human harassment of breeding cetaceans has arisen and the urgent need for sanctuary: protection of the whale habitat.

"Anti-harrassment notice: Humpbacks: Maui

"Swimmers, divers and boats may stay 300 yards or more from cows, calves in designated breeding grounds. In other cases they may approach no closer than 100 yards. Aircraft must maintain an altitude of at least 1000 feet within 300 yards of the whales, may not hover, circle or buzz the animals."

"My stay with Jim has given me a deep and sobering insight into this aspect of the human/cetacean interface and the problems that can arise when self-centred human curiosity unintentionally oversteps the bounds of ethical conduct. Like the yachtsmen who shove their super-eight cameras at people in atoll villages. These aspects of the interface will need sensitive consideration before any major development can be made in our relationships with cetaceans. It would be very nice if, as the

Mobius Group suggest, we could ask first through psychic channels, and always ensure that we are not by our actions and documentation, unleashing a flood of inconsiderate tourists upon them.

"Play may be the safest, most unexploitable avenue for communication with cetaceans. It has to be spontaneous and can't be forced on them. Some sort of safety valve or perhaps even a venturi is needed to ease grasping humanity towards this new symbiosis without too much culture shock. Interspecies joy-sharing could be the rosetta stone to translate the barrier between us and other life forms; people and cetaceans. Just as we learnt from the atoll-dwellers of the South Pacific (see *Islands of Survival*), creative play is the key to man's ecological niche: the quest for diversity and avoidance of monotony.

"During a taped interview with Jim Hudnall today I asked him a question which I'm finding of increasing interest with people dedicated to cetaceans: the primal experience is often something of an elevating nature.

"'How did you get drawn towards cetacean research, Jim?'

"'Well, I first became really intrigued by cetaceans in 1963 while a geologist at Scripps Institute of Oceanography. I was working in a little cottage on a cliff overlooking the sea at La Jolla. During a coffee break one morning I was sitting out there on the cliff edge with my secretary watching some dolphins body surfing about half a mile up the coast. They'd been riding the waves for about fifteen minutes when we saw a grey whale heading along the coast very close in. It swam through the Scripps Pier and became entrapped by a reef diagonal to the shore below us.

"'The dolphins left off surfing and headed down the coast. They lined up on the shore-side of the whale near its head and either pushed it or were very close. If touching at all, it would only have been a gentle nudging. They oriented the whale towards the opening of the "trap" and accompanied it out. When the whale began curving shorewards a little north of the reef they got on the inshore side again, near the head region and seemed to guide it out to sea. Last seen, the whale was on course for the northward migration. I looked at my assistant. "Did you see what I saw?" And she said "yes" and we both decided it would never be believed, so we mentioned it to nobody.'

"Jim went on to explain how he had then done his draft stint with the Navy, in sonar work, as an anti-submarine warfare officer during which he learnt to distinguish various whale sounds and understand acoustics. Later he got involved with guiding tourists out to see whales up on Vancouver Island and became increasingly interested in cetacean behaviour. This led him to Hawaii and his humpback study."

Full circle day

21 May: "Those sleek spinner dolphins at Lanai seem like a dream to me now that Jim Hudnall has brought us back to Maui after two days with them. When I set out on this journey from New Zealand to Washington I hadn't the least inkling it would lead to interlock. I'd steeled myself for a world of words and cities.

"On Sunday Jim's inflatable whisked us over the eight-mile stretch of indigo blue ocean between Maui and Lanai. Three of us: Ingrid Orbom,

222

the girl who makes such vital ceramic dolphin busts but had never met a live dolphin, Jim and myself.

"During the crossing I kept a hopeful eye open for humpbacks but most have left these waters by now. As the steep cliffs of the volcano island drew near Jim followed a hunch and took us straight to the dolphins: the black fins of eighty spinners, *Stenella longirostris* cruising slowly in a bay where they pass the daylight hours quietly. At dusk these dolphins move offshore to feed on squid 1000 feet down during their rise with the night-time plankton swarms of the deep scattering layer, until by midnight there is a feasting near the surface.

"Leaving the inflatable adrift on a sea anchor, we dived straight down and the dolphins came around us. I felt as if I were already back home, in a dream involving a strange species with extra long beaks and salmon pink bellies, yet so similar in their body language and responses to our presence. How I longed for our catamaran and all the communication gear that enables us to interlock more intensely, but at least these dolphins accepted us in their midst, circling tightly within arm's length and maintaining eye contact. Jim saw one trailing a piece of plastic or tatty seaweed from a flipper. I remembered Simo.

"We wore no wetsuits and I found the Hawaiian waters not quite tropical enough to avoid chilling. After three warm-up spells in the boat Jim and I decided to hang back and let Ingrid meet the dolphins alone. As the pod advanced over the surface en masse towards the boat, Ingrid swam into their path. They circled her very slowly, including the *Zodiac* in their course and then circled her again. Full circle day: the dolphins showed themselves to the girl who had been sculpturing their forms with such devotion. Ingrid said when alone with them her residual fears emerged and were overcome.

"On the beach at Lanai Jim introduced me to Joan McIntyre. It was Joan who compiled the momentous book *Mind in the Waters* on cetacean consciousness and put such energy and insight into establishing Project Jonah. She told me these days she leaves the organisational scene alone for island life."

Jim Loomis

27 May, Maui: "Both Jim Hudnall and Ingrid insisted I should not leave Maui without meeting Jim Loomis, director of the Cetacean Relations Society. This morning I found him in his office, on the edge of town, where he sells solar heaters. Without a moment's hesitation Jim shut his desk and I spent a very pleasant day getting to know him.

"Jim Loomis is *Homo delphinus*: a former maths teacher, owner of four ocean-front wilderness properties on various Hawaiian islands, a tall dreamer/philosopher with the physique of a Greek athlete (6ft 3in, 180 pounds). At forty-five, Jim is in his prime: a perpetual sea boy who rows from one island home to another with a sixteen-foot dory.

"Since founding the Cetacean Relations Society in 1973 Jim has established six centres which offer a variety of facilities for the human/cetacean interface: from the Dance Centre on Maui to the Cetacean Observation Station on Molokai, boat and dock facilities at Lahaina and Lanai and the Sensory Enhancement Centre over at Malibu.

"Jim whisked me out to his Hoolawa valley property, the Wingdoor Cave-pool. He led me along a string of pools and waterfalls to a vast poolside cavern and down there we lunched and swam together. I learnt that Jim has been struggling towards similar goals to our own for a slightly longer time but his plans are ambitious and hard to finance. He is a man totally inspired with a vision of the dolphin/human interface that makes my own dreams seem timorous. For Jim dolphins are divinities and our greatest teachers if we wish to join the cosmic dance.

"Warming ourselves on the volcanic rocks beside the pool Jim told me his plans:

"'I'd like to see all my twenty acres in fruits, gardens and flower and no paths, and full of active, healthy people engaged in the common goal of living with dolphins and like dolphins when ashore. A community of divers, dancers, actors, singers, musicians, artists, scientists, gardeners; futurists whose aim is to celebrate cetacean consciousness.'

"As we talked young people began to come down to the pool from small cabins dotted through the bush and dive from the crest of the waterfall. Jim believes that as extramarestrials we should adopt a dolphin viewpoint to see ourselves more objectively.

"'The contemplation of cetacean consciousness leads to a new perspective. Away from the anthropocentric position and towards biocentrism, essential for continued survival upon this planet. Modern man seeks more and more technology to solve his distresses. From the viewpoint of a highly encephalised, large-brain mammal that's evolved with no need of technology, the tool has become a crutch for human survival. Did you know "whale" derives from wheel? They became their technology rather than use it as we do.'

"In the pool by the cave Jim is training with a group of swimmers to achieve synchronous dolphin-swimming in readiness for an interspecies ballet. He already knows that dolphins respond when humans approximate their breathing and diving patterns.

"'Man is *Homo ludens*, the playing mammal. At his best when at play. Dolphins are the masters of play. When we approach them as our friends and teachers, the drama of interspecies ballet will begin.'

"Members of Jim's 'School of Humans' must have 100-second breathhold ability and feel at ease sixty feet below, moving like dolphins and following their breathing schedule. He believes such delphinic formation swimming is too dangerous to attempt unless the swimmers develop a new perception, a total watching and awareness of one another underwater such as dolphins possess, instantly ready to offer mutual assistance.

"'This generalised buddy system is imperative,' Jim insists. He showed me the little shrine above the pool in which his son died. 'Its lack cost Gannon his life.'

"To develop the necessary group consciousness Jim plans to use a circular isolation tank that will take six trainees in a spoked wheel, head-to-head within a twelve-inch diameter. 'Water is a better conductor than air for sensitizing yourself to group perception.'

"I told Jim of my recent contact with Jacques Mayol, the world's deepest diving human, who reaches depths of 100 metres using yogic techniques. Jacques has just written a book in Italian titled *Homo delphinus*, and I showed Jim the yin yang symbol Jacques designed, so like our own. 'Jacques sounds like a vital key,' he said.

"Then Jim told me about his favourite bottlenose dolphin, Guruthgill who seems to wear a halo of bodily radiance, and showed me photos of a bow-riding dolphin from his portfolio. Some may consider it is just the bulge of water over the dolphin's body forming a convex lens but I have never seen anything like it in a great many dolphin photos.

Dating back to December 1976, meetings with Guruthgill have made Jim think deeply about the implications of ESP communication or visualization transfer. He gave me a detailed account of one such meeting wherein the bow-riding dolphin responded to a sequence of four spontaneous questions with explicit answers right on cue. Many dolphin-lovers have had these experiences and wondered about them.

"Jim has written: 'There are at least four modes of viewing reality. They are complete within themselves, but contradictory taken together. All satisfy different parts of our being. Those parts that aren't fed starve. No explanation is complete. All the lists of axioms of the perception structures include as their bottom lines, "All the above statements are true, all other realities are false." *That* is what is false. A total human wouldn't be bound by any of these perception structures, but would feed the parts of her/his being that was needing the sustenance these structures were making available. All structures are incomplete models of reality. What's more, the notion of there being a reality which holds still while we study it, is false. Reality is created-discovered much more than it is perceived-reacted to.

"'So what is the reality that you would like to experience? Tune in.The reason that people get so sure they are looking at *the* reality rather than *a* reality is that the world does perform "as if" *the* reality were so. And it contradicts other realities at face value, which they lack the flexibility to experience. Seems so simple. Is. There is a great revolution in human thought close at hand. I think Kant began this one. It holds more potential than anything that I have considered for years.'"

Hawaii, the big isle

28 April: "By some wizardry, a couple of phone calls from Hudnall's house, a little machinery, eighteen minutes in the sky and here I am on the island of Hawaii — the 'big isle' as it is called. Paula, a dolphin research student, met me at Kailua airport in a small truck and rattled me along the foot of a soaring volcano cone over a cinder black lava flow, an inert moonscape crazy with hibiscus flowers, to the seafront house where I now write.

"Dr Bernd Wursig, whom I'd met in Washington, was here to welcome me. My main purpose for coming is to meet Jody Solow, the dolphin girl. Bernd tells me she flies in from Los Angeles late tomorrow so I'll be very lucky to see her.

"Sitting here at dusk, in a chair on the sea wall, watching a six-man outrigger canoe cross the bay I am astonished to find this is the very spot Dr Ron Nolan, back on Oahu, had wanted me to visit: Kealakekua (meaning "The Way to the Ancestors"), the Kona-coast bay where Captain Cook was killed in 1779. The beetling cliffs curve around to Ka'awaloa Point, a low promontory where a white monument stands at the sea's edge.

"Nor had I realized Bernd was running a fullscale dolphin research project here. With eight students from the University of California, Santa Cruz, under the supervision of Dr Kenneth Norris, the diurnal behaviour of spinner dolphins is being studied. (It was here that Dr Gregory Bateson observed wild dolphins in 1970 following his famous study of a captive group at Sea Life Park, Oahu, as described in *Mind in the Waters*.)

"Bernd has just been telling me some of their findings and we compared notes. There is an estimated population of 200 to 300 spinner dolphins along this western coast and anywhere from four to eighty spend the day in Kealakekua Bay. From a transit site 245 feet up the cliff researchers have been following them using a surveyor's transit telescope and plotting their general movements on a map to provide an accurate picture for comparison with the bay's submarine topography.

"A more intimate view is gained using the Boston Whaler *Maka'ala* which has been fitted with a sunken well and plexiglass windows. Student Christine Johnson lies in this and has been observing the social behaviour of dolphins on the bows. Then, further along the coast, Jody Solow swims out with dolphins, attempting to gain acceptance much as the chimpanzees of Gombe Stream accepted Jane Goodall.

"Research so far shows that the spinner dolphin day falls into several phases of activity. They usually enter the bay quietly just after sunrise. A period of active socializing ensues with vigorous leaping and spinning, somersaulting and tail slaps. During this time the dolphins rub and roll over each other, push each other in the middle with their beaks, chase each other just beneath the surface, and copulate.

"Then follows a quiet period when they draw close to each other in groups, diving and surfacing together. In the afternoon they socialize again with even more spectacular leaps than in the morning. Finally comes the 'zigzag swimming' period when they speed towards the mouth of the bay with abrupt changes of direction and slowly cruise back in. This may be repeated several times before they finally leave.

"Each day there is a change in the individuals that return. The researchers have been recording the dolphins' underwater sounds and find that they become very noisy during the socializing periods — 'It's like a news bulletin jabber in a foreign language.'

"Bernd tells me that, like us, they have noticed the way distinctively marked individuals often take the initiative in approaches and suggests these may be dominant animals. I'd wondered if they can sense that our attention is directed to more easily recognized individuals. He says some photos of dolphins in their spinning leaps show they have remora adhering to them and thinks the leaps may be to displace them. Christine tells me Jody studied the Lanai dolphins two years back, before coming here and had remarked on an individual that habitually carried a plastic bag around.

226

"The girl researchers are very glum. There have been no dolphins in the bay for several days. They are refusing to ride on the bows of *Maka'ala*. Some other researchers recently captured a spotted dolphin and attached radio gear. A clear example of the clashes that arise between benign research methods and the more traditional approaches for which, it appears, it is much easier to obtain funding from industry. They plan to track the dolphin using satellites. I wonder how much we have learnt about alien cultures since Captain Cook was killed?"

Kealakekua Bay — clifftop reverie

29 April: "At dawn tomorrow my homeward flight begins to New Zealand from Hawaii, the volcano island, this bay where a seaman from the west took his last breath, this anchorage strewn with ship bones where the tourist boat comes daily to see the Captain Cook monument out on the point; where the dolphins come on their coastal visits to pass the hours till squid night.

"And now I sit here on these massive tumbled rocks, an ocean surging over seaworn boulders, my body fresh from scuba diving for Frank's anchorlines and all the brooding spirit of this island arises around me — our mother, 'Papa' to the Maoris, 'Gaia' to the old Greeks, who mightily moved this month at Mt St Helen on the Pacific rim, her life force welling from the planet heat, a primal birth process. Our mother, Papa, palpable. *Touchstone*. Earth me here —.

"As I wrote these words I entered a reverie that invoked all the people I'd met in the past thirty-five days wandering in the American wilderness. I think it started when I noticed a couple along the shoreline gazing out to sea just as I was and felt a common bond. I wrote on my pad:

"One ocean rims this world
And on its shores
Who hear its surging breath
From self to one
Unfurled. . ."

"A string of names follows, arranged in playful patterns. Somehow this verbal game induced a state of trance, an abstracted state in which I was fully conscious but my writing finally petered out.

"The next words on my pad are : 'a canoe passes, I wave two men. Dolphins appear in their wake.'

"There ensued the most elevated interlock I have ever experienced. Something I find very hard to articulate other than the basic facts. For at least an hour, possibly two, six spinner dolphins gambolled below me. There was a mother with a baby and four others. They came in quietly behind the canoe from the direction of Ka'awaloa Point and the Captain Cook monument and moved over to an area directly opposite me and adjacent to a pair of moored yachts. In all their activity they kept these yachts between them and the houses at the head of the bay. The initial move was that typical spinner dolphin gesture, milling close together with their long beaks and heads waving around above water. This they did on the seaward side of the trimaran hull. Then began a session in which they leapt and tumbled in synchrony with my thoughts and questions. Something which is really too much for me to believe afterward and yet so distinctly remembered, like freeze-frames in a movie.

"At times I would glance over to the dolphin research centre, and *Maka'ala* moored out front, wondering whether the students would notice the dolphins had returned. Then I wondered whether the dolphin movements were being masked from that angle by the boat hulls. In mid-afternoon they left the bay quietly along with any doubts I still harboured about mind links.

"As I returned along the shore I suddenly noticed the massive stone walls of the Polynesian temple in the corner of the bay. With my thoughts on the sea I'd walked right past it this morning. At the house nobody had seen the dolphins today.

"Then, still fresh from her long flight, Jody Solow arrived — every inch a sea girl. At a glance I knew what I'd come here to learn. The dolphins could not want for a more devoted and sensitive student.

"Jody has a camp out on the Kona coast near the airport but spent the night at the research centre where we were able to project slides and exchange notes. She was pleased to hear of the Lanai dolphins and the plastic bag dangler. We felt a tremendous empathy and had so much to compare. This is the first time I've met anybody else trying to gain the trust and acceptance of free-ranging dolphins. She swims out with them each morning in the nude, making delphinic noises, observing individual markings and trying to understand their social patterns.

"Jody's problem is finance: lack of academic qualifications makes it hard to get a study grant. Jody will have to leave her dolphins soon and attend college on the mainland until she graduates. I hope she may manage to return during vacations to maintain contact and give her study the benefit of time."

My journal closes. Over the winter of 1980 an injured arm tied me to the desk, and I wove together all that has happened since Jan and I started our dolphin study. Now spring is coming, my arm is getting strong enough to return to sea and there is so much we have to learn from our friends out there, the ocean dancers.

Postscript: The summer of 1980-81 saw an exponential increase in interlock reports from around New Zealand's coastline: a growth in complexity, intimacy and range which quite exceeded our expectations. These we would like to share with readers in a later book. Our biggest question is: would similar dolphin/human development occur in other parts of the world if a global feed-back system were organised? We are sure this book will contact others having cetacean experiences (and dreams) and would dearly welcome accounts and photos for our files. Address to Project Interlock, Box 20, Whangarei, New Zealand. (See report form page 168.)

Appendices

The following seven pieces are offered as appendices in that, while they belong in this book, they could not be filled into the main structure without interrupting the flow.

A Strandings
B Care of the dead
C Dog/dolphin episodes
D Iki: a lesson for mankind
E Scientific revolutions
F Reading list
G The Interlock theory and Gaia hypothesis

A

Strandings

INTERSPECIES communication can play a valuable role in whale strandings. While it is not my intention here to go into the complex problem of why cetaceans strand, two episodes occurred near us during our study period which indicate that cetaceans respond to a communicative approach from rescuers. Both strandings were in 1978, in tidal harbours in the northern part of New Zealand, and both were near the sites of existing or intended thermal power stations.

In the early hours of Friday, 31 March 1978, a pod of pilot whales became stranded with the receding tide on the extensive mudflats of the Manukau Harbour. When they first beached the group, some 250 whales, was tightly bunched. Local people tried to help by pouring water over them to minimize sunburn and dehydration. The whales were crying like babies and sighed in response to the cooling.

With the incoming tide as many as 160 were refloated by members of Greenpeace, Project Jonah and Friends of the Earth, but they restranded again at low tide. They resisted attempts to tow them by the tail. One returned twice to a dead companion but on the third rescue attempt continued away from the stranding. Many were floating on their sides. They were righted, their balance restored by rocking, and encouraged to swim in groups. Most of these were juveniles and in quite good shape apart from sunburn. Social cohesion was strong with healthier animals supporting and assisting the injured. They resisted attempts to separate them and herding them out was more successful when close bonds were respected. As the tide fell rapidly they panicked, swimming erratically and restranding. The total mortality was estimated at 253 with a body count of 190. Those dissected had empty stomachs.

We obtained a personal account of the stranding from Greenpeace member, Deborah Bailey. Deborah told us, "The whales seemed to sense we were trying to help them and offered no resistance or harm. When we reached them most were exhausted, but when they felt us lifting them up and pushing them out they put all their energy into swimming and blowing. They were like confused children out of their own environment and nuzzled nose to nose to keep company and protect dying mates. They all seemed to have different personalities. We were whistling and clicking to them. They listened and returned these sounds. One lifted its head and stared at us with one eye. Another was taken out and released. At first she went well, but then became confused and began to swim in the wrong direction. From behind we whistled to her repeatedly. She stopped and appeared to listen and think, then slowly turned around and followed me for some distance. In the shallows they seemed able to sense the presence of our boat exactly, when beneath it and always surfaced to one side. One nuzzled it as if for companionship and I leaned over and stroked and talked to her. She looked up and blew several times in my face, as if she knew.''

On the opposite coast, a little further north, another pilot whale stranding occurred that year. It started beside the fuel jetty in Whangarei Harbour late on Friday, 29 September 1978. When fisheries officer D. Young arrived there, he found three dead whales on the beach and the remainder of the pod some 150 metres offshore, milling around in a confused manner. Local people had already assisted a number out into deeper water as the tide receded. The whales moved further up the harbour and began to strand again. Local people assisted the fisheries officers to refloat them. In his report Mr Young said, ''We noted the whales were very easy to assist and made every effort to cooperate. One of the larger whales, when stranded, was attended by several juveniles apparently trying to assist, rubbing their bodies against its head. All the time the animals were uttering what seemed to be cries of distress or alarm.

''This situation continued for some hours. We found the whales could be deterred from stranding by wading into the water and shouting and splashing in front of them.''

Next day Mr Young learnt of another stranding further up the harbour at McLeods Bay and with three others went there by jetboat. They found some twenty-two to twenty-five whales thrashing around in bloodstained water. Eleven were dead. Local people had already assisted a number out. Mr Young and others manoeuvred about seven back into deeper water. After wallowing aimlessly for a few minutes they swam slowly away to join the rest of the pod milling about in the channel some 150 metres away.

Taking the jetboat out to inspect them Mr Young found most appeared extremely exhausted, having difficulty breathing. Many were floating on their backs, their undersides completely exposed.

Then, about 400 metres away, he noticed a school of dolphins. They decided to try driving the whales towards the harbour entrance but found them reluctant to move, just milling about. A group of larger whales, who seemed to be the leaders, would break away from the pod and strand on a shallow sandbank. Using pressure from the jetboat they managed to redirect these whales.

''After several minor strandings and aimless blunderings by the herd leaders we decided to try to incorporate the dolphins, who were still swimming some 400 metres away out in the channel, with the school of whales. We rounded up the dolphins with the jetboat, guiding them back to the whales. We found the two species integrated well and had little trouble keeping them together. The jetboat was used to get the herd moving and slowly we shifted out.

''The dolphins seemed quite at home, split up among the whales as individuals or at times reforming as a group and swimming ahead of the whales, leading the way down the channel. There were two set nets in the channel area but due probably to the dolphins guiding the whales, all passed safely around the ends of both nets. The whales were now making slow but much steadier progress. Some were still swimming on their backs. This, we concluded, was to ease the pain from sun and windburn sustained while stranded earlier.

As we neared the main channel at Darch Point we noticed the whales breathing much more easily and deeply, swimming steadily, no longer on their backs. About this time the dolphins left the whales, diving deep and returning to the harbour."

In his conclusions the fisheries officer remarked that talking to the stranded whales had the effect of calming them and reducing their thrashing about. He felt that, in all cases, the whales seemed able to interpret the desire to assist them and that the dolphins appeared to be aware of the needs of the whales. "Is it likely," he asked, "that the two species can communicate?"

This account comes from the report: "Stranding and Mortality of Southern Pilot Fish at Marsden Point and McLeods Bay, Whangarei Harbour 29/9/78 and 30/9/78" by D. Young, Supervising Fisheries Officer, M.A.F., Whangarei.

B

Care of the dead

IN 1942 Syd Raines was serving with the Royal Navy, based at Malta. While on a fishing trip with two Maltese friends they sighted three dolphins near Gozo Island. One had a dead juvenile draped across its back, just forward of the dorsal. The Maltese were familiar with the custom and told Syd they do this when they have a stillborn or birth death, taking turns to carry the dead baby and feed, until it completely decomposed.

Then, around 1975, when Syd was master of the launch *Tokoroa* in the Bay of Islands, New Zealand, he came across a similar situation. It was mid-afternoon when his launch and the *Waikare II*, with some 200 tourists between them, sighted three dolphins near Poroporo Island. The middle dolphin looked as though it had a shawl draped across its shoulders.

When the two launches came together around the dolphins they sounded, leaving the dead juvenile afloat. All that remained was the outer skin. When the launches drew apart the dolphins returned and resumed their burden. (Many of the tourists had cameras. Photos of the incident would be of great value to Project Interlock, Box 20, Whangarei, New Zealand.)

In the late sixties, Syd had another strange dolphin experience in the Bay of Islands. It was a flat calm day when he sighted a lot of thrashing dolphin bodies and took his launch over to see what was happening. He found a circle of turbulent dolphin activity some fifty yards across, surrounded by two rings of dolphins at intervals beyond. He and others in the area concluded there was some special mating ritual amongst those in the centre with "guards" surrounding them.

Further such observations would be of great value to Project Interlock.

This is from Project Interlock files.

C

Dog/dolphin episodes

THE DAY Elsa came to our river (Chapter 6) Jan and I noticed the strange way a pair of beach dogs behaved towards the visiting dolphin. As the children stroked Elsa the dogs fell silent. They were fascinated but totally passive —

almost mesmerised by the dolphin's presence. Yet we have seen dogs go mad with excitement when a net full of fish and the occasional shark was dragged up the beach.

In a letter telling us of dolphin sightings Murray Brighouse, an Auckland scuba instructor, mentioned his poodle's excitement when she first saw dolphins. "One holiday my wife, Tony our poodle and I cruised north in our yacht *Xanadu,* with no set plans. We reached North Cape on the fourth day and then took two weeks to wend our way home to Auckland. Our fourteen-month-old dog had never been on a boat before and as we were sailing from the Mokohinaus to Great Barrier she became very excited, running the length of the boat, barking and trying to climb the steps to get on deck. If I remember correctly she was down inside asleep before this happened. When we put her on deck, she scampered up to the bow barking her head off, leaning over the side and almost falling in.

"We looked and found dolphins on the bow. They seemed to play and roll on their sides more than I have ever noticed before. They stayed with us for about an hour. It seemed the more the dog barked the more they jumped and played. Again off Coromandel, a few days later, the same thing happened. Tony heard them coming while she was down below. Our concrete boat is a good conductor of sound and I have heard the dolphins myself while inside, when superficial noises were at a minimum.

"Our poodle was still only a puppy at the time and I could not sense any real communication in her act, but it was noticeable that she could hear the dolphins through the hull of the boat from a long way off. On deck, when she ran from the bow to the stern, they would follow her."

Then, from Awanui in New Zealand's far north, we received our second anecdote that showed an unusual response to dolphins by a dog. Cliff Knight wrote:

"My family and I usually take our spaniel bitch Sugar on our steel yacht *Lady Oh.* Whenever we sight dolphins Sugar gets very excited making many extremely agitated, whining sounds. She trembles violently and we usually restrain her as we think she may jump overboard! She is normally a very quiet dog, only barking occasionally at strangers at home. When there are no dolphins around she paces the decks constantly searching the sea for 'something.' Possibly she thinks small waves may be dolphins arriving, but she never becomes agitated by these. Several times we have boated large kingfish but Sugar never takes much interest in them even when they are very close to the boat and breaking water.

"When we see dolphins we say 'Look at the fish' or 'Here come the fish' (of course we see them further away than the dog). She immediately runs about in a most excited manner but only really gets 'turned on' when dolphins actually arrive.

"Recently we got near a large whale (our boat weighs 30 tonnes plus) but Sugar didn't seem to take much interest. At the end of a day at sea she is usually exhausted by her constant vigil for dolphins."

By this stage our curiosity was aroused and we opened a new Project Interlock file titled "Dog/dolphin episodes".

Val Walter, the lighthouse keeper's wife, sent us the story of Kim, a dog belonging to Bruce Wiig, skipper of the launch *Tio*:

"Bruce tells me Kim always seemed to know when dolphins were around and she would sit right up on the bow of the boat and bark madly at them. The day she went in with them, he can't say for sure whether she jumped or she slipped as he was in the wheelhouse. It was quite a surprise to him. He said he did notice that her barking became several octaves higher than normal just shortly before she went over the bow. By the time he turned the boat about Kim was well astern with the dolphins swimming around her in a tight circle. He couldn't actually see the dog until he got close but he could see the dolphins going round and round. They stayed with Kim until the boat was about fifty feet away then moved off while he fished Kim out of the sea. This occurred between Little Barrier and Mokohinaus in open sea. Kim was a small 'Bitza', predominantly foxie. Shortly after Bruce picked Kim up she was back in her favourite spot on the bow vocalizing at the dolphins again.

There were many other tales about dogs of all kinds in various predicaments. Wilf Mason sent us a tape from Monkey Mia, Western Australia, telling how his dog often swims with the dolphins:

"Our dog Pluto is in the water most of the time trying to catch fish. Every now and again while the dolphins are around he'll go out and actually swim with them. He swims in a circle and the dolphins follow him around. They'll give him a touch, turn and go around the other way. He'll play there for an hour with the dolphins swimming all the time, but this only happens every so often. There are days when both dog and dolphins are there and nothing happens."

"In a subsequent letter Wilf told us about a kelpie dog staying with people at the caravan park:

"I think he must be in love with the dolphins. He stands in the sea, the water just covering his back, the whole time they are there. He doesn't try to molest them and I've never seen him swimming with them. He just stands and stares. The dog will be shivering with cold but he will not stay out of the water if there is a dolphin about."

Then came a dog/dolphin anecdote from California that capped them all. Ted Boehler is a top scuba diver with twenty-four years' experience and is national director of the Underwater Instructors' Association (N.A.U.I.). He had been receiving our interlock newsletter and not long after I arrived back in New Zealand Ted sent us the following account:

"In June of this year I was crossing in my twenty-four-foot powerboat to Santa Catalina Island. About ten miles out we encountered a school of dolphins, thirty to forty Pacific Whiteside dolphins, *Lagenorhynchus obliquidens*. I've encountered the species fairly frequently on this trip and on two other occasions had dived in with them. This time I really hadn't intended to enter the water, as the most frequent response of the dolphins is to move away. However, the boat was stopped in the water and the dolphins sped past it.

'My small dog Oro, upon seeing them, became quite excited, whining as when he wishes to approach another dog to play and is on a leash. Much to our surprise he suddenly took matters into his own hands (paws?) and leapt out into the water. The next moment we all stared in awe as Oro swam off towards the open sea with dolphins cavorting all around him.

"I began donning my gear, shouting orders and loading cameras with reckless abandon! For the next twenty minutes or so Oro and I free dove and filmed in an absolutely incredible encounter in the wild. Actually Oro had the encounter and I madly filmed the amazing rapport that seemed to be developing between a dog and these marine mammals. The dolphins seemed fascinated by Oro and circled him, jumped alongside, doing barrel rolls under him and generally trying to engage him in their play. Oro, who loves the water and other animals, was delighted and completely ignored my calls to return to the boat!

"Fortune certainly smiled on me that day as I had taken my 16 mm movie camera along just for the heck of it. The footage arrived yesterday. Only 100 feet of it but absolutely incredible! I've enclosed a still shot for you to see. Truly an inspiring adventure, difficult to share in words and indeed one of the highlights of my twenty-four years of diving.''

D
Iki: a lesson for mankind

"WHY," PEOPLE are asking, "when dolphins are so intelligent, do they still go to Iki where they must know they will be in danger of being killed?''

We have a great deal of knowledge about the intelligence of dolphins, from analyses of their complex brain structure, studies of behaviour in captivity, and that of lone dolphins like Opo, Sandy, Donald and Horace in the wild. We now have another angle: the growing number of stories on Project Interlock's files in which dolphins have assisted mariners in distress. All this builds up to a picture of very complex behaviour beyond that of any other living creature, even man. For dolphins will not, under any provocation, retaliate against human persecutors even though they are among the most superbly equipped predators in the ocean.

The question arises then: why did they return in 1979 to the Japanese island of Iki, and to sure death at the hands of fishermen, after the 1978 massacre?

First we should reflect a little: a lot of human behaviour is difficult to interpret as the action of a reasoning being, unless we understand the total context in which it is performed. Take warfare as an example. . . Until we know the full context in which the dolphins are acting we should reserve judging their 1979 return to Iki as a stupid, blind response. We do know that Japanese waters are severely overfished, reclaimed (23 percent of coastline) and polluted. In many ways the Japanese population is reaching the limits of growth before the rest of the world: it is the cutting edge of the western-style consumer civilisation. Tokyo traffic smog, Minimatta disease (from heavy metal pollution), the insatiable, worldwide quest for resources, even the first two urban populations to suffer the atomic holocaust. If mankind is at the turning point, the fulcrum seems to be Japan.

Would an intelligent, ocean-dwelling creature stand aside to let things deteriorate beyond the point of return?

If cetaceans face the threat of being hunted for food, let us not forget that they also risk being starved to death through the heavy industrialisation of fishing on a global scale, or poisoned gradually through the build-up of toxic and radioactive wastes in the inshore marine food chains.

Just as for man, if we spoil this planet, there is nowhere left to go, where else could the dolphins of Japanese waters live without displacing other populations elsewhere in the Pacific?

At Iki some 1400 large, modern fishing vessels (average forty feet) now operate from one harbour, to fish an offshore bank where each spring there *may* be an aggregation of fishes. With a two-man crew they are happy if they get four or five fish in a day, such is the value of freshly caught fish in Tokyo, where it is a luxury item for wealthy businessmen. Many of the fishermen are from fishing villages elsewhere in Japan that have now become dry land, reclaimed for the expansion of heavy industry.

Just as these fishermen have been displaced by industry, pollution and over-fishing, it may reasonably be concluded that the dolphins are obliged to feed at Iki — or perish.

Furthermore, unless they make a stand at Iki, sticking out for their right to share the ocean, the steamroller of modern technology will continue to displace them from every other niche on this planet. We are offered the justification: "It's the livelihood of the fishermen versus the dolphins." But where does this stop? How long before the same cry is heard in other parts of the world?

Let us ponder: is the latest dolphin reaction to the 1978 Iki massacre that of a lemming-like beast, or could it not be that of a being with 15 million years of ecological culture, one that has managed its own population and its food niche with expertise for thirty times longer than man's entire existence? One that has demonstrated a willingness to share the oceans with us, to cooperate with us in fishing when we use ecological methods. (Polynesian, Aboriginal and North African cultures provide examples of joint ventures: human/dolphin.)

Iki could be seen as an object lesson for man; a gesture that Mahatma Gandhi would have understood. A powerful protest at the stupidity of our short-term, dead-end approach to planet housekeeping by an ancient and alien culture: the cetaceans.

On my recent visit to the United States I found that Iki is not the only place in which humankind is coming into food competition with cetaceans — it is an increasing problem in today's world. There are many examples in earlier pages.

In Tasmania orca are annoying fishermen by robbing set lines in Bass Strait — a newly exploited fishing ground where man is expanding his territory into that of the orca. Does it ever occur to us why orca and dolphins don't do this more widely? They could easily ensure that no trawl net caught a fish. Fair is fair.

In Hawaii big-game fishermen impale live baitfish on their trolling hooks. Dolphins remove them. Some irate sportsmen shoot the dolphins to maim them and lead the pod away.

The killing of dolphins by purse-seiner still continues in the Eastern Pacific. The latest mortality figures include between 17,000 and 20,000 in 1979. First three months of 1980: 6493. Pirate whaling is rife and now the Antarctic krill are up for grabs. The battle to save the whales will be futile if we destroy their foodstocks. In all our major fisheries the long-term, rational approach has been sacrificed for the shortsighted reasons of economics — boom and bust — because we have not yet progressed beyond our nomadic ancestors except in the dinosauric scale we now operate.

The cetaceans have been waiting for half a million years for homo "sapiens" to wake up. There is a significant change in our thinking about the sea just beginning — it is the offspring of the scuba age. Will it be too late? Since World War II, thanks to Cousteau, man has re-entered the ocean. He has started to think as a planetarian. If cetaceans cede to us all the food in the ocean with no passive resistance as at Iki, it will only be a brief time before we destroy these resources, eliminating the whales in the process and ultimately ourselves.

But there is a faint glimmer of hope as human awareness expands.

E

Scientific revolutions

AS OUR dolphin research became more complex several people urged me to read the book *The Structure of Scientific Revolutions*, by Thomas Kuhn (University of Chicago Press).

Eventually I was given a copy and found it an elegant masterpiece on the philosophy of science. It explained the essential conservatism of most scientists and their rejection of novelty and new insights, so important to other creative fields.

Now professor of philosophy and science history at Princeton, Thomas Kuhn wrote his extended essay on scientific revolution in 1962. It has since become a basic text in virtually every modern university.

Examining the history of scientific thought Kuhn found that scientists work intensively within a conceptual framework, a "paradigm" or world view, and gradually become more and more specialised until the boundaries of the known world are reached. At this point anomalies in the paradigm begin to appear more and more frequently, and the accepted world view begins to crumble.

Kuhn believes that scientific revolutions such as the Copernican, Newtonian and Einsteinian, began with a growing sense that an existing world view had ceased to function adequately in the exploration of some aspect of nature.

For an anomaly to provoke a crisis and lead to revolution in scientific thought it has to be of such a nature as to call into question the very foundations of the existing world view, or, as with the Copernican revolution, lead to practical applications of such importance that a crisis is provoked. Thus, in an age of global exploration, new ideas about astronomy attracted the attention of more and more of the field's most eminent men until a new paradigm emerged.

Kuhn discovered that, almost always, the men who achieve the fundamental invention of a new paradigm have either been very young or very new to the field whose model of reality they challenged. Being little committed to the traditional rules of normal science, such people are particularly likely to see that the existing rules no longer define a playable game and so they conceive another set that can replace them. The result is a scientific revolution following which the scientists work in a different world and a host of new discoveries emerge.

Kuhn claims that quite often "the new paradigm, or a sufficient hint to permit later articulation, emerges all at once, sometimes in the middle of the night, in the mind of a man deeply involved in crisis."

Thereafter the scientific community is an immensely efficient instrument for solving the problems or puzzles that the new paradigm defines.

To me this all seemed to point directly to the modern crisis in humanity's relationship with other life forms. I saw the great thrust towards a new conceptual model given us by people like Gregory Bateson and Buckminster Fuller, or Jim Lovelock (the Gaia hypothesis) and John Lilly.

I saw the crisis expressed succinctly in Bateson's words: "The organism that destroys its environment destroys itself." And I realized why, in coming to terms with the convergent evolution of terrestrial and oceanic intelligence, normal science is hamstrung. This will continue while potentially intelligent creatures are assessed according to rules whereby it is presumed the researcher and the experiment can be isolated from affecting each other except in controlled and understood ways; rules which expect that the experiment, if valid, can be repeated by any other researcher and that the conditions under which it was carried out can be duplicated. From the very frontiers of hard science, the world of the particle physicist, such assumptions are no longer acceptable. We are, right now, in the throes of a scientific revolution with crucial implications for life in this part of the Universe.

F
Reading list

WE ARE frequently contacted by somebody who has had an extraordinary experience with a dolphin or whale. We often find such people have little more than a vague general knowledge of cetaceans but they are fired with enthusiasm and eager to learn more.

All too frequently people have not realized the significance of a cetacean gesture because they had nothing to relate it to. In the hope that it will help to fill a gap for some readers, this is the range of books we found of most value.

To start with, species identification is essential if observations are to relate to an existing body of knowledge. For this we have found *New Zealand Whales and Dolphins* (Baker) a handy little guide, with occasional recourse to the much weightier tome, *Whales, Dolphins and Seals* (Gaskin). For readers in other parts of the world a recent treatment is *Whales, Dolphins and Porpoises* (Lockley).

Then there are books which provide a good general background knowledge of cetaceans, including the fossil record and a historical review of early Greek and Roman writings. The classic in this field is Alpers' *Dolphins*, with Stenuit's *The Dolphin: Cousin to Man* providing more scientific depth. The Cousteau volumes *Dolphins* and *The Whales* are also useful, especially when recounting the actual adventures of the *Calypso* crew, such as the chapter on the symbiotic fishing relationship between the nomadic Imragen and dolphins of North Africa.

For the reader wishing to explore the subject deeply, Dr John Lilly provides a wealth of scientific material on dolphin physiology, sensory capacities and captive behaviour. His book *Lilly on Dolphins* is a compilation of *Man and Dolphins* (1961) and *The Mind of the Dolphin* (1976).

Of course, these books are biased towards dolphins, as is most of our cetacean knowledge, by reason of the sheer immensity and physical apartness of the larger cetaceans — a situation now changing as people learn to meet them on their own terms.

For sheer inspiration and the extension of cetacean knowledge on many fronts, there can be no more important or delightful book than *Mind in the Waters — A book to celebrate the consciousness of whales and dolphins*. This is a compilation of scientific research, anecdotal experience and creative thought which Joan McIntyre assembled in 1974 for the Sierra Club. Even as an example of the art of publishing, it sets a standard worthy of the beings it explores.

In 1979 Robin Brown took our knowledge a stage further. His *The Lure of the Dolphin* reviews in very readable form the existing knowledge gained from studies of captive dolphins and cries loudly for benign study of free-ranging cetaceans.

That same year Tom Wilkes of Los Angeles brought out a superbly illustrated book, *Project Interspeak*, which seems like a prolongation of Joan McIntyre's work, bringing us up to date on recent developments, such as Dr Roger Payne's research into cetacean sound.

The scientific content of Joan's book is also extended by the two volumes of *Whales and Whaling*, proceedings of the Australian inquiry 1978, which includes scientific papers on the cetacean brain and intelligence potential, by scientists Jerison and Morgane and a review of whale harvesting strategies by Dr Sydney Holt.

For visual delight Bill Curtsinger's photographic exploration of cetaceans,

Wake of the Whale provides rich fare, extending the colour plates of *Mind in the Waters*, as photographers have learnt to get closer to cetaceans.

At this stage the reader may care to turn to books about individual cetaceans, such as *Follow a Wild Dolphin*, Dr Horace Dobbs' account of Donald's adventures along the English coastline over a period of years.

A Whale for the Killing is a tragic tale of man's inhumanity to a fin whale. Entrapped in a frozen harbour at the mercy of gun-happy locals, it dies of blood poisoning, riddled with bullets. Farley Mowat's grim story has had a positive spin-off though: when a similar incident occurred in 1978 in the same region of Newfoundland, the public response was totally reversed and the whales were saved.

Killer Whale, the Saga of Miracle is the story of a young orca injured by human hands, and after an immense human effort, restored to health.

In *Feet Upon a Rock*, due to be published in 1981, Rosamond Rowe tells the story of her life's struggle with physical disability and the inspiration she had from empathy with other living things. When the lone dolphin Horace visits her home town in Napier, New Zealand, despite her weakness Rosamond and her whole family share an adventure with a wild dolphin few would not envy.

In the course of our own reading, interest expanded along several paths. We read widely about animal behaviour and found *Among the Elephants* (Hamilton), *In the Shadow of Man* (Goodall) and *The Year of the Gorilla* (Schaller), all studies of other large brain mammals in the wild, provided useful perspectives. *Apes, Men and Language* (Linden) reviews work, now considerably advanced, in teaching sign language to chimpanzees, while in *Communication between Man and Dolphins*, John Lilly explains his Project Janus experiment with a computer interface.

Anthropology is another worthwhile field for the cetacean student. Two books I found particularly fascinating. *Wizard of the Upper Amazon* (Lamb) presents a picture of our own species living almost as dolphins: rain-forest Indians, who rely on hearing as much as vision in their hunting, project "visualizations" of their prey to instruct novices and communicate with whistles and animal mimicry. *Seven Arrows* (Storm) provides insights into the nature of a non-materialistic American Indian culture which emphasizes interior life and self-realization through human relationships. This gave me some inkling as to the possibilities of a cetacean culture.

My own two books, *Sharks and Other Ancestors* and its sequel *Islands of Survival* recount experiences in Melanesia and Polynesia exploring living patterns of the coral reef community, including the villagers who are part of it. During this time ideas were forming about the ethics of interspecies communication.

Undersea exploration in both tropical and temperate worlds developed a strong interest in ecology. This led to my reading the works of scientist Gregory Bateson, *Steps to an Ecology of Mind* and *Mind and Nature — a Necessary Unity*. Bateson had a deep interest in cetaceans and both books include useful passages on the subject, in an illuminating context. Buckminster Fuller's *"Synergetics"* is a massive tome that provides a mindboggling new vision of the Universe from a non-egocentric viewpoint and one within which it is easier to find a place for cetaceans. Fuller believes they may have stored in their huge brains such a knowledge of Earth history through successive ice ages that they are sensitive to this planet's slower rhythms of cyclical change, while we, with our ant's-eye view of time, ignoring the warnings of climatologists, geologists and the like, destroy Earth's forest, change its atmosphere and pollute its oceans. The book *Gaia* (Lovelock) brings this concept a step forward, providing a holistic view of Earth as a living entity. With his final lines scientist Jim Lovelock speculates: "Perhaps one day the children we shall share with Gaia will peacefully cooperate with the great mammals of the ocean and use whale power to travel faster and faster in the mind, as horse power once carried us over the ground."

As our dolphin experience deepened in complexity I began to read more widely into the literature of human consciousness. I enjoyed all of Carlos Castenada's works, exploring the nature of a separate reality. John Lilly provided another avenue with his *Centre of the Cyclone, The Deep Self, The Dyadic Cyclone* and *The Human Biocomputer*, all of which explore the inner spaces of the human mind using a variety of unorthodox techniques from the isolation tank to LSD, in an attempt to expand the human side of the new cultural interface. Having reached a point where he felt he could get no further in his study of dolphins based on captive animals, Lilly closed down his research facility and explored his own mind.

In *Gifts of Unknown Things* Dr Lyall Watson gives his personal experience of strange events that ensued in an Indonesian village after a whale died on the beach. This provides dramatic insights into his more general treatment: *Supernature*.

Space scientist Dr Carl Sagan speculates on the evolution of human intelligence in *The Dragons of Eden* and provides ideas about interspecies communication in *The Cosmic Connection*.

Seeing with the Mind's Eye (Samuels) and *Creative Vizualization* (Gawain) explore the possibilities of mind/body control in the maintenance of health, both physical and mental. *Roots of Consciousness* (Mishlove) is a history of parapsychology, and in *The Secret Vaults of Time* Stephan Schwartz assembles a range of archaeological studies which have involved psychics. Frank Robson's *Talking Dolphins, Thinking Whales* explains how the former dolphin trainer used ESP or visualization in his pool work.

The Tao of Physics (Capra), *The Silent Pulse* (Leonard) and *The Roots of Coincidence* (Koestler) are all titles exploring the cutting edge of western science in areas such as particle physics and its relationship with multiple realities and ESP theory.

As we go to press (July 1981) two new books have arrived: *The Dolphins' Gift*, Chi-uh Gawain's heartwarming account of the Monkey Mia dolphins, and *Save the Dolphins*, in which Dr Horace Dobbs updates the Donald story and many others.

In fiction, writers have imagined themselves into the bodies of whales, to present a whale's eye of the world. In so doing Victor Scheffer, *The Year of the Whale* and Vincent Smith, *Musco — Blue Whale* have woven into their narrative a wealth of accurate cetacean knowledge in a readily assimilable form, just as in *Boy and the Seabeast* Anne de Roo has told the story of a human/dolphin friendship in words which will inspire children.

Science fiction writers speculate from the basis of what is known to provide an internally consistent view of a possible reality. So, in *Cachalot* (Foster) we visit a planet where cetaceans are supreme and in *The Day of the Dolphin* (Merle) and *The Voice of the Dolphin* (Szilard), scientists learn to communicate with dolphins when on the verge of planetary disaster. Wishful thinking?

Finally, two periodicals which provide valuable cetacean material: *Oceans* magazine, and *Whalewatcher*, journal of the American Cetacean Society.

G

The Interlock theory and Gaia hypothesis

IN CHAPTER eleven of his book *The Human Biocomputer,* Dr John Lilly discusses interspecies communication as a coalition between two biocomputers for which he coins the phrase "computer interlock."

He proposes an approach in which the theorist establishes interlock with a non-human biocomputer by whatever modes are possible, programming himself with open-ended hypotheses so as to encourage communication.

If communication attempts by one side are blocked by the other in a certain area, search tactics may be used until an open channel is found or a channel developed suited to both. He discusses mimicry as evidence of interlock between bottlenose dolphins and humans:

"Early in the interlock mutual rules are established regulating the muscle power and force to be used, and areas considered dangerous, the absolutely forbidden areas. . ."

Then comes the sentence that activated the Project Interlock research programme: "Dolphins, correctly approached, seek interlock with those humans who are secure enough to openly seek them (at all levels) in the sea water."

Lilly points out that anatomical differences limit the channels, as do human social taboos. He outlines a variety of possible channels for communication. From his research into the sound production/hearing channel he suggests that the wish to communicate may be demonstrated by mimicking the other's sound signals even though for the time being these signals make no sense, and that one should insist on having one's own signals mimicked on the same basis. Then another key sentence: "This leads to mimicry of our swimming patterns by the dolphins when we have mimicked theirs."

Thinking about that led to our invention of the dolphin suit. Now the dolphins have copied us as we try to swim in their mode. We made the first move as they could not possibly mimic our bipedal style of swimming.

The Gaia hypothesis postulates that the Earth can be regarded as a single living system including the biosphere, atmosphere, oceans and soil.

According to one of its leading proponents, Jim Lovelock*: "The air we breathe can be thought of as being like the fur of a cat and the shell of a snail, not living but made by living cells so as to protect them against an unfavourable environment."

That the oxygen in our atmosphere is of biological origin has long been accepted, but Lovelock claims the same is so for atmospheric nitrogen, ammonia, methane, nitrous oxide and a whole range of gases which are the products of the metabolism of various micro-organisms. Thus the atmosphere is a highly sensitive regulating mechanism maintained by Earth's life forms, making the whole planet, in effect, one life.

Gaia — A New Look at Life on Earth, J.E. Lovelock. Oxford University Press: 1979.

Epilogue

"All the neurological evidence is not in, regarding the whale brain and intelligence. However, enough is known to lead us to believe we are dealing with special creatures with remarkably developed brains. Major riddles of nature and relations between species may indeed be answered by study of these brains, and these opportunities may die with the whales if we do not act now. They could have taught us much if we had only listened. Their kinship with man at the level of neurological development holds us in awe and fascination. It is unthinkable for us to sit idly by and let such unique beings wantonly be destroyed by selfish and short-sighted men. This is a resource and kinship that belongs to us all. Our very training and deepest feelings make us respect these wondrous creatures. Would that the brains of men could lead them to live in harmony with nature instead of ruthlessly plundering the seas that nurtured us... We must continue to be haunted by such solitary beings, with amazingly complex brains, wending their way through the seas, wondering, perhaps, what manner of men are hunting them down to destroy them forever."
— Dr Peter Morgane, Worcester Foundation for Experimental Biology, Worcester, Massachussetts.

Index

Persons and Named Cetaceans (italicised)

Adair, Chris 123
Adams, Graeme and Joyce 184
Alpers, Anthony 115
Amazing Grace 201
Amphlett, Mike 172
Anderson, Don 134
Ayling, Drs Tony and Avril 15, 148, 172, 195

Baker, Donna and Mike 180
Bateson, Dr Gregory 226, 236, 238
Beamish, Laurie 179
Beamish, Dr Peter 202, 210
Bennett, Quentin 91, 99, 104, 108
Bentfin 57, 80, 88
Berzin, Dr Alfred 208
Bingham, Margaret 108, 112, 113
Bradstock, Mike 153
Brett, Laurie 178
Briggs, Ian 34, 124
Brighouse, Murray 62, 232
Brown, Robin 159
Buckley, Karen 87
Busy Bee 144-145, 148-149, 153-154

Cate, Dexter 211
Chapman, Hal 69, 74, 78, 83-84, 87
Charlie (Scot.) 99, 116
Cotterill, Ross 76
Cotton, Dr Simon 160, 191, 205
Cousteau, Jacques 18, 116
Cropp, Ben 124
Crossland, Des 186

Day, Gundi and David 202
Denzler, John 117
Dobbs, Dr Horace 99, 104, 117
Dods, Gary 193
Donald 99, 105ff
Drew, Cathy 14, 17

Earle, Dr Sylvia 123
Elsa 101-103
Feigel, Bob 55, 61, 81, 84, 87
Fenn, Barry 74, 83, 87
Fortum-Gouin, J.P. 208, 209, 213
Fouts, Alan 135
Fox, Dr Michael 212
Fuller, Buckminster 176, 236, 238

Gawain, Chi-uh (Elizabeth) 125, 129
Giddings, A1 121, 123
Goodall, Jane 18

Goodall, Terry and Alison 90, 99
Grey, Les 14, 172
Grimble, Sir Arthur 16
Guruthgill 225

Hartog, Dirck 123
Harvey, David 19, 21, 56
Herman, Dr Louis 208
Holeyfin 127
Horace 104ff, 141
Horn, Paul 54
Hudnall, Jim 176, 198, 209, 221-223

Jerison, Prof. Harry 206
Johnson, Mrs 100, 102
Jones, Hardy 176, 211

Kempthorne, Roger 133
Khan, Pir Vilayat Inayat 95
Kircher, Eric 42, 75-76, 87
Kleiman, Ray and Mikki 215, 217
Kodituwakku, Les 120
Kuhn, Thomas 68, 235
Kupe 115

Lilly, Dr John 16, 18-19, 60, 208, 212, 214, 218, 236, 239-240
Linden, Eugene 209
Lockyer, Christine 117
Longsworth, John 81
Loomis, Jim 223
Lovelock, Dr Jim 236, 238, 240

McCaffery, Edwin 154
McHarg, Sam 89, 180
McIntyre, Joan 223
McKenney, Jack 121, 176
McKenzie, Meda 181-185, 195
McLaughlin, Chris 118
McMath, Witi 141
Mandojana, Dr Ricardo 204
Mason, Hazel and Wilf 125, 233
Mayol, Jacques 129, 224
Mishlove, Dr Jeffrey 215
Mitchell, Maura 118
Moitessier, Bernard 130
Morgane, Dr Peter 130, 241
Morris, Eric 203
Morrison, Alan 145, 173, 179
Mosen, Graham 42, 72, 75, 143
Munro, Peter 29, 78

Nicky 127
Nina 99, 115, 118
Nolan, Dr Ron 220, 225
Nollman, Jim 191, 193-195, 201, 211, 214-217
Notchy 199

O'Keefe, Timothy 122
Old Charlie (Aust.) 124
Olivier, Jason 81, 84, 87
Opo 19, 99, 102, 115, 141
Orbom, Ingrid 222

Papillon (Henri Charriere) 137
Patterson, Lynn 124
Payne, Dr Roger 17, 210
Pelorus Jack 99, 115, 141, 182
Pink Floyd 30, 56, 149
Pita, Waipu 85, 141
Pitt, Malcolm 29, 70-72, 78
Plutarch 114
Puthoff and Targ 216

Raines, Syd 231
Renoir, Jacques 116
Rippon, Peter 74
Ritchie, Lew 102
Robinson, Neil 175
Robson, Frank 104
Rowe, Rosamond and Allan 108ff

Saayman, Dr Graeme 209, 213
Salleres, Luis 116
Samuels, Dr Michael 216
Sandy 118ff
St. Pierre, Lin 133
Saul, Peter 75
Selby, Pat 123
Shanks, Bill 15, 145
Shields, Belinda 183

Sideband 77-78, 94-95
Simo 152, 154, 156-162, 223
Slark, Cindy 181
Solomon, Robin 28, 44, 143
Solow, Jody 199, 226, 228
Speckledy Belly 126
Spong, Dr Paul 53, 76, 192, 194
Stander, Kobus 132
Starck, Dr Walter 26, 38, 68, 74, 148
Stenuit, Robert 18, 114
Stewart, Ramari (Dusty) 146, 175, 184-189
Stumpfin 154
Sullivan-Meads, Te Rina 142
Surgerson, Ian 180
Sutphen, John 17
Swartz, Dr Steve 200, 210

Thomas, Claude 33
Thomson, Graeme 107, 168, 171
Treloar, Tom 119
Triplenick 149-153

Vasquez, Jose 116

Walter, Val 156-171, 232
Watson, Dr Lyall 17, 20, 196, 205, 239-240
Watson, Dr Richard 131
Webb, Dr Nicholas 117
Wellgreen, Pat 105
West, Marilyn 62
White Patch 36-39, 44
Whiting, Penny 193
Wiese, Michael and Morgan 175, 195, 214-215
Woollacott, Rob 133
Wright, Bernie 81
Wursig, Dr Bernd 214, 225

Yablokov, Dr A.V. 207
Young, D. 230

Places and Subjects

Akaroa 180
Aldermen Is. 193
Apes, Men and Language 209
Atoll-dwellers 222
Auckland Harbour 193

Bahamas 174
Bay of Islands 231
Benign research 206, 227
Boat towing 118
Body language 16, 21, 26, 31, 34, 51, 75, 80, 95,
    104-106, 118, 150-153, 167, 174, 176, 182, 187
Bolinas 193, 201, 215
Bonding 16, 78, 92
Bottlenose dolphin, Tursiops truncatus 14, 30, 72, 99,
    104, 115, 118, 132, 134, 141ff, 161, 171, 179-181,
    207ff, 219, 240
Bryde's whale 202

Cape Rodney 196
Care of Dead 231
Catamaran, James Wharram 53, 68, 70-72, 78-79, 83,
    90, 92, 165
Cetacean rights 212
Ceta Research Inc. 202
Christchurch 180
Common dolphin, Delphinus delphis 30, 60, 67, 70,
    72, 81, 89, 99-102, 144-145, 161-162, 171-173, 180,
    183-189
Cook Strait 181
Cornwall 117

Defaecation signal 31, 34-35, 57-58, 68, 73, 153, 170
Delphinid Research Institute 206, 209
DINTs 99, 114ff
Dog/dolphin episodes 231-233
Dolphin: Cousin to Man, The 18, 114

243

Dolphin-kick 15, 30, 35, 52, 146
Dolphin-swim 28, 43, 49, 51, 93
Dolphins (Alpers) 115
Dolphins (Cousteau) 18, 116
Dolphin suit 13, 22, 24, 28, 69, 74, 78, 87, 92-93, 95, 146, 149, 240
Dolphin warnings 130-137
Dorsal fins 40, 43, 55, 57, 67, 73, 75-78, 90, 93-95, 101, 147, 167-168, 186
Dreams 84, 86, 88, 112, 143, 219
Dry Tortugas 197

El Torito 16, 21, 26, 29, 48, 84, 148
Encephalisation theory 207
ESP 16, 57, 71, 154-155, 159-160, 174, 176, 208-210, 216, 219, 221, 225, 227, 238-239
Ethics 16, 53, 60, 62-63, 211-213

Falmouth 119-120
Farallon Islands 201, 216
Fishing mortalities 186, 202, 221, 235
Follow A Wild Dolphin 99, 117

Gaia hypothesis 240
Galapagos Islands 202
Gifts of Unknown Things 17, 20
Goat Island 146, 148, 154
Great Barrier Island 62, 145, 181, 191, 232
Great Mercury Island 171, 191
Greenpeace 229
Grey whales 199, 222

Hanson Island 194-195
Harassment 166, 204, 221
Hawaii 220-228
Hector's dolphin, *Cephalorhynchus hectori* 180
Hippo 99, 115
Hokianga Harbour 19, 115
Houhora 133
Humpback whales 32, 198, 202, 210, 221

Iki 174, 193, 211, 234-235
Intelligence 119
Interlock theory 240
International Whaling Commission 205
Islands of Survival 14, 83, 222
Isle of Man 116
Isolation tank 218, 224, 239

Japan 234

Kaikoura 203
Kapiti Island 173, 182
Kealakekua 225

La Corogna 115-116
La Jolla 222
Lanai 222-223, 228
Leigh Marine Lab. 195
Lilly on Dolphins 18, 60
Long Way, The 130
Los Angeles 215, 217

Luaniuans 28, 83
Lure of the Dolphin 159

Malibu 81, 217
Manukau Harbour 229
Maori traditions 26-27, 83, 85, 89, 114-115, 141-142, 182, 202
Marco Polo 27, 76, 95
Matapouri 15, 68, 92, 103, 141
Maui 176, 198, 221-225
Maui Whale Research Unit 199
Message tape 20-21, 30, 37, 50-51, 60, 62, 75, 147, 150, 166
Mimicry 14-16, 18, 22, 26, 34, 44-45, 56, 58, 60-63, 69, 77, 80-81, 104, 105, 149-152, 167, 174, 176, 194, 199, 240
Mind in the Waters 192, 223, 226
Mobius Group 216, 219
Mokohinaus 156-171
Monkey Mia 123ff, 218, 233
Music 16, 18-19, 21, 26, 29, 34, 48, 52, 54, 60, 69-70, 79, 83, 111, 166, 174, 176, 181, 194-195
Mutual trust 79

Napier 91, 99, 104, 108, 142
Newfoundland 202, 210
Newsletter, Interlock 165
New Zealand Dive 165
Ngatiwai people 85, 141
Ngunguru 14, 15, 68, 70, 84, 99, 126, 146, 173, 175, 191

Opononi 115
Orca 53, 67, 118, 189-195, 235

Pacific Whiteside dolphin, *Lagenorhynchus obliquidens* 233
Paper nautilus 22, 31, 36, 40-41
Parapsychology 215-216
Patagonia 17, 204, 210
Pattern of Islands, A 16
Pilot whales 229-230
Pirimai 203
Play 222
Pliny the Younger 115
Poor Knights Islands 13, 20, 22, 30, 45, 51, 82, 141, 148, 168, 184
Possession 111-112, 118
"Programming and Metaprogramming in the Human Biocomputer" 18, 240
Project Janus 208, 218
Project Jonah 131, 223, 229
Project Interlock 99, 130, 137, 165, 192, 220, 240
Pseudorca 90, 102-103, 197, 221

Questionnaire, Interlock 168

Recurrences 95
Reef fishes 22
Right whales 17
Rikoriko Cave 14, 26, 42, 45, 49, 84

Sandy Bay 178
Sandy Point 120, 123
San Francisco 125, 174, 214
San Salvador Island 120ff
San Ignacio lagoon 200, 204, 210
Scotland 116
Sei whale 195
Sexual arousal 107, 112, 116-121, 198
Sharks and Other Ancestors 26
Shark Bay 123
South Africa 132
Southern right whale 203
Sperm whale 203
Spinner dolphin, *Stenella longirostris* 176, 222-223, 226
Spotted dolphin, *Stenella plagiodon* 121, 176, 227
Strandings 90, 102, 229-230
Structure of Scientific Revolutions, The 68, 235
Surfers' anecdotes 178ff
Symbiosis 222, 237

Tasmania 235
Tiny Dancer 107, 109-111
Torres Strait 135
Three Kings Islands 133
Tuamotu Islands 203
Tukaiaia, seahawk 86, 143-144
Tutukaka 30, 36, 41, 47, 55, 82, 104, 134-135, 145-147, 153, 184

Valdes Peninsula 196

Whale Island 186ff
Whales 17, 27, 32, 53, 74, 191
Whangarei 134, 230
Whangaruru 85, 88
Washington D.C. 205
Wellington 172, 179
Whakatane 186ff